Philosophy of Music

Philosophy of Music

An Introduction

R. A. Sharpe

McGill-Queen's University Press
Montreal & Kingston • Ithaca

© R. A. Sharpe, 2004

ISBN 0-7735-2927-6 (hardcover)
ISBN 0-7735-2928-4 (paperback)

Legal deposit fourth quarter 2004
Bibliothèque nationale du Québec

Published simultaneously outside North America
by Acumen Publishing Limited

McGill-Queen's University Press acknowledges the financial support of the
Government of Canada through the Book Publishing Development Program
(BPIDP) for its activities.

National Library of Canada Cataloguing in Publication Data

Sharpe, R. A.
    Philosophy of music / R.A. Sharpe.

ISBN 0-7735-2927-6 (bound).—ISBN 0-7735-2928-4 (pbk.)

    1. Music—Philosophy and aesthetics. I. Title.

ML3800.S532 2004   780'.1   C2004-906106-2

Designed and typeset by Kate Williams, Swansea.
Printed and bound by Cromwell Press, Trowbridge.

Contents

Acknowledgements

Many of my fellow writers on the aesthetics of music will recognize some of their ideas in this book. I am deeply indebted to Stephen Davies, Lydia Goehr, Peter Kivy, Jerrold Levinson, Derek Matravers, Colin Radford and Aaron Ridley, even where I disagree with them. Stephen Davies read the draft manuscript and made many helpful criticisms. I have too a general debt in matters of the philosophy of art to another old friend, Colin Lyas, and to the late Frank Sibley. My wife, Dr Lynne Sharpe, brought her inimitable sense of grammatical propriety as well as her philosophical nous to the text. My colleague, David Walford, helped me with the translation of Hanslick.

Some parts of this book were presented in a more technical form to audiences at the universities of Leeds, Limerick and Wales, Lampeter, at the Bolton Institute and at the annual conference of the British Society of Aesthetics. I thank all the audiences for their criticisms. Some of the reflections on profundity appeared in a different form in *The British Journal of Aesthetics* anniversary issue 2000 and some of the arguments on functionalism in the *International Yearbook for Aesthetics* 1998. Finally, I thank an anonymous reader of this book and my publisher, Steven Gerrard, who suggested that I write it and made its arrival as free of birth pangs as can reasonably be expected.

R. A. Sharpe

Schubert, "To Music", as written in the album of Albert Sowinski

Introduction

"People always think something's all true."
(Holden Caulfield in J. D. Salinger, *The Catcher in the Rye*)

Since you have opened this book, let me guess at what motivated you to do so. You may, like me, be interested in the philosophy of music because of your life with music. You may find it puzzling that your taste should be sometimes idiosyncratic, sometimes different even from that of people with whom you share many enthusiasms. Music you love bores some others. You may wonder whether you are right or wrong about it. You may wonder on what basis some music is thought to be more significant than other music. You might have reflected on whether or not music means anything. You may wonder at its power to excite us and move us to tears. You might have been bemused by some of the things you read in the newspapers. Could putting fireworks into a piano and then setting fire to it really count as music? I, too, have found these matters puzzling, and they have led me to consider some of the answers that have been proposed. For it is music and our reactions to it, rather than the prospect of another area on which philosophical training can be practised, that sparked my interest in the first place. The questions I raise are, predominantly, questions about the value of music, about the individuality of our assessments and about the way in which we prize music for its power to move us. Even with other issues, such as what makes something a piece of music, questions of value are in the background. It is initially hard to see how setting fire to a piano could be of value; indeed, for a pianist, it is a crime, since pianos have their own individual character. So we are led, inevitably, to the lengthy discussion of artistic value that constitutes the last chapter of this book. For the notion of art and the notion of value are, I believe, connected. This

1

remains so even if most music is mediocre. Responding to it and assessing it remains at the heart of our encounter with it.

Sometimes these questions can be answered, and sometimes they seem to have no answers. Where they have no answers I try to show why. But first some general reflections. Music is ubiquitous. Go into a shop or a restaurant and there is background music. Since the 1930s, films have been accompanied by a score of greater or lesser distinction. Increasingly, announcements or continuity on radio or television are accompanied by a beat. Think how various it is – rock music, rap, country and western, gospel music, hymns, football songs, traditional jazz in pubs, contemporary jazz in jazz clubs, world music and so on. Yet philosophers have written almost entirely about Western classical music to the exclusion of the music that most people are familiar with. I suppose it is related to the fact that most philosophers are either from middle-class homes or climb into the middle class, where a passion for such music is part of what is required for a good life, in the sense in which Aristotle understood that idea. The educated and well-rounded individual is interested in classical music. The assumed pre-eminence of Western classical music is, as well, hardly just a matter of the appropriation of a certain type of music by the haute bourgeoisie, and its consequent elevation above other forms of music is not merely the whim of the dominant class. It is arguable, after all, that nothing in the rest of the musical world compares with it in depth, subtlety and its capacity to engage with the rest of our lives. This is partly a matter of sheer scale. A symphony may last for well over an hour. If other music goes on that long – as a work song might – it is likely to be repetitious. Perhaps only in Indian classical music can we find elsewhere organized sound at this length. At the end of *The Valkyrie*, Wotan bids his beloved daughter farewell, sending her to sleep, ringed with fire. The text is not hugely eloquent. Combined with the music, it becomes unbearably moving. It is followed by a transcendent passage for orchestra, whose slow-moving length is requisite for the depiction of an age-long sleep. This is a famous passage, lauded even by those who find Richard Wagner resistible. Let me quote another example. At the climax of Schumann's infrequently heard *Scenes from Goethe's Faust*, Faust sings of a moment of beauty that the ages cannot efface, reflecting the fact that the transitory nature of human experience does not cancel its value. Schumann underlines this with an orchestral tutti of tremendous power. Perhaps Schumann is an overrated composer, but he was, as this shows, capable of greatness. Such a climax would be out of place save in a work of length. These are both examples of music with a text. For a third and last example, illustrating a very different feature of Western classical music, consider a purely instrumental movement. Prokofiev's Fifth Symphony is probably his finest (although a case could be made for the Sixth). Its second movement is a whirlwind of a scherzo full of memorable and striking ideas. Yet the Fifth Symphony is a war symphony; it was composed rapidly in 1944 and the first movement is weighty and serious. The scherzo can sound flippant, but its surface is, I suspect, misleading. Its frenetic motion easily turns to hysteria; fear is only just below the surface. It is the forced jollity of those in mortal danger. To understand this movement, and there are many parallels with his great contemporary Dmitri Shostakovich, is to understand the significance of masks. In a tyranny these are essential, but they may also be a form of courage when something other than tyranny threatens; namely, death in wartime. Only an art capable of profundity can elicit reflections that bear in this way on our life outside that art.

In other cultures, music may serve other purposes. The degree of repetition that is largely absent from classical Western music may be part of what is required to generate a trance-like absorption in the listener. Listened to in the appropriate cultural context, its significance may become clear. What Western music shows, to a greater or less extent, are analogies with the novel, with a narrative that moves to a dénouement, and it is only in fairly recent music such as that of Steve Reich and other minimalists that we see an exception to this.

This, perhaps is the moment to anticipate another conclusion. On the whole philosophers have tended, although perhaps not consciously or explicitly, to fall in with the Hegelian notion that "absolute" or "pure" music or "music alone" is the pinnacle of the art towards which Western music, in its long history, has progressed. The sonata, the symphony or the string quartet are "higher" forms than song, dance or opera. Their beauties are the beauties of form. This forms part of an ideology that is deeply embedded in thinking about classical music. However, despite its attractions, I do not think it easy to defend what is known as "formalism": the idea that the merits of music are no more than the aesthetic appeal of beautiful patterns. I suggest that music is surrounded not only by texts, dances, dramatic situations, liturgies and narrative programmes but also by associations that may not be merely personal but may form connections with the landscape and history of the composer's native land, with the Zeitgeist and with a social and political context that form an aura, a rich backcloth, in terms of which we "read" the music.

If this draws music closer to the other arts that are generally representational (drama, fiction, film and painting represent people and places, real or imaginary), it is worth reflecting on some of the differences. One striking

3

and, I think, infrequently observed feature of the arts is that different individuals place differing requirements upon them. I don't know how much I differ from others in this but I listen to the same piece of music or read the same poem far more often than I re-read a novel and I re-read a novel more often than I see films again. I suppose some people watch a film on video as often as I listen to a favourite piece of music or some people re-read Jane Austen's *Persuasion* equally often. But even if this is the case, music does make rather special demands. In the case of most of the finest Western music, we have an art form where the performer has to practise over and over again. The requirements of quality are thus very stringent indeed if a player is not to tire of the music as a result of this constant repetition. Of course, we should not assume that the rewards the player gets from practice are strictly comparable with those the passive listener gets from hearing. For the pianist, the physical exercise involved in playing the piano, the intimate connection with the instrument, the dance of the fingers across the keyboard, is very important. This daily contact with the keyboard is a necessary part of life, "bodily gesture as well as sound", as Charles Rosen says. He concludes his recent book, *Piano Notes*,[1] with the remark that the physical pleasure of playing will, if anything does, ensure the survival of piano music. Nevertheless, although I think that the interest in mastering a piece, in solving problems of fingering and tempo, is, to an extent, independent of the interest the listener takes in the music, even when we allow this the main point remains untouched. Music of stature can be played over and over again with interest and satisfaction and the realization of what can or what should be done with a particular movement or a particular passage may only become clear after dozens or even hundreds of repetitions. It is true, as well, that repeated hearings or repeated readings are required to understand much of the greatest music and poetry. Indeed, a mark of greatness has always been that we need to re-encounter and constantly reassess. With fiction, however, it is often enough to remember the gist. If somebody hands me a copy of a Shakespeare sonnet I won't dismiss it by saying that I've read it. The only excuse for not reading it would be that I could recite it from memory. But fiction is unlike this. There are exceptions; the philosopher Gilbert Ryle read the Jane Austen novels every year and my music teacher reads the Charles Dickens novels every year, or at least a selection of them. He evidently does not regard this as some sort of mortification of the mind. But even so we re-read and are expected to re-read fiction far less often than poetry. So the brush-off "I've read it" is generally applicable to fiction even though it would make sense to say "Well, its worth reading again" if it was an outstanding novel. This is a non-trivial remark in this context but it usually would be otiose if it were a poem. Likewise with music.

Now music may be changing. There is talk of "disposable art" and a belief abroad that old assumptions about the "eternal value" of the arts are outmoded. I wonder if younger concert-goers look for an interest that does not go beyond the performance. They expect to be stimulated or entertained for a short while, but they may not want to hear the music again. It may be becoming a more ephemeral art. So, for at least some, the point of listening to new music is not to see if there is something that may become a significant part of their lives, a piece to which they will return with admiration and pleasure and in which they will expect to discover new subtleties the more carefully and frequently they listen. Listening to a contemporary piece may not mean any more than a single reading of a contemporary novel, something to interest you *pro tem* but to be then cast aside and not read again. If so, the nature of the reception of music is changing. Improvised music is the norm rather than traditional Western music, where a notated work is performed over and over again.

Be that as it may, traditionally the arts do vary and the consequences for judgement have been stark in their differences. I might go to a concert of new music and enjoy it in a way. But if I say I do not care whether I hear it again my judgement is somewhat damning. Normally we expect of music, if it is of the highest quality, that it will repay many re-hearings. And we usually do not desire to re-read a novel we have just read and enjoyed in the way we may ache to hear a piece of music over again within an hour or two of first hearing it. Poetry can, of course, be memorized, but we might want very much to read again or hear again a verse that we half remember. Painting and sculpture are rather different cases again. I imagine that people to whom painting matters a lot are suddenly convulsed with the desire to see something that is, unfortunately, half way across the world. If this is so, life is more frustrating for them than it is for the lover of books or music or even films, for reproductions are no substitute for the real thing.

All this evidently bears on the role the arts play in our lives. The relationship we have to art to some extent, and this I wish to explore later in this book, resembles the relationship we have with family and friends. In both cases the requirements vary. Some of our family we see frequently and would be unhappy at seeing them rarely. Some we see seldom but "keep in touch", while others we see or write to occasionally. Likewise with the arts, although, as I have said, the arts vary in the extent to which they permit this intimacy. It is a contingency that a man who was a close friend lives in Malta or Brisbane and that I have not seen him for years. It is a contingency also that a favourite painting is in The Hague and that I have only seen it once in the flesh. But for rich Westerners, books and music are rarely the victim of such contingencies. Only if they are out of print or deleted are they inaccessible.

This book is a mixture of the general and particular. My experience in teaching music is that the philosophical issues that arise most frequently are, first, what distinguishes music from noise or ambient sound and, secondly, how can the quality of music be anything else than a matter of individual taste? It is thus difficult to write about the philosophical issues that arise out of music without encountering problems that constitute the philosophy of the arts more generally. Chapter 2 begins with a general discussion of what it is for an artefact to be a work of art before going on to consider some of the more specific questions about the nature of music. Chapter 4 is perhaps more general than any of the others in that nearly all the questions I raise about the nature and measurement of artistic value arise equally for the other arts. Only when we consider performance are the questions more narrowly focused. So some of the questions I shall raise in this book are questions that are equally a source of puzzlement in literature or drama or film. But most are specific to music; questions about the status of a work of music and its relation to performance do arise with respect to the other performing arts such as dance, but because music's relationship to its notation is far more significant than is the relationship between dance and its notation, the analogies with mathematics that have so often been canvassed have a greater pertinence here. Chapter 3, in particular, discusses a question that is peculiar to music and has always been central to philosophical discussion of it: can music have a meaning? If so, what can it be?

I must issue a few warnings. I discuss differing theories about the nature of the musical work and its meaning and value. I have tried to represent fairly both the strengths and the weaknesses of the views that have been put forward. Very few positions in philosophy have nothing to be said for them. But I make no pretence of impartiality. A decent philosophical book puts forward various positions and the positions, of course, are my own, even where I share them with other thinkers. What I have tried to do is to say clearly when a view is my own and when it is likely to meet with opposition. I strongly suspect that what I have to say towards the end of the chapter on value is the most controversial part of this book. However, these are conclusions that are the result of long thought about verdicts on merit, and they seem interesting to me. But I expect some readers to disagree strongly.

Secondly, some of my musical judgements may seem rather eccentric to the reader. I have some strong likes and dislikes. I have tried to tone down the idiosyncrasies of my judgements but they will keep "toning up" again. I have therefore given up, in the conviction that the best I can do is to warn against them. Unfortunately, as far as this issue is concerned, many of my arguments require that I consider cases where opinion sharply varies. It seemed, then, that the best course is to take real cases rather than fictional cases. Were I to take an imaginary case, such as the supposition that Beethoven's middle quartets are not much good, or that Miles Davis was a rotten musician, the consequent astonishment and irritation would only get in the way of an appreciation of the issues. So I have taken cases where some of us seem to be at odds with much musical opinion. I think it was probably puzzlement over the peremptory nature of our tastes that caused me to become interested in aesthetics in the first place. I have always been troubled by the way that people differ in their judgements of value. In my last book, *Music and Humanism*, I wrestled with this problem of diverging tastes, attributing what conformity there is to the existence of an ideology, embodied in the canon, that directs our judgements. Thus classical musicians think of the central tradition as Austro-German and regard music from other countries as marginal or provincial to a greater or lesser extent. Our ambivalent relationship to this official history explains in part the difficulty we have with musicians outside this canon and our defensiveness about them once we have recognized major talents who do not belong to the dominant tradition. But I did not consider the possibility of divergent judgements within a common taste. These, and the difficulties they raise, are discussed in Chapter 4.

Thirdly, as my own philosophical life nears its end I have become increasingly disenchanted with the tradition of philosophical analysis, not because few analyses have been successfully completed but because, when the concepts are interesting, they cannot be. Philosophical analysis is the programme that attempts to provide necessary and sufficient conditions for the application of a concept like "knowledge" or "truth" or, relevant here, "work of art". Chapter 2 gives some reasons why I think this exercise is futile. Again, this is a judgement that will not find too much general acceptance and it is no good pretending otherwise. For many philosophers, conceptual analysis is their *raison d'être* and to challenge it is to challenge something deeply lodged within their philosophical ideology. On the other hand, as I said earlier, I am not in the business of writing a book that does not state the truth as I see it.

To reject the programme of analysis is not to object to the tradition of analytic philosophy. This book is in that tradition. I am interested in positions that can be stated clearly and defended by argument. Ideally, I want to know what the world must be like if a philosophical claim is to be true. Otherwise, I do not think philosophy is an intellectual discipline and there seems no very good reason to practise it. This means that the ideas introduced by some writers on music find no place here, writers such as Arthur Schopenhauer and Suzanne Langer.[2] I readily admit that I do not understand what could be meant by the former's observation that music is the image of the will itself, and nothing I have read has made this much clearer to me, although Schopenhauer was probably important in raising the status of music among the arts. But although I find analytic philosophy a fascinating and worthwhile task in itself, nothing, of course, that a philosopher can do enriches our lives in the way that the best of art does. No philosopher, however eminent, who is realistic about his subject and his achievements would think them worth the value of a minor but lasting lyric, an unforgettable carol or a comic masterpiece in film like *The Blues Brothers*. Towards the end of his life, Benjamin Britten grouped a collection of settings under the title *Sacred and Profane*. One of the choral settings is of a carol, "Maiden in the Mor Lay", and it lasts just a minute and a half. I have studied, taught and written about philosophy for fifty years. I have been fortunate. The subject has always absorbed me. But I venture that, compared with the genius displayed by Britten in this tiny piece, the genius, undoubted genius, displayed by Kant in his *Critique of Pure Reason* is minuscule. This is not even one of Britten's greatest works, but its sheer invention takes our breath away. Such is the disparity between the creative artist and the philosopher. Only when, and how rarely, a philosopher like Hume in his *Dialogues Concerning Natural Religion* brings to philosophy the sort of literary elegance and moral passion displayed by Samuel Johnson in his *Review of Soame Jenyns* can the claims we make for the philosopher be remotely comparable to those that we can make for the creative artist.

What I attempt here is the next best thing. I can try to interest those of you who have thought, with puzzlement, about this wonderful art. I hope to clear up misunderstandings that block our appreciation of the art of music and some of these misunderstandings are philosophical in nature. They may distort our judgement of music. Here a philosopher should aspire to be what Locke called "an underlabourer". The only way he can hope to enrich our lives in any way remotely comparable to that of the creative artist is to succeed in what Horace mistakenly thought was the task of the poet: "to please and instruct".

Chapter 1

Overture and beginnings

Philosophical reflection on music is more than two thousand years old but it is patchy. Beyond a handful of names, beginning, perhaps, with Plato and Aristotle and leaping two thousand years to Eduard Hanslick and Edmund Gurney, most of what has been written is only of interest to historians of ideas. But the past two decades have seen an extraordinary flowering in the aesthetics of music that has eclipsed earlier speculations. This philosophical activity has been predominantly analytic in style. It prizes and expects clarity and detail in argument. There are other philosophical traditions but I am not aware that there has been any sudden efflorescence in writing on the aesthetics of music in these other provinces. The newcomer to analytic philosophy may easily form the impression that a great deal of it is devoted to the invention and solution of rather arcane problems requiring considerable intelligence but rather remote from the rest of humanity and life as we know it. There is some substance in this but it is not an entirely just verdict. Analytic philosophy can have implications for our lives by making us reflect upon unconsidered presuppositions; sometimes it may lead us to reflect on our lives and our values and cause us either to value things differently or perhaps more directly to alter our conduct. If utilitarians persuade people that they should grade their actions solely on the principle of what maximizes happiness, then people will change. At the other end of the spectrum, the issue of whether the concept of truth is evidence-transcendent, which has occupied many philosophers for much of their time over the past three decades, does not strike me as one that is likely to have any immediate results for the way we live our lives. It has its fascinations, of course, but these do become rather close to the fascinations of doing a crossword without the satisfactions afforded by finding an answer. The distinction is not, of course, absolute. Even the most arcane issues leave eddies in their wake that may make imperative certain more mundane decisions, and we shall see that this is true, perhaps surprisingly, of the question of realism in music. In writing about the philosophy of music I shall try to concentrate on issues that illuminate musical listening and practice. Although I shall write about apparently esoteric topics such as what a musical work is, these all eventually debouch into more practical issues of playing and listening.

My reason for taking this approach is that philosophy is, I think, important when it is a cultural critique or an originating force in culture. Most often a philosopher picks up ideas that are in the air and elaborates them into some sort of system. Individualism was in the air in the Renaissance, as we can see from the essays of Montaigne or from *Hamlet*. In both of these, in their different ways, there appears a persona that strikes us as utterly idiosyncratic. But it was a philosopher, Hobbes, who elaborated this conception of the individual as a self-contained unit concerned with satisfying his or her own desires, an individual who competes with others; he considered its implications for the body politic in what has been called his "possessive individualism". Descartes's picture of the self-contained individual whose claims to knowledge need a grounding and a justification, I suggest, equally "rationalizes" ideas that were in the air in Western European culture. The greatest and most important philosophical achievements either "rationalize" and render explicit what is implicit in the culture of the times or "deconstruct it", as Hume did, paradigmatically, in *Dialogues Concerning Natural Religion*. In this way philosophers may be both contributors to and critics of what is often thought of as the "ideology" of a society. They contribute to or subtract from a cultural hegemony. Many of the philosophical issues that arise about music arise because music has been understood in terms of those ideas that dominate in the culture, ideas whose origins do not necessarily have much to do with purely musical issues. Thus the central feature of reflection on music between, say, 1750 and 1950 was the idea that music is a language, specifically a language of the emotions in which the composer expresses his mental state and communicates it to the listener. Such an idea owes much to Romanticism, indeed it is hardly thinkable without a general romanticism, (recall Wordsworth's famous remark about "emotion recollected in tranquillity"[1]). Equally, nineteenth-century reflection in the Hegelian tradition led to the idea that music evolves into an art that owes nothing to a text or programme. "Pure" or "absolute" music is the pinnacle of the art, perhaps even the art to which all others aspire.

Pertinent to the rest of this book is the question of what happens when philosophers introduce ideas that are rather more obliquely related to the stock of everyday concepts. The invention of a technical concept is partly a piece of hubris on the part of a writer; she expects her reader to expend time in memorizing its significance and, possibly, looking back through the pages to remind himself of the definition. Of course, sometimes the labour is not great. Everybody can see what is meant by "mentalese"; it indicates an internal mental language, a language of thought. Neologisms can be well chosen. More significantly, in a philosopher it is a danger sign. More often a writer takes an existing word, such as "utility" or "person", and, quite often unawares, delicately adjusts the meaning. Where "person" was both a legal term and used to describe a role-player, philosophers use it to describe the human beings that people our globe and any putative rational aliens, and with that shift and replacement come problems. Sometimes their usage adds to or modifies the ideology of their culture. If their invention or adaptation is picked up by others, the way we think may change. An example is Thomas Kuhn's use of the word "paradigm", which has become widespread outside philosophy. It is possible that words like "soul" or "spirit" originated in this way.

This picture of philosophy as both a cultural force and critique is very distant from that which prevails in academia. Aestheticians have concentrated instead on the programme of philosophical analysis. Analysis is the programme of giving necessary and sufficient conditions for the application of terms like "law of nature", "morally good action", "work of art", "truth" and "knowledge", to name just a few. Thus, in the middle of the twentieth century, "knowledge" was defined as "justified true belief", only for counter-examples to ruin this analysis. Such is the dominance of the model of science in our culture – understandably – that when doubts arose about analysis, refuge was sought in the idea that philosophy is a kind of science, acknowledging the ways in which great scientists have sometimes seemed to be involved in philosophy of science. Thus many philosophers now claim that their discipline is some sort of branch of science, a view that I believe to be a grave mistake. The style of argument in philosophy is different and the "facts" appealed to are familiar and banal. Philosophical refutations depend not on experiments but on reminders; very characteristically the cut and thrust of philosophical debate depends on adjusting a thesis in the light of apparent counter-examples to it. The characteristic philosophical error is that of overlooking something that is in front of you. How else can we explain the persistence of philosophical theories that present infanticide as no crime or claim that animals do not feel pain because they do not talk about it?

The project of analysis has lingered on in the philosophy of art. Indeed, much of the history of the subject since its coming of age as a subsection of philosophy four decades ago has been the attempt to say what a work of art is. In parallel, we have the attempted "analysis" of the concept of the "work of music", a generic term not much used by musicians. What does its advent portend? The fact that it is comparatively recent and that its use is conspicuous in the talk of philosophers and in general talk about music rather than in the conversation of practising musicians or music-lovers ought to give us pause. It suggests a certain artificiality; perhaps "work of music" was coined in the course of general reflection about the place of music in our culture. There is certainly a well-argued case for regarding the concept of a work of music as one that developed in the nineteenth century when the status of music as one of the fine arts was still not entirely secure. Works of music were posited as analogues of the works of art found in art galleries and museums. To talk of a work of music was to draw an implicit comparison with sculptures and paintings. The concert hall was the "museum" where such items were displayed. Thus the concept of a "work of music" plays a role that we need to consider.[2] I believe that when we do we shall feel less sanguine about either the possibility of an analysis of the concept that will command general acceptance or about the utility of such an analysis.

Now if it is true that "work of music" is a rather late arrival, a term used by thinkers about music rather than by practising musicians or the general public, there is a dilemma here. To the extent that the concept up for analysis is quasi-technical (that is, coined by specialists as a term of art to use among themselves) it is, to that degree, private property. Questions raised in analysis may indeed have answers but those answers will arrive directly or by few steps. It is a self-inflicted solution. Compare this with everyday concepts used by many; these may have fluctuating senses or delicate gradations of sense. Examples are aesthetic concepts like "elegant" or "beautiful", or moral concepts like "decent" or "a good man". That different speakers apply them to different objects suggests that there may be overlapping usages rather than an identity of meaning in such words. These differing shades of meaning can reflect quite important differences between people and the ways they think about music or morals or anything else. For it is how our usages differ from others' that reveals what is distinctive about ourselves and, more generally, our culture. Philosophy, then, in so far as it reflects the latter, becomes a sort of a priori cultural anthropology. It shows us how we differ in the ways we think. But this philosophical task, of course, is incompatible with the ideal of analysis, for that shows the essence of a concept, such as the concept of knowledge. Analysis possesses a generality. What I find interesting here is how analysis so often privileges one sort of knowledge, such as the logical or mathematical over others. Of course, analysis reflects the philosopher's wish to universalize. But in many areas philosophy, born from the urge to find general patterns, has to learn that sometimes generalization is fruitless. For example, what is called "music" differs. To endorse and privilege one sort of music, the Western classical tradition of an increasingly fully notated music, is to simplify and distort, as I shall try to show. There are many varieties of music. This in itself will not preclude analysis; there would simply have to be many different analyses, one for each variety of music. Rather, it is the loose fit of such concepts, the fuzziness of the boundaries and the significance of such fuzziness that makes analysis impossible.

Early speculations

I remarked that philosophizing about music is over two millennia old.[3] We know much more about what the ancient Greeks thought about music than about how their music sounded. The Greek word we translate as "music" is more inclusive than ours, as well. It is associated with dancing and, in particular, with poetry and physical exercise as well as with singing and the playing of instruments. Indeed, one aspect of philosophical discussion about music we would do well to bear in mind is the fact that, even though we may accurately translate a word as music in the sense that it refers, in its original language, to what we think of as music, singing and the playing of instruments, it may have implications that our word "music" lacks. There is good reason to think that the nuances of our word "music" have shifted even over the past three centuries.

In particular the Greek conception of music was dualistic in two ways. First, and very strikingly, the Greeks conceived of the celestial world as in harmony. Music described the mathematical relationships that held between heavenly bodies. Indeed, it was assumed that there was a music of the spheres and there was discussion as to why human beings could not hear it; was this a consequence of our being used to it from birth so that by habituation we no longer heard it – much as you may not notice the ticking of the clock – or were exceptional individuals, like Pythagoras perhaps, able to hear it? This mathematical conception of music as abstract intervals, perhaps best translated as "harmony", a matter of harmonic relationships expressed numerically, was to play an important part in European thought up to the Renaissance. As late as Jean Philippe Rameau, we find the idea that the pleasure music offers is a consequence of the way it imitates the divinely ordered and mathematical structure of nature. Additionally and separately, for the ancient Greeks music was what was heard, sung or played on the lute or aulos, as it still is for us. The second way in which the Greek conception of music is dualistic has its modern progeny. Music was seen as having very opposed aspects, one of which was ecstatic and frenzied and the other civilizing and educational. We are familiar with Nietzsche's distinction between the art of Dionysius and the art of Apollo: the one intoxicating and orgasmic, and the other calm, reflective, ordered and balanced. We even see the contrast in the music of a single composer, Stravinsky, in *The Rite of Spring* on the one hand and *Apollon Musagète* or *Agon* on the other. The first aspect is what older people have found alarming in rock music, beginning with Bill Haley and continuing with the Rolling Stones. Finally, it is worth remarking the Greek emphasis on the pleasure that music gives, which is particularly striking in Aristotle. Aristotle's emphasis on the fact that music involves movement is also anticipatory. We will need to consider in more detail later on both the idea that music brings pleasure and the idea that music's power comes from the way it moves people. It speaks to the hearts of men. But the distinction between music as an abstract business of tonal relationships and music as heard is a contrast that is still evident in contemporary discussion.

These varying conceptions of music lasted well into the Middle Ages. For medieval thinkers music was in part a theoretical branch of knowledge, a science of numbers, and in part an aid to mystical experience. But it was also an aural attraction: a seductive matter of the senses that presented a temptation to indulge in those worldly pleasures that divines regarded with considerable suspicion. All these ideas were rooted in Greek thinking about music and were transmitted to medieval thinkers through the immensely influential writings of Boethius. The belief, too, that the life of the mind was of superior value to the work of the artisan implied that the dexterity required of the performing musician was considered a poor thing compared to theoretical understanding. Medieval writers would often scoff at the singer ignorant of the theory that underlay the music he sang. This prejudice certainly has not vanished. There are relics of this attitude in modern anecdotes about the ignorance of orchestral musicians and singers. Recently an eminent conductor who conducted the Vienna Philharmonic in Vaughan Williams's "Tallis Fantasia" said that the orchestra admired the music immensely and enquired whether Vaughan Williams had written much else and whether Tallis was still alive; and a flautist with a leading American orchestra who was regarded as a bit of an intellectual by his colleagues was approached with the question "Who came first – Mozart or Verdi?" These may be apocryphal – indeed it is hard to think otherwise – but their relevance lies in the attitude they enshrine.

With the early Renaissance, a greater emphasis was placed upon the pleasure that music brings. We read of the "sweetness of music" – perhaps the main descriptive phrase to be found in late medieval writing is "dulce" or sweetness – and of the importance of "moving the affections". But this did not rule out a very considerable interest in the mathematical proportions that underlay the stringing of instruments. A case was made for a return to nature, a reaction against the complications of late medieval polyphony. At the same time, improvements in the technology of keyboard instruments required great attention to the issues of tuning and temperament. Musicians became theorists as well as composers and performers and the gap between theoretical understanding and practical competence narrowed. Theory, too, had less and less to do with the supposed celestial harmonies. Rather, the Pythagorean doctrine transmuted in the hands of later thinkers like Rameau into the idea that music, like nature, was under the sway of laws. It was an enterprise of reason.

These seeds came to fruition in the Renaissance in two ways. First of all the concept of what is "natural" became a sort of talisman. Anybody reasonably widely read in Renaissance literature will be aware of its ubiquity. Both the church and secular composers were uneasy at the earlier custom of setting a single word to such cascades of notes that the sense of the word was lost. Theorists and composers (and they were usually the same individual) began to consider what sort of music was appropriate for the setting of a particular text and music as accompanied monody began to seem "natural", a weasel word if ever there was one. Theorists justified their preferences as a return to the ideas of the Greeks. In both sacred and secular music, the music was seen as subservient to the text, an idea that constantly resurfaced in the time of Claudio Monteverdi and in the arguments of Raniero Calzabigi, Christoph von Gluck's librettist, and, of course, with some degree of anachronism in Richard Strauss's opera *Capriccio*. Music, it was thought, should move the affections, and it did so by the choosing of music which served the emotional features of the text. The German doctrine of the *Affektenlehre* developed the idea that music is linked with the passions. Descartes wrote in *Les Passions de l'âme* that the purpose of music is to arouse certain emotions in us, a doctrine reminiscent of those philosophical theories that advocate "arousalism", which is an idea we shall examine in detail later. The second legacy of Renaissance thinking about music, then, is the notion that, as speech is the language of the mind, so music is the language of the heart.

Eduard Hanslick

There are philosophers, and Schopenhauer springs immediately to mind, who have been thought to have influenced composers. Wagner was certainly influenced by Schopenhauer, although whether he would have composed differently if he hadn't read Schopenhauer is as debatable as the question of what precisely Richard Strauss owed to Nietzsche beyond the programme of *Also Sprach Zarathustra*. I am much more interested in philosophers of music who have influenced the way music is received; they may do this by encouraging us to pay attention to certain features of the music, say its form as opposed to its expressive qualities of lightness or gloom; consequently they may directly or indirectly suggest a canon of music that causes us to privilege certain composers or certain national schools at the expense of others. Thus a view that regards "pure" or "abstract" instrumental music as the pinnacle of the art tends to elevate the symphony, the sonata or the fugue at the expense of opera and song or promote certain types of symphonic writing over others. Thus a preference for Brahms over Tchaikovsky may be partly explained. Of course such prejudices, if that is what they are, can also be a product of certain national biases and they can vary. I recall an eminent Russian pianist saying that as a young man he was led to think of the Russian school as having a sensitivity and soul lacking in the more arid intellectual products of western and central Europe, and particularly the first Viennese school, a school that most Westerners are educated to see as the pinnacle of musical achievement. These latter considerations apart, the thinker about music who had done as much as any to influence ways of listening is, at the same time, one of the two thinkers who have most influenced the analytic movement in the philosophy of music: Eduard Hanslick.

Where modern philosophizing about music is concerned, the first important figure, probably the most important figure prior to the extraordinary developments in the subject in the past two decades, is Hanslick (1825–1904), the Austrian music critic familiar to music lovers through his skirmishes with Wagner. He has been thought of as the arch-formalist, a formalist being somebody who thinks that the value of music lies in its formal properties of design and line and not in its expressive capacity, but he never denied that music "calls into life sorrow and joy". What formalism is we shall need to consider in a little more detail here and more fully in Chapter 3.

Hanslick seems to have planned his *On the Musically Beautiful*[4] as a prolegomena to a fuller treatment of the subject; however that more expansive work was never published. What we have instead is a discussion of what he thinks of as misconceptions about the art current in his time. In fact, he supplies in an appendix a sort of rogues' gallery of quotations from various writers, many of whom maintain forms of the thesis known as "expressionism": the thesis, first, that the purpose of music is to express, represent or arouse feeling, and, secondly, that feelings are the content of music and that music is the language of feeling. Both claims are, he thinks, false; it is not the case that the purpose of music is to arouse the feelings and feelings are not the content of music.[5]

Hanslick's book is, in fact, tricky. It is, despite its brevity, not very well organized, sometimes inconsistent and, in places, pretty obscure, and this explains the fact that most writers on Hanslick manage to miss some of the salient points or misrepresent some of his ideas while getting others right. (His account of imagination is difficult to comprehend and to persevere with this on the assumption that there are some specific ideas here that a temporarily inarticulate author has failed to get across is, I think, premature.) Nevertheless the importance of the book is undeniable, firstly because it contains some arguments that are remarkably sophisticated for its period, and, secondly, because Hanslick expresses, mostly implicitly, what we might call an "ideology" of music in which instrumental or "pure" or "absolute" music is seen as the pinnacle of the art, a view that has only been seriously challenged by musical thinkers in the past few decades. This is related, as we shall see, to what has been described as "formalism": the idea that music is essentially a matter of patterns in sound that have no meaning or reference to the world beyond music or that, if they do, these connections are irrelevant to its value. (Part of the remit of formalism is the encouragement of a suspicion of instrumental colour. Music that relies on ear-catching timbres was assumed meretricious. If music could not be played without loss in a piano arrangement or "reduction", as it is usually called, it was suspect. Its merit must lie in the aesthetic appeal of its patterns of sound.) In some respects Hanslick was a formalist, but what is meant here by "formalism" needs spelling out.

If formalism means that music cannot be described properly as having expressive features such as gravity or joy, then Hanslick, despite what he says at some points, is not a formalist. He allows that music can be expressive, although he does think these descriptions are figurative. What he argues is that this has nothing to do with its beauty.[6] The constant harping on beauty is an unfortunate feature of Hanslick's discussion. There is great music, as there is great painting, that is ugly. If we make the discriminations required, we can see that beauty is a feature of some art of quality, but not of all. Even Mozart sometimes wrote music that it is simply a perversion of language to describe as beautiful; the splendidly craggy

17

"Eine kleine Gigue" K.574 is an example and in work by composers such as Bach, Bartók, Stravinsky or Shostakovich we find quantities of wonderful music that cannot accurately be described as beautiful. So let me substitute for "beauty" the unsonorous "artistic merit". Is Hanslick right in the claim that expressive features are irrelevant to the artistic merit of music? Up to a point. There is plenty of music that has expressive qualities and is of no aesthetic merit. Further, possessing expressive features is not, in general, a positive reason for value. For sometimes the expressive features music has count against its value. It might be sentimental, for instance, although we can easily imagine situations where sentimentality might be a merit (for example, in an opera where a character is required to display sentimentality). But, on the other hand, to say that music expresses joy is to give a reason for valuing the music *ceteris paribus*. What we can say, and Hanslick would probably deny this, is that music would be an impoverished art if it did not have expressive features for then it would cease to reflect or comment on our cultures in the way it can, something that I illustrate later in this book. Part of the value that great music can have for us lies in its expressive features and then it is not surprising that some have thought that possession of expressive features must be a prima facie merit. But such expressive features are neither necessary nor sufficient for its merit. Such features can always be defeated by other considerations. The music might be lively but poorly organized.

I remarked earlier that what is sometimes overlooked is the fact that Hanslick allows expressive descriptions of music, if a little grudgingly. Music can be "arrogant, peevish, tender, spirited, yearning". "We may use such epithets", he says, "... provided we never lose sight of the fact that we are using them only figuratively and take care not to say such things as 'This music portrays arrogance'".[7] In fact most writers will agree that when we say that music is yearning we use language metaphorically, although, as I shall explain later, there are some difficulties here. His reasons for denying that music can be literally yearning are generally sound and represent the most advanced part of his case.

First, he argues that music is incapable of representing any specific feelings because no judgements can be detected in the music.[8] When I yearn it is for something; there is, to put it in modern parlance, an object of my yearning. We nowadays think of emotions as having "intentional objects"; if I am angry, then I am angry about something and this "directedness", associated with the work of the philosopher and psychologist Franz Brentano, characterizes human mentality to a great extent. Admittedly there are mental states that do not have any specific object and often these are used, with less metaphorical weight, to describe music. But

Hanslick is right to claim that the specificity of emotions depends largely upon the objects they have. Judgements enter the picture because of the significance of beliefs in this equation. I have beliefs about the object that are highly pertinent. That is, if I fear something or somebody, setting aside cases where we speak of irrational or mistaken fear, then it is because I correctly judge that that person or object threatens me. The difference between fear and anger has more to do with the judgements about the objects of these respective emotions and less to do with the "feeling-tone" of these psychological states. It may not feel very different to be frightened rather than angry but the judgements about the objects in view are very different. In one case we are typically threatened and in the other case characteristically injured in some way or other.

You may have noticed the use of the word "represent" here. Hanslick is not particularly careful; sometimes he speaks of representing and sometimes of expressing.[9] Music can represent, although its powers to do so are limited. Haydn's *Creation* begins with a famous representation of chaos, largely through some highly unorthodox harmonic shifts. But we do not naturally say that sad music "represents" sadness. Our misgivings about the viability of this locution are partly due to the fact that "x represents y" is usually a move in a discursive process: "Let this salt cellar represent Wellington's army and this pepper pot Napoleon's, then ...". Undoubtedly paintings represent their objects and there is no discursive process there, save in interpreting the painting, which, as we shall see later, involves further issues. But music is a temporal art and the analogies that are relevant to any attempt to introduce the concept of representation into music are discursive. So if we are told that a violin passage represents the wife of the composer, we are inclined to say "And then what?" But since music does not make statements, the point of representation is somewhat oblique. All in all, we are better off with the vocabulary of "expression".

A second argument offered by Hanslick is that some music seems to have no expressive content. Bach's *Forty-Eight Preludes and Fugues* is the example he offers.[10] You might be a little uncertain as to whether this is so, but no doubt examples can be found of music that it is very hard to characterize in expressive terms. You might consider some parts of Bach's *The Art of Fugue* to be music for which it is hard to find a suitable expressive description. Or you might find examples in Pierre Boulez's *Pli selon pli*.

Thirdly, he argues that there is music on whose merit we are agreed, although we may differ on its expressive content. His example is the music of Mozart, which is characterized differently by different critics;[11] indeed, he might have cited the fact that the expressive qualities of the great Symphony in G minor are described in ways that are not mutually compatible by a single author, Schumann, on different occasions. There are other examples. Haydn's "Military" Symphony might have sounded ferocious and threatening to its contemporaries; to us it is inclined to sound jolly. Of course, it will be said that this does not preclude one of these descriptions being correct and the other incorrect, but that reply does not cut the mustard. Where we have, as we do, a difference of judgement about the expressive features of a piece of music by two equally attentive and well-equipped critics, we have grounds for accepting both. Yet they cannot both hold. In Chapter 4 we shall look in some detail at difficulties of this kind.

Finally, the same music can express different feelings in different contexts. The borrowings of Bach and Handel[12] offer examples of secular music being re-used to set sacred texts. The expressive nature of the text differs radically but the music was deemed equally suitable for an erotic or a religious text. This, of course, might not be an objection to the idea that music is expressive. For if both of these texts express a more generic state, say, contentment, then the music would be suitable for both texts and its use in the two contexts unobjectionable. The argument does, however, have purchase upon those who claim that music is very precise in its expressive features. Mendelssohn famously said that what music expresses is "too precise for words" and, to this thesis, Hanslick's argument is an effective counter.[13] If erotic satisfaction and religious peace are different emotions, then they cannot both be true descriptions of the expressive features of the music. Now Bach and Handel, who after all should know, thought the music appropriate for different texts. If they were right the character of the music is only appropriate because of its more general features such as contentment.

Of these four arguments, it is the first that has the most weight. In Chapter 3 we shall consider how it may be answered.

The expression of feeling is not, Hanslick concludes, that which gives music its merit, contrary to what many previous thinkers claimed. At most music can "depict" the motion that attends an affect like love.[14] The beauty of music is a beauty of tones. Tones are its content and music is peculiar in that content and form cannot be separated.[15]

So far we have been considering Hanslick's reservations about the idea that music can represent feelings. But what about the thesis that music's purpose is to arouse feelings? It is, after all, possible that music might arouse feelings while not representing them or having them as content. Now this cannot, in Hanslick's view, bear on the quality of the music. We need to distinguish the quality of the music from the feelings that it produces. In fact, he thinks of the appreciation of music in very different terms from the mere occurrence of feelings stimulated by it. We grasp the music when we follow it. In a justly famous description, Hanslick refers to "the mental satisfaction which the listener finds in continuously following and anticipating the composer's designs, here to be confirmed in his expectations, there to be agreeably led astray".[16] This is what is involved in hearing the music for its own sake; it is not a matter of being in a warm bath of sensations and feelings stimulated by the music. What Hanslick scorns is an ecstatic wallowing in rather than a following of the music. If it was only the sensations that mattered (and here Hanslick anticipates a famous observation by Wittgenstein), then they might be obtained in some other way, perhaps by a fine cigar.[17] Curiously, he does in fact think that the performer may lose herself in the act of performing so that the cliché of the artist as "possessed" by a mental state that she cannot but articulate in the form of a work of art, holds of the pianist, say.[18] In fact, such a picture is equally silly as a description of the performer; she may not feel the emotion the music expresses; indeed, an over-indulgence in the sentiments of the music may distract; she, too, has to think about what she is doing, work out how a piece should be performed and consider the technical implications for fingering, etc. So Hanslick brusquely rebuts the view that music's purpose is to arouse feelings; he remarks that beauty has no purpose; it is mere form and remains beauty even if no feelings are aroused. It is here that his position seems most resolutely formalist.

Hanslick is right to stress the difference between the properties of the music and our response to it and the distinction certainly matters when we come to those questions of value that are his main concern. There is a difference between the value of the music and the value of the experience we get out of it, for a start. We might think, and a surprising number of people do, that the main purpose of composing music is to give others pleasure, yet any thoughtful individual will recognize that there is music that we admire very much but from which we don't get pleasure, unless the word "pleasure" is to be stretched or substantially redefined. It seems hard to deny that *The Merry Widow* offers its audience more in the way of pleasure than the *Goldberg Variations* yet it would be absurd to rate the first higher than the second. Equally, there isn't much doubt that *Kind of Blue* is a superior work of art to "Everybody Needs Somebody to Love" as sung by the Blues Brothers, but it seems pretty likely that the latter offers the greater pleasure. Of course, this simply starts a debate. Perhaps there are different sorts of pleasure. You will go on listening to *Kind of Blue* for the rest of your life at regular intervals; you think about it, about Miles Davis's use of modes, and you keep noticing new things about it.

21

"Everybody Needs Somebody to Love" does not offer rewards of that sort. These questions arise again even if I take two pieces of music that are more comparable in stature. How do I compare the pleasure I take at the subtle harmonic structure of Ravel's Trio in A minor as against the intense and intoxicating effect of Bach's Mass in B minor? (I return to some of these issues in Chapter 4.)

Hanslick hoped to begin an exploration of music that would use the methods of the natural sciences.[19] Now the word "science" is often used in a very general way; we speak of the "human sciences" and may not want to commit ourselves to the idea that they follow the same procedures and methods as the natural sciences such as physics, biology and chemistry. But Hanslick unquestionably has the natural sciences as a paradigm; he thinks of physiology and chemistry as models. If you think, as he does, of a movement in music as developing from a melodic germ, then the model of a crystal developing is perhaps a half-decent analogy. Hanslick emphasizes the fundamental importance of melody. All of this sits rather uneasily with his remark that it is the spontaneity of art that makes it different from physical experiment.

I suspect, although these things are difficult to demonstrate, that Hanslick was an influence on the formalism of such musical thinkers as Heinrich Schenker. Intellectual relationships are often mysterious and we can be influenced indirectly through intermediaries even when we are familiar with the origins of an idea. Schenker tried to demonstrate that the unity of a complex movement can be displayed by showing it to be the elaboration of a basic cadence, something he called the "*Urlinie*"; he did this by stripping a movement down to its essentials so that a complex movement such as the first movement of Beethoven's Fifth Symphony can be shown to be the elaboration of a basic triad of the home key. Hanslick believed in the autonomy of music; his privileging of the tonal combinations as the locus of artistic merit is what makes us want to call him a formalist. He opposes any idea of music as a "mixed medium" and views the music as what is important in the setting of words.

Edmund Gurney

The other major figure, prior to the developments of the very recent past, who rewards study is Edmund Gurney (1847–1887). His *The Power of Sound* is not read as much as it should be, partly, I suspect, because of its sheer length. It is also repetitive and not well organized. Readers who have managed the first couple of hundred pages may not be encouraged by the observation "it seems better to encounter the charge of tediousness than of obscurity".[20] Gurney was a Fellow of Classics at Trinity College, Cambridge for a time and tried his hand unsuccessfully at careers in music, medicine and law before becoming interested in the paranormal. He spent the years before his premature death working on ways of testing theories about telepathy, spiritualism and the like, although music seems to have been a steady passion. This experimental bias made Gurney an acute observer, a rather neglected merit in a philosopher. Remarks like his observation on melody show this: "a common (though very far from universal) feature of a simple melody which is strongly approved on first acquaintance is that, while it seems perfectly natural and easy to catch, one cannot quite get hold of it afterwards ...".[21] Try playing "by ear" one of Prokofiev's more catchy melodies; even if you are skilled in this particular art, it is pretty difficult to land in the right key. Consider, too, the remark that when we remember a tune we don't usually recall it in its instrumental colour.[22] His prescient observation, following Hermann Helmholtz, that "the modern predominance of dissonant chords, and of perpetual modulational change, threatens to destroy the all-important feeling for tonality"[23] anticipates the musical developments of three decades later. His scientific interests also surface in the way he so often alludes to evolutionary explanations, albeit of a speculative form. He was, I think, puzzled by the development of the ability to discriminate pitches to a degree that is not required in the natural environment, although putting this down to the pleasure it gives hardly qualifies as a Darwinian explanation.

Like Hanslick, his discussion tends to make the unquestioned assumption that what matters is beauty and that beauty is a matter of form. But to a greater degree than Hanslick he anticipated contemporary interests in the philosophy of the arts. For example, his discussion of what a work of art is is very modern sounding. He proposes that a work of art is something designed by man with pleasure as its end.[24] This leads him to discuss what are nowadays called "negative emotions", such as horror or dread of death, whose stimulation by the arts seems a counter-example to the claim that pleasure is what art is designed for. He is not very successful in handling these issues, but he is hardly alone in this: "What is partially true of all the arts is wholly true of this one – that it must be judged by us directly in relation to pleasure, and that pleasure is the only criterion by which we can measure the relative worth of different specimens of it."[25] He is sceptical about the possibility of getting a consensus on musical value; all there is, it seems, is the pleasure of the individual. (I have already suggested, and will elaborate later, the view that such emphasis on pleasure is a mistake; but his emphasis on the primacy of the individual judgement is well founded.) Eventually he offers what we would now call a "functional theory of art" by defining art in terms of the intention of its creators to bring about particular states in its audience. He writes perceptively on the importance of originality and on the creative imagination. The work of art is "in the most literal sense a creation" and it possesses an organic unity. He observes, like Hanslick, how different the arts are from one another; indeed, he regularly compares and contrasts music and architecture. Gurney is at pains to point out dissimilarities and certainly is sceptical of the close parallels suggested by the adage that "architecture is frozen music".[26]

Musical analysis in the twentieth century was dominated, it is fair to say, by the ideas of Schenker and his followers. Of course, Gurney knows nothing of these later developments but it is easy to see that he would disapprove of them. Melody is central to Gurney's conception of music and, in this respect, he differs from Schenker. For harmony, thinks Gurney, is subsidiary, whereas in Schenker the harmonic cadence is basic. (Gurney is closer to the theoretician Rudolph Réti on this matter.) Our interest, he says, is in the surface of the music. What matters is "cogency of sequence at each point",[27] the enjoyment of the parts moment after moment. Overall structure, musical form and design are less significant in the pleasure of music. We learn, he thinks, very little from being told that a piece is in sonata form or that this, that or the other is the second subject other than having our attention drawn to "noticeable points" that may strike us. This extreme view is not very plausible; not only does it deny what seems to be the case, that our understanding of music is often conducive to our appreciation – and that holds even if we no longer admire it as much as we did before the flaws were pointed out – but it leaves Gurney with a reduced role for the judgement that we often make, that a piece has cogency and a satisfying overall structure. Consider the opening movement of Haydn's Quartet in D minor op. 76 no. 2, which is an exploration of what can be done with a bare fifth: two notes five tones apart. The answer is a very great deal indeed, in the hands of a master. But if you are not aware of the way the music develops from this tiny germ, much will pass you by. And what you lose is not merely an intellectual grasp; this awareness enters into your very excitement and interest in the progress of the music. Conversely, the overall effect of a piece may be disjointed and to see this, and to make that judgement, is important. Furthermore, one's judgement of the structural integrity of a piece may involve noticing thematic, harmonic or rhythmic relationships between movements as well as within a single movement.

Gurney introduces a rather unhelpful technical phrase to describe the way a succession of notes (or tones or pitches, if you prefer) forms a unity in which the parts are felt as indispensable, such that one has a sense of movement from the beginning of the melody to its end. He calls this musical process "Ideal Motion".[28] In this, the sense of movement and rhythm is essential. Indeed "some continuous groundwork of satisfied expectation is a necessity". This aspect of music is obviously central and has, as we shall see, been discussed by later thinkers. By contrast, harmonic progression makes sense in the absence of rhythm.

Perhaps the best known and, probably, the most widely read section of *The Power of Sound* is the chapter entitled "Music as Impressive and Music as Expressive". It is worth reading even if you find the rest of the tome indigestible, although rather typically it is disorganized, the crucial arguments appearing in comparatively terse prose at the end. Although Gurney read widely, I have found no evidence that he knew Hanslick's work, to which his own views show some resemblances. Like Hanslick, he did not think that the beauty of music was in general a product of its expressive features. Music may impress us while lacking expressive features. In a footnote (like Edward Gibbon in *The Decline and Fall of the Roman Empire,* the best of Gurney is often in his footnotes), he observes that the way we characterize music may be distinct from the effect it has on us, something on which I shall elaborate later in this book. Elsewhere he remarks perceptively, "mournful music, if sufficiently beautiful, may make us happy".[29]

Gurney attacks the idea that music is an art of expression, as he puts it, "the reproduction in tone language of the feeling in the mind of the composer", reproducing these feelings in the listener. It is not, in the familiar phrase, "a language of the emotions". He offers a battery of arguments that counter the idea that the beauty of music comes from its expressive features, several of which are familiar from Hanslick.

- Much beautiful music has no definable expressive character. In general, the character of music is extremely indefinite.[30] It cannot express pity, let alone the sort of pity we feel for Antigone as opposed to the kind we feel for Hamlet.
- Where it does have a definite character, it may have no effect upon us.
- People differ over the expressive character of music. The opening of Schubert's Piano Trio No. 1 in B flat is variously described by different critics as, on the one hand, energetic and passionate and, on the other, as girlish and confiding, although they may concur that it is enjoyable.

25

- If music produces in us a definite emotion and if this "stirring of the emotion is the whole business of [it]",[31] what is to be gained by listening to other music with the same character?
- If the stirring of emotion is the point, why not by some other person than by music? If we want to experience an emotion, there are all sorts of other, more foolproof ways of experiencing it.
- There is no reason to suppose that the character of a piece of music depends on the mental state of its composer. A musician may compose a funeral march without losing his good spirits and the prolonged labour involved means that it is implausible to suppose that he is in that state for the entire time of composition.[32]

How, then, do we describe, perfectly aptly, music as stormy, tragic and the like? Gurney suggests that the connection between music and its expressiveness is most easily seen in the matter of pace. A slow pace is often solemn; on the other hand, confidence is expressed by a strong rhythmical outline at a quickish pace. Pace is so characteristic of emotional speech that the corresponding features in music owe some of their quality to it.[33] The higher registers of the voice are more penetrating and so have been used to attract attention or give force to an utterance.[34] But Gurney does not think that such expressive features are that important. Our interest lies elsewhere and we have to force ourselves to consider those aspects of the music that are expressive. Indeed, although we can describe music in such terms, the excitement that music creates in us is something *sui generis*. For how could mournfulness or exultation explain or guarantee the beauty of a tune?

This conviction that music is a non-representational art existing in comparative detachment from the others is what is most striking about Gurney's position.[35] He is an autonomist. The musical mood is unique; about the most we can say of it is that it is "simply that unique one which we can but describe as the mood of musical exaltation".[36] He frequently remarks on the isolation and uniqueness of our experience of music and his reservations about the value of musical expressiveness underline this. If Hanslick is a formalist, Gurney is one too.

We shall return to these issues later. For now let me say that I think music is more deeply involved in the culture from which it emerges than autonomism suggests. Certainly Victorian music doesn't tell us about Victorian life and culture in the way that the novels of Dickens or George Eliot do. You won't find any helpful diagnosis of the limits of utilitarianism in Edward Elgar's early music. But the range of expressive descriptions is constrained by the culture of origin; and remember that neither

Gurney nor Hanslick deny the aptness of such descriptions. It matters to us that we can object to the sanctimoniousness of Elgar's early religious music and it is significant that this is a description that we could not properly apply to religious music of the sixteenth century.

The legacy

Hanslick and Gurney bequeathed to us what nowadays is called, rather pretentiously, a "problematic" and this sets the scene for Chapter 3. Historically the central question in the philosophy of music over the past two and a half centuries has been this: is music a language and, more specifically, is it a language of the emotions or is it an art of form alone and its merits merely those of artfully composed patterns? In attendance come a series of subsidiary questions. How does the beauty of music relate to its expressive power? How can we explain its capacity to express? If it is not by expressing the mind of the composer or producing correlative effects in the listener, then what entitles us to call it "grave" or "spirited"? But the most fundamental difference lies between those who think of music as an autonomous, abstract art form, and those who think that it draws its importance for us from connections, no matter how tenuous, with our lives outside the world of music. On the whole I side with the latter.

Chapter 2

The work of music

"Beethoven was more important than whoever was playing him."

Phil Spector

For the philosopher, two questions about what it is for something to be a work of music spring to mind. First, music is described as one of the fine arts. So what is it that makes music – or, to be precise, some pieces of music – works of art or examples of fine art? This is our first question. The second is what is the work of music *per se*? Is it just what we hear, the performance, or is it something over and above that? Is it something we invent or something we discover? These questions occupy the second part of this chapter.

Now you might ask why we should need to answer the question: what is a work of art? This is, after all, a book about the philosophy of a specific art, music. "Work of art" and "fine art" are used in quite broad and not very well-differentiated senses. Music is sometimes described as one of the fine arts, but the fine arts also cover Fabergé eggs, Staffordshire pottery and the sort of things found in the Victoria and Albert Museum. If we describe the latter as "works of art" then we are likely to be grading them not only as exceptional examples of their type but as something more. For works of art have expressive features such as sadness, optimism, joy and such like. Works of art may be loosely said to have "meaning". Paradigmatically, they are "about" something in the sense in which, for example, *Jane Eyre* is about the moral growth and liberation of a young woman. This makes works of art something far more than decorative. They have implications for our lives and the way we judge others. We learn morality in part from works of fiction, plays and films. If music is to be included in the family of "works of art", then we need to think about what "work of art" means and whether it can be extended to an art that seems not to have moral content. We need to distinguish music that is "art music" from hymns, advertising jingles, work songs and football songs. Once we use the term "work of art" to describe something, the range of descriptions that are appropriate is immediately expanded. A jingle can be jolly, but once we describe it as ironic we are already in the foothills of art.

What makes music art?

Hard cases

To begin at the beginning, why do we think of some pieces of music as works of art? The question is quite general. What, after all, makes a painting or a sculpture a work of art? The question is very familiar in recent writing on the philosophy of art; it has been the centre of attention over the past four decades. Yet it might strike you as strange, largely because the question as put is contextless (as philosophical or, perhaps more accurately, metaphysical questions characteristically are): in some contexts, at least, asking such a question would be absurd. Certain sorts of contexts are surely required for the question to be sensible. We certainly cannot imagine somebody *au fait* with the English language and who is not a philosopher asking of a Gainsborough "What reason have we for calling this a painting?" any more than she is likely to ask "What reason have we for calling this blue?" It would be equally odd to ask the question "What reason have we for calling this a work of art?" of an exhibit in the National Gallery, although it might be less puzzling if we were looking at something in the Museum of Modern Art.

Why has the question "What is it to be a work of art?" taken centre stage? I believe that it is because of what I shall call the "problem of the hard cases". It is the hard cases – concept art, aleatoric music (music involving the selection of sounds by chance) and the like (notably cases in the visual arts and music rather than examples from literature) – that have caused a massive academic industry to be employed in trying to analyse the concept "work of art", one consequence of which is that philosophy of art has rather edged out general aesthetics in the past few decades. There has been comparatively little written on the aesthetics of natural beauty or fashion, or on the decorative arts and crafts, compared to the concentration on the notion of art. The difficult, or what I shall continue to call the hard cases, begin with the use of unfamiliar materials. And here the problems are, I think, less striking. If you make sculptures out of elephant dung instead of marble, there seems less reason to hesitate about calling the result "art" than there is when you "recycle" bicycle parts. One reason is connected with a deep-rooted assumption that skill is a requisite in the production of art; the amount of skill required in the latter seems minimal whereas I presume that moulding elephant dung requires technique, although I suppose the fact that elephant dung is more malleable than marble makes the technique less exacting. Certainly a mistake is more easily corrected, although the same is true of some other forms of art; corrections are easy in writing poetry or music and paintings have *pentimenti*.

But the standard examples that take pride of place in modern discussions seem to require no technical ability at all. Thus Marcel Duchamps's *Fountain*, an inverted urinal signed "R. Mutt", does not require the technical ability of a Rodin or Bernini. Tracey Emin's *My Bed* and Andy Warhol's *Brillo Boxes* are other examples, as, indeed, are most of the shortlist for the Turner Prize. Let's turn to music. Takehisa Kosugi's *Micro I* requires paper to be wrapped around a microphone. The crackles created as it unfolds constitute the music. But the standard example in music is John Cage's *4'33"*, the celebrated "silent music", which has come again to public attention because his estate made some legal enquiries about a silent track on a disc by another musician:

> In June, after the British musical group the Planets introduced a 60-second piece of complete silence on its latest album, representatives of the estate of composer John Cage, who once wrote "4'33"" (273 seconds of silence), threatened to sue the group for ripping off Cage (but failed, said the group, to specify which 60 of the 273 seconds it thought had been pilfered). Said Mike Batt of the Planets; "Mine is a much better silent piece. I (am) able to say in one minute what (took Cage) four minutes and 33 seconds. (*Independent*, 21 June 2002)

In Cage's "composition", it seems that the "music" is supposed to be whatever ambient sounds occur during this interval. Perhaps this is a new kind of music that somehow replaces and at the same time challenges traditional music. Cage's general justification of his position suggests that he might have benefited from the intellectual rigour that a first-year philosophy course can offer.

> I said that since the sounds were just sounds, this gave people hearing them the chance to be people, centred within themselves where they

actually are, not off artificially in the distance as they are accustomed to be, trying to figure out what is being said by some artist by means of sounds. Finally I said that the purpose of this purposeless music would be achieved if people learned to listen; that when they listened they might discover that they preferred the sound of everyday life to the ones they would presently hear in the musical program; that that was alright as far as I was concerned.[1]

I suppose this is hardly worth arguing with (although connoisseurs of fashionable egocentric twaddle will love the idea that hearing sounds "gave people hearing them the chance to be people, centred within themselves where they actually are"). But, of the last few sentences, where Cage deviates into sense, I am inclined to say that few would travel miles and pay good money to hear everyday sounds and for very good reason. Of everyday sounds, a few most of us like, many we dislike very much and most we don't care about. I like the sound of birdsong in my garden. But, like other people who are comfortable living in the country, there is much I don't like: the sound of crows and jays, the bleating of sheep and the roar of low-flying aircraft. I don't like the sound of vomiting either. Cage does not give us any reason for preferring other sounds to music and, indeed, we should be surprised were he able. He wants us to direct the concentrated attention normally required of music to these everyday sounds but, although it is conceivable that people might come to prefer these sounds, he gives no grounds for supposing they would nor any for supposing this is not a dereliction of taste rather than any sort of advance.

The problems of silent music hardly stop here. Could it be performed? Each "performance" would probably sound very different from the previous one, so that whereas I can easily recognize two different performances at different tempi of Beethoven's "Eroica" Symphony as performances of the same work and not of Beethoven's Fourth Symphony, I certainly would not be able to distinguish a performance of *4'33"* from the performance of another piece of silent music that lasts 4 minutes 34 seconds unless I knew when it started and stopped and was equipped with an accurate chronometer. (Could the performer of silent music opt for a slower tempo?)

In any case, the aesthetic appreciation of ambient sounds is closer to the appreciation of natural beauty than the appreciation of art. We might be struck by the beauty of one oak tree among a group of less interesting trees just as we might be struck by the beauty of one man or one woman in a crowd of less attractive people. But in all sorts of ways this diverges from our attraction to art. Where are the roles of education and the development of taste? How does our preference here connect with other preferences through our lives? Our taste in opera, say, or drama or painting, will probably show some consistencies with our moral values and religious opinions, for example. A love of Ravel or of Thelonius Monk says much more about somebody than her love of gherkins and rather more than her love of the Yorkshire Dales as opposed to the Scottish Highlands.

A potent objection to conceptual art might very well be that these artists just cannot do the technical stuff, one sign, perhaps, of the problem of the fraudulent that Stanley Cavell thinks, is both so significant and so elusive when we are considering the contemporary arts.[2] Even David Hockney is sufficiently mystified by the draughtsmanship of Holbein and others to suggest they must have used the *camera obscura* to produce such verisimilitude. We know that Picasso, for example, was more than competent in the traditional skills and that makes us ready to accept what strikes the uninitiated as the apparent crudities of some of his work. I have heard it argued that a sculptor getting somebody else to do the modelling that he cannot do himself is no different from the fact that, in all probability, much of Michaelangelo's work was produced by an army of apprentices working in his atelier. (Hogarth objected to the creation of artistic "factories" and took a pride in doing everything himself, including priming the canvas.) No doubt, but there is also no reason to think that Michaelangelo could not also do the job had he time and every reason to suppose that he went around touching up and correcting the work of his employees. Unless he could and did, we might as well credit Pope Julius with the Sistine Chapel ceiling. Composition technique is something that composers need; harmony and counterpoint have to be learnt. Of course, it is true that they cannot play all the instruments they write for – Mozart was a brilliant pianist and good violinist but he did not play the horn, as far as I am aware – but orchestral technique requires knowing the possibilities and limitations of the instruments written for. It is difficult to think of a significant composer who was not competent in this and only a few come to mind who were not decent keyboard players. For a start, all major composers have been able performers. Certainly, there is music that seems to require no skill at all in composition such as aleatory music or silent music (if you count this as music), but most of the music found "difficult" by the contemporary non-specialist listener is music that requires a great deal of technical mastery to compose, such as the music of Elliott Carter, Pierre Boulez, Karlheinz Stockhausen or Harrison Birtwistle. It is music that is difficult because we find it hard or impossible to "follow" in the way in which we follow earlier music. Even minimalist music usually turns out to be a more complex business than it at first appears. It certainly can be difficult to perform since it requires enormous rhythmical precision. Most contemporary music does not constitute hard cases in the sense in which I have used the term. On the whole, anxiety as to the technical competence of the creator is less a consideration in the case of contemporary music.

It is a familiar point that the term "work of art" is used in a special way in philosophical discussion. Outside philosophy, we would use it of painting, sculpture and things like Greek vases. We also use it to describe what we find in the Metropolitan Museum of Art or the Wallace Collection. We don't normally use it to refer to individual pieces of music and poetry. (It is also worth noting that German *lieder*, French *mélodies*, or the English school of song writing is described as "art-song", presumably in distinction from folk song.) But the "philosophical usage" is justifiable. We need some generic term to cover the group of man-made objects whose fuller appreciation requires special preparation and which we value above most other things that man makes or does. That the use of "work of art" as a generic term by philosophers is not an entirely arbitrary or idiosyncratic usage is shown by what is covered in the arts pages of the broadsheet newspapers, and by the existence of various organizations for the arts.

So this usage is not purely down to philosophers. But neither is it wholly down to people who write about and finance the arts rather than create art. Although Cage was prone to speak of "the music" he and others created, he also spoke of "art" and himself as an "artist", significantly in the context of his silent music or in one of a set of variations where the audience is told to wander away and listen to ambient sounds. Robert Rauschenberg spoke of his erasure of a drawing by Willem de Kooning as a "work of art".[3] So, and perhaps this is significant, "work of art" is often used to describe the hard cases by those who produced them. The salient fact is that both the extension and the intension of "work of art" differ from the extension of "pieces of music", "poem", "painting" and so on. I shall suggest later that the decision to count music as "art" has pretty profound implications for the way we treat it.

I said that only some music would count as art. Nobody would quarrel with the suggestion that Mozart's *Don Giovanni* or Bach's *Forty-Eight Preludes and Fugues* count as what we might call "art music". So does Indian classical music, Miles Davis's *Kind of Blue*, the music of Thelonius Monk or the Modern Jazz Quartet (MJQ). What about the Beatles? Well, probably most of "Sergeant Pepper" counts: certainly "A Day in the Life". What about the operettas of Gilbert and Sullivan? Do we include *West Side Story* but exclude *South Pacific*? *Porgy and Bess* gets in. Muzak certainly does not. We won't include football's World Cup songs, advertising jingles, most hymns and nursery rhymes. Do we include music by Dire Straits or folk songs? That is somewhat moot.

"Art music" and philosophical analysis

In the next part of this chapter I am going to examine some general accounts of why something counts as a work of art to see whether the question of when a piece of music counts as "art music" can be clarified thereby. But perhaps I should say in advance that I don't think this enquiry will, in the end, help us to decide on the hard cases. I am going to discuss four approaches: procedural, functional, historical and recognitional. My conclusion will be that each of them explains *some* cases but that none of them work for *all* cases and that problems remain with the hard cases.

All of these are attempts at analysis. The goal is to produce a set of necessary and sufficient conditions by reference to which we can establish when something is a work of art and when not. This programme of analysis has been part and parcel of the tradition of philosophizing in the twentieth century; for instance, there have been attempts at analysing the concept of knowledge so that we can see how it differs from belief. (The initial suggestion was that knowledge is belief that is true and justified. That thesis has been shown to fail.) Now there are some reasons to be wary of attempts at analysis. In the case of art, we have to say that despite years of activity there is no agreed analysis. This does not show that analysis is impossible, of course – somebody may always turn up with the goods – but it suggests that we should be cautious about the prospects of success. It may be that art is an "essentially contested concept",[4] one that is always going to be the locus of debate in part because its function is to serve as a battleground for disputing parties. There is, for example, always likely to be conflict between conservatives and the Young Turks as to whether a certain piece of avant-garde art counts as art at all. We can see this process in action in the debates over the hard cases I mentioned earlier. Indeed, I suspect that understanding the concept of art is as much like understanding the sorts of arguments admissible in a court of law as it is knowing what the verdict is. That is, you understand the concept of art when you understand what considerations lead people to call something art.

Secondly, there are cases where it cannot be clear whether the concept applies or not. Usage gives us no idea how to classify these cases so the concept is indeterminate at this point. It is pretty evident that there are many hard cases where we are not sure whether we are dealing with art or not. Nor can we be quite sure where the boundaries lie that distinguish art from entertainment, kitsch or pornography. I am not sure whether the griffin handles that are all that remain of a seventh century BCE Greek pot count as art or craft. We might give reasons either way but these reasons will culminate in a decision if they culminate in anything at all. We might even make an arbitrary decision. But in both of these latter cases it will be a decision and not an analysis and that rather defeats the point of the enquiry. Wittgenstein puts it well: "It is only in normal cases that the use of a word is clearly prescribed; we know, are in no doubt, what to say in this or that case. The more abnormal the case, the more doubtful it becomes what we are to say."[5]

Proceduralism

A distinction is currently made between what are called "procedural" and "functionalist" accounts of art.[6] The distinction roughly is between those theories that make arthood a status that is conferred upon artefacts by those qualified to do so (which may include the creator or *bona fide* critics) and those theories that view art as a group of artefacts that have a special point or function (they do something for us). The two may not be independent. For example, we may classify something as art because it is already seen to have a function of the sort common in art or it may be that the act of classifying it as art leads us to look for these sorts of functions or even that, as a result of classifying it so, it takes on some functions (it becomes an object whose meaning and significance we debate, for example). For the time being I want to concentrate on proceduralism.

What is called "proceduralism" differs little from what was previously called "institutionalism". Roughly speaking, and a rough characterization is all that is needed for the moment, the idea is that art is art because the art-world or, in the limiting case, a member of it, decides so. *A work of art is an artefact presented to the public for their appreciation by a representative of the art-world or an agent for it.* This account has been variously modified and has aroused a great deal of comment. I shall not repeat the excellent discussions available elsewhere. What I am more interested in here is the way the weaknesses of institutionalism reflect more general problems in the programme of attempting to secure an analysis of the concept of art.

The two difficulties with the institutional theory that are most often aired are: (i) the problem of circularity; and (ii) the problem of what is called "first art". As far as (i) is concerned, it is argued that it is hard to see how we can get the notion of the art-world off the ground without a reference to art. Since art is then defined in terms that refer to the art-world the circularity looks both inevitable and dangerous. To some, the question is not important, especially for those who reflect on the parallel difficulties of defining "moral" or "religious" or "spiritual" in terms that are entirely independent of the original notions. After all, perhaps we can build up a concept of the art-world via examples and instances that may be sufficient for us then to be able to specify the concept of art well enough. I want to spend a little more time on the question of "first art" because it is both a more interesting question and somewhat germane to subsequent discussion.

"First art" covers those artefacts that were created before anybody possessed anything like our concept of art. The Altamira cave paintings (in France) are standard examples. They were painted 11,000–19,000 years ago. It is unlikely that those communities had our concept of art. We count these as art although their creators might have counted them as having magical powers and created them for that purpose or as votive offerings. There is certainly no reason to suppose that they thought of them as "works of art", although it is highly likely that their contemporaries were as struck by their grace and beauty as we are. At some point in the history of the West, probably in the Renaissance, the modern concept of art began to emerge and, from the outset, gathered under it those artefacts, paintings, sculptures, poems and so on that were created shortly before and during its emergence, together with a selection of classical sculptures and plays. The notion of music as a fine art seems to have developed in the eighteenth century as a response to the development of what used to be called "pure" or "absolute" music. The problem for the proceduralist is that we want to say that a Mass by Josquin des Pres dating from the early sixteenth century counts as art music even though there was then no concept of art as we understand it and, *a fortiori,* no concept of art music. How, then, can its status as art music depend upon its being so christened?

Functionalism

"Functionalism"[7] seems to avoid the difficulty of first art. What the functionalist will say is that the artefact is intended to produce a specified result; and such an account neither needs reference to previous works of art nor seems to require the concept of art to get off the ground. Function-alism may also have a condition of success built into the rubric; then works of art are works of art because of a certain function that they fulfill. However, I shall concentrate on versions that build in the notion of "intention". We need a concept of art that allows that some works of art are failures. The most obvious candidate for this has seemed to be pleas-ure. The old phrase "to please and instruct" gives the basis for a functional definition of art. Concentrating on the first part of this rubric, music counts as art if it was intended to please. Another function it might serve is that of being intended to generate aesthetic experiences. But then, of course, we must define "aesthetic experience" before this analysis has any value. So the threat of regression is not immediately banished. (In as much as institutional theories speak of "appreciation", they introduce a functionalist element. They say the work of art is intended to be appreciated; indeed, the relative thinness of the characterization of "appreciation" in institutionalist theories has aroused some adverse comment.)

So far, the discussion has been very general; as I have described it, functionalism is a theory that applies to any of the arts. But in talking about functionalism, we have focused on an aspect of particular interest in music and for this reason I propose to devote more space to it in this book. More than in any other art, in my experience, the value of music has been seen as a matter of the pleasure it gives. Pleasure has thus been taken to be central to this art. But the supposition that pleasure is basic to assessment certainly raises problems in the other arts. Recent work for television by Rob Brydon (*Marion and Geoff*), Ricky Gervais (*The Office*), Steve Coogan (*I'm Alan Partridge*) and others is rightly admired but exceedingly uncomfortable to watch; we squirm with embarrassment. We watch these dramas for their brilliant characterization and timing, but not, I think, because they give pleasure. We admire the achievement but find it difficult to watch all the way through. Because the other arts have traditionally been thought to have, *inter alia*, a moral purpose and may be good for us, that we do not enjoy a play or a novel seems to present no particular difficulty. But this consideration has never been very plausible in music, which cannot, even indirectly, embody a homily. Perhaps partly as a consequence, music has, in my view wrongly, been thought to aim at and be justified by the pleasure it gives. In Chapter 4 I shall argue that we need a contrast between taking pleasure in and taking an interest in music.

As far as functionalism is concerned, we can look outside the philosophy of art for clear guidelines as to how to approach this theory. For the paradigms of function are to be found in biology and in man-made machines. The function of the heart is to pump blood around the body. The organ has this function within a larger unity: the body of the creature. If it fails the creature dies; if it fails to function properly, then the creature's capacities will be much impaired. It may find that it cannot move quickly enough, for example. In the car, the function of the carburettor is to mix petrol and air so as to form an explosive mixture. If it fails to function properly, the car will not run evenly or, in the last event, not run at all. Importantly the concept of function has been extended to the social sciences with the claim that the way to understand social practices and institutions is to understand how they operate in keeping society in being.

There are some analogies in the arts, although these analogies do not play any role in the present debate about functionalism. W. H. Auden used to teach schoolchildren about poetry by replacing a word in a line with a near synonym: the most effective way of showing the work that a particular word does. Change damages. The perceptive critic of music will show me how a particular harmonic shift operates in the course of a work as a whole. Its absence may damage the work or render a passage incomprehensible. But, as I said, these are not considerations that the functionalist in philosophy of art is concerned with. For he is concerned with the function of the work of art as a whole. (In fact he removes functionalism from the area in which it might have some insights to offer into an area where it does not.) Given this, the most plausible reading of functionalism as a theory of art is to conclude that individual works of art are analogous to tools. Their specific function has been variously described as being to reward disinterested attention, or to produce aesthetic experience or aesthetic pleasure.

Now for the objections. If we define the function in terms of either aesthetic experience, disinterested pleasure or aesthetic pleasure we have an unduly narrow view of what the creator might have intended his work to do. According to some recent writers, the intention of Wagner in "The Mastersingers of Nuremberg" was to call German people to an appreciation of their community. Certainly Dickens and Émile Zola had social reform in view. Some of Bach's church music was, we are told, intended to harrow the souls of the congregation.

But even if we could find a more plausible general account than one in terms of pleasure or aesthetic experience, we face a major obstacle. A tool has the proper function its maker intended. But the thesis that a work of art has the function its maker intended is too close to the thesis that it has the meaning that its creator intended. We shall point out that on many occasions a work of art comes to function in a way or have a meaning that the creator might not have known about and so could not have intended. Bach would have been surprised to find audiences in concert halls listening to his cantatas. The problems are even more obvious in literature. Lewis Carroll would have had second thoughts about publishing had he known the Freudian interpretations placed upon the "Alice" stories (and these interpretations can certainly be defended). If Stanley Fish is right, *Paradise Lost* was intended to recall backsliders to a firmer faith in Christ; it was intended to have a didactic function. But it is not read that way now. Should Britten's *The Turn of the Screw* be seen as a warning against submitting to the sexual attractions of children? If it is, it won't have a very wide application.

Of course, I can use a tool in a way the inventor did not intend; a tyre lever can be used as an offensive weapon. These are, of course, "improper uses". There are also improper uses for art. To play *The Rite of Spring* very loudly to annoy the neighbours, or to pick a Howard Hodgkin to complete the decor or to use the full score of *Der Rosenkavalier* to stop a table wobbling are all improper uses. But these are peripheral cases and the admonition that the work of art is being "used improperly" is presumably jocular. But it is not an improper *use* of a work of art to interpret it in a way that its creator did not intend, even if the interpretation is indefensible. The problem, then, with the analogy between a work of art and a tool is that whereas it makes perfect sense to say of any use of a tool that was not intended by the creator or manufacturer that it is an improper use of that tool, if the work of art was intended, like Bach's church cantatas or Milton's verse, to have a certain function, the setting aside of that function is not regarded as an improper use of the work of art. (An improper use of a tool, of course, might well be justified if nothing else is available and the matter is urgent.) In saying all this, I am not down-grading the liturgical or didactic use of art; the point is that *qua* work of art, considerations other than utility enter.

Still, where an artefact does not belong to the central forms of the arts, the decision to classify it as a work of art may be a consequence of the fact that it "works" in the same way as standard works of art. When we decide to include jazz and some world music or some musicals (a very few) as works of art, we do so because we find that we respond in the same way to them as we do to standard works of art. Thus a basically procedural account may employ elements of functionalism. In some of these cases we may be too ignorant of the culture in which they originate to be able to talk intelligently about their meaning. For instance, we may know very little about the significance of some African music and its place in society. Critical debates over its interpretation cannot even begin. So it is, as a matter of fact, very likely to be our sense of the aesthetic qualities of balance and design, melody and shape that matter here. We then naturally infer that the creator intended to appeal to that sense and, in very many cases, we are surely right to do so. So functionalism certainly covers some of the cases where works of art become accepted as art, but only some, I think.

But perhaps the most striking problem is this. Good art, and especially great art, is valuable precisely to the degree its qualities are non-generic. It is a criticism of, say, poetry, that its effects are generalized. What we look for in art is the individual and idiosyncratic. Even where we think of a painter like Raphael or a composer like Mozart as displaying the qualities of the quotidian style in a canonic way we still note their individuality. Classicism does not exclude it. Mozart's best works are undoubtedly Mozart's. Nobody who really knows about classical music would mistake a piece by Mozart for one by Haydn; even where Haydn, in tribute, seems to imitate Mozart's style, we still know it is the authentic Haydn manner we hear. So it is a criticism of a work that it merely shares the general features with others of its genre. What we look for in art is the individual and those writers who stress the effect of art upon us rightly emphasize how important it is that the response mirrors the uniqueness to be found in the work. Indeed, if you are going to embrace any form of functionalism, you must emphasize the idiosyncrasy of the work and of its correlative effects. These are insurmountable obstacles in the path of a general account of the function of art, especially when one is dealing with what is outstanding and in the philosophy of art it is what is outstanding that is of overall importance in determining the nature of art and of our response to it.

There is a parallel with familiar thoughts elsewhere in the philosophy of art. We shall see later that the notion of judging the value of a work of art with reference to criteria fails because, if the critical standards are to be of general applicability, they are too vague to be of help. The more precise we make them, the easier it is to find counter-examples, works of agreed accomplishment that infringe these standards. Equally, any plausible account of the function of art will be too generalized to be informative; make it more exact and many successful works of art will be omitted by the formula.

Turning, then, to our experience of art, I remarked that the functionalist has the problem of describing the experience in a way independent of the work of which it is an experience. This is something quite widely acknowledged. Wittgenstein famously observed, "If I admire a minuet I can't say: 'Take another. It does the same thing'".[8] This is a counsel of perfection though. A celebrated musician once suggested replacing some of the weaker movements in early Haydn with some of the stronger movements in the same set of quartets. Whether anybody would have the nerve to do so in the current climate I rather doubt. However, Wittgenstein's point was not about what liberties we may or may not take in classical music. It has been taken as suggesting that our experience is an experience of one particular and individual piece. The strong individuality of artistic experience comes out in the way that the experience that the work produces is thought to be unique to that work. Now that view is not quite accurate. It is not that our experience is different on every occasion; it isn't. The sense of exhilaration produced by one Haydn finale may not be much different from that produced by another. Wittgenstein's aphorism should be taken differently; it is that what should matter to us is the work of art itself and our attention should be focused upon it and not upon our experience. The thesis should be understood as a covert thesis about the attention we pay and the attention we pay should, ideally, enable us to recognize the individuality of the work. And we won't know what the peculiarity of the work is until we see, read or listen to it. Now, we select a tool for a certain job and any other tool will do as well providing it does the same job. But art is not like that. Indeed, what we find here reflects the thesis associated with the philosopher R. G. Collingwood. He argued that the creator does not know what he accomplishes until the work of creation is complete, and that this distinguishes art from other activities like craft. It is the conceiving of the work of art that is the real creative act. My suggestion is that, in parallel, you don't know what the character of a work is until you experience it. Having it described to you is, as we all know, no substitute. This holds whether or not the phenomenology of listening to the Minuet of one of Haydn's "Paris" Symphonies is identical with the phenomenology of listening to the Minuet from another. The quality of our conscious experience may not vary. (The study of phenomenology is the study of the nature of consciousness in abstraction from what it is consciousness of.) And with great works, it does not stop there; you might think that when we read or hear or see it again we know what to expect, but this is not necessarily so; when we encounter it again we may see different things in it. What I have described is, of course, a feature of outstanding music. Plenty of mediocre music sounds like other uninspiring music. Perhaps unfairly, Vivaldi is said to have composed the same concerto six hundred times. Whatever is the case here, there is competent music, like that of Telemann, that shows no strong individuality. Haydn, Bach, Mozart and the like are different, and it is the individuality of their voices that we prize. While we continue to prize art for this, our concept of art will not be one that can be satisfactorily defined in terms of function. For the best we can say is that the function of this piece of music is to be just what this piece of music happens to be.

I have no overall purpose in settling down to listen to some new music. Indeed, it is the work itself that calls for my attention, not what I experience when hearing it. This is just what it is to be interested in music. Certainly, on occasion, you may look forward to a performance, anticipating pleasure, and be disappointed if you are bored, but not all encounters are like this. It is not to be doubted that an individual piece of music or an individual poem may be designed to please. It may be produced with that function in mind. The point is that this is implausible as a general thesis. Not only do most major works of art not set out to please, but the creator nowadays will probably expect divergent reactions from the public. In any case, whether or not he or she expects it, that is going to be the case, and the greater the stature of the work the more likely it will be. If it pleases and is good, there is usually more to be said. Even *Die Fledermaus* has an edge.

Indeed, setting aside the composition of music merely to entertain, it is often a grave charge against a work of art that it has a function. When artists have such an intention then we are alarmed. What we resent is propaganda. The ideologically or religiously loaded work can offend although much depends upon its social and cultural background. I don't object to Mariolatry in a fifteenth-century English composer but find the religious sub-text of Elgar's *The Dream of Gerontius* or the work of Olivier Messiaen or Arvo Pärt, John Taverner and other "holy minimalists" somewhat rebarbative.

An "historical" account

Consider now a third account. Suppose an artefact counts as a work of art in as much as it was intended by its creator to belong to a tradition of artefacts. We can describe this as an "historical account".[9] This could even incorporate a functionalist element so that the artefact is expected to have the same sort of function as its ancestors did. This theory accounts for art in terms of the intentions of the creator, intentions that themselves are controlled by an historical sequence or tradition of works of art; a work of art is something made for regard or treatment as previous artworks have been regarded or treated. An immediate objection is rather obvious. The account looks either regressive or circular for it seems to be a fault in the historical account of art that it, too, cannot cope with first art. The first work of art cannot aspire to the status of its predecessors for there are none. But if all that we require is that when an artist intends to produce an object that has the functions that previous works of art have, he thinks of his work as belonging to the tradition to which these sculptures, painting and poems belong, then there is no especial problem. It is not required that the artist has the concept of art as opposed to some concept of the genre in which he works. And he may very well even have a concept of the genre without fully articulating it. So somebody fashions a flute from a bone and finds that covering holes in it allows them to alter the pitch. At this stage we have something that could be called "music" but we don't have anything that contemporaries call a "work of art" or "art music". They

43

don't have those concepts. These are concepts that evolve as other factors begin to intercede. Players practise and the art becomes more complex. (Imagine how revolutionary it must have been when somebody found that practice makes perfect!) Masters take on pupils. A tradition develops. Now one important advantage of this account is that it connects closely with the way creative artists work, something certainly lacking in the first account I discussed and, I think, in the second as well. For it is a fact about art that artists add to a tradition of art; they learn from, modify and add to the achievements of their predecessors. The Hegelian idea of *aufheben*, frequently translated as the neologism "sublating", catches something of this.

What an historical account won't do is explain the addition of new genres once the concept of art is launched. How can photography, film and even music become accepted? They come under the banner of "art" or "fine art" once these concepts are already understood as applying to painting, sculpture and literature. Additionally, we need to take into account the situation where what was once dismissed as entertainment or craft becomes accepted as art. Thus world music, primitive art and jazz joined the lists in the twentieth century. But this cannot be explained in terms of the accretion of individual works of art to a tradition consisting of other works that are more or less similar. This is a matter of new genres or, at least, sub-genres, being accorded the status of art. Here, something like a functional account appears to be a plausible description of why these classes were given the status of art. Jazz had many of the functions of classical music. It was noticed that it moved and excited people and was discussed and criticized in terms that were familiar. The move to include it under the heading of "the arts" thus seemed a natural and defensible one.

A "recognitional" account

So far I have mentioned three accounts of what it is for something to be a work of art. I add to these a fourth account of art, the "recognitional". (The neologism is ugly but has the important virtue of being transparent.) This has not been much discussed in the literature, although there are strong hints of it in a paper by Terry Diffey, albeit embedded within a form of institutionalism.[10] It has much to recommend it, even though I shall eventually reject it as a satisfactory general account. Its distinctive feature is that it emphasizes what would now be called "the reception" of art: how it is appreciated, understood and, above all, valued by its public. An artefact may become art because of some perceived quality seen in it by qualified people. "Work of art" is a category that marks out, *inter alia*, some of mankind's greatest achievements. The point about arthood is that in order to understand the concept we need to understand this feature and we really need no further elaboration of why we should think "recognition" is important. As Wittgenstein said, man is a ceremonious animal; we need no further functional account of funeral rites over and above their procedural description nor of the exchange of rings beyond what is ritual. No more need we a justification of the business of "recognition", even though we can imagine, at least in the case of art, how such a justification might run. We might say that the greatest of human achievements are objects that repay study and attention and that we find we can return to on many occasions, often with added rewards. Then "recognition" would have a functional justification. Thus you may feel impelled by the sheer power of a piece of music to re-describe it as a "work of art". Hearing Ray Charles singing "Yesterday" or Dire Straits performing "Love over Gold" or "Sultans of Swing" may induce this reaction.

So what a "recognitional" account will offer is something like the following. There are certain objects that human beings make that we describe in terms like "expressing the human spirit". This sounds pretentious but is, I think, defensible. We talk about what these works mean and we describe them in expressive terms largely borrowed from our vocabulary for describing people. We speak of what *Hamlet* is about and we can describe a late painting by Rembrandt as expressing love or resignation. I think Kenneth Clark was exact when he described "The Jewish Bride" as a "picture of grown-up love, a marvellous amalgam of richness, tenderness and trust".[11] As we shall see, it is important that music, too, can express tenderness, resignation or opulence. It is this, it is worth repeating, and the capacity of music to be something that can be followed, that make it a fine art and not merely an art of ornament. There is, of course, also technical mastery. In celebrating all this we acknowledge that the human race has managed to produce Bach and Proust as well as Stalin and Napoleon. However vain and difficult creative artists can be, they can have a devotion to what they make and what they make can be of the greatest intrinsic value, and that can give us solace in our darker moments. At least, cultivating the arts can help to give us a balanced outlook on our species.

You might ask how a recognitional account differs from others. Obviously it contains elements of functionalism and proceduralism. I have discussed the effect that some music may have such that it persuades us to count it as art music. I have referred also to the role of the expert in welcoming it in; he would then be operating like an agent of the art world. But, standardly, procedural accounts claim to be value-free. They are an account of what it is for something to be art, not for it to be art of distinction. The recognitional account, however, claims that what is involved in making something a work of art depends upon a judgement of value. The value may or may not be narrowly aesthetic. Aesthetic features are not first and foremost in the fiction of George Eliot, for example; here it is the psychological insight that matters. Music may be ugly but fascinating. I mentioned Mozart's "Eine kleine Gigue" K. 574 earlier; Charles-Valentin Alkan's Gigue op. 24 shares its character; both offer us *une belle laide*. Music can also be repulsive and brilliant and certainly not to be avoided because of the former quality; Bartók's *The Miraculous Mandarin* is a good example. Secondly, unlike a functional account, the recognitional account does not demand that a work of art is or was designed to produce a specific effect in the audience. No such intention may be present. The recognitional account differs from the historical, too; for although an artefact may well stand in a relation to a tradition of music-making or painting, that relationship alone does not make it a work of art. Indeed this account has the merit of explaining how we may decide that a work outside a tradition counts as a work of art; it has to have outstanding quality. Recognition is one more element in a concept that, I am more and more convinced, is very convoluted indeed.

Some writers argue that our experience of music owes little or nothing to any technical knowledge we might have. But, again, a recognitional account puts this into perspective. "Pleasure" seems a little anaemic for the ecstatic effect that music such as Tallis's *Spem in Alium* can have on the listener. The knowledge, as well, that it is written in forty independent parts and the astonishment that music so spontaneous and free sounding could be written to such constraints makes it seem a miracle. Hardly anybody who hears it will be unaware that it is written in forty parts, although they might be unaware of just how difficult an accomplishment this is without a constant din of dissonance, let alone the production of music of such consistent melodic and harmonic interest. Music is to be admired for all sorts of reasons, and the fact that it is the result of extra-ordinary gifts and accomplishments ranks very high among them. Such achievements are astounding in a mere mammal. The principal reason why silent music is such an odd case is because nobody could admire the skill, the technique, the years of honed accomplishment that go into this; there isn't any. So the account I have dubbed "recognitional" has this advantage over its rivals: it registers something intrinsic to the way we value music.

What are the problems with a "recognitional" account? There is an obvious one; there is bad art. It cannot be the case that what counts as art is only what is greeted as of outstanding quality nor even (a weaker thesis that brings it close to proceduralism) that it is thought by some agent of the art-world that it is of outstanding merit. Even in the art-world there are sharp operators.

Conclusion

My conclusion is not difficult to guess. Of these four accounts, as in Lewis Carroll's caucus race, all have won, but by the same token they have all lost. That is, I suggest, there are works of art whose place in the canon can be accounted for by one or other of these theories, possibly in combination, but that none of them account for all cases. They may be best regarded as describing, *inter alia*, the various routes whereby something becomes art rather than as offering an analysis of "art". Some of the familiar difficulties that have attended the various accounts are straightforward consequences of ignoring the ragged nature of the concept of art. This, of course, provides further reason for being sceptical about the possibility of an analysis. So the various philosophical theories have been regarded as competing when in fact they are dealing with different cases.

Most composers are uneven; they sometimes produce poor work. The acceptance of inferior stuff as art music can be accounted for in proceduralist terms. I am inclined to think, although you may disagree with me, that Michael Tippett's work, both early and late, was uneven. Yet there is no question that the music he composed counts as "art music". By the end of his life, Tippett was himself a "grand old man" of music and his status meant that he was an "agent of the art-world" and therefore in a position to give the imprimatur to his own work. A procedural account also fits the situation when a new genre is recognized, such as photography or film or latterly, perhaps, pop videos. To recapitulate a little, the sort of considerations that come into play might be the following. Thoughtful people found cinema to be interesting and discussable and realized that it raised issues of the sort that arise when we talk about paintings or about theatre. Gradually a body of critical opinion developed and it became increasingly clear that we were dealing with works of art. Questions of meaning and value became important and then a canon began to form. In this way, although critics do not make the artefacts, they certainly make the artefacts count as art and this, I believe, is one truth behind the procedural account. It is, however, noticeable that functional elements seem to be playing a role. Perhaps we are prompted to call film "art" because we find we react in the same way as we do to theatre or photography. We are moved. However, such functional elements may well recede into the background as the form of art develops. As film matures, idiosyncratic aspects of the form, such as montage and so on, draw our attention. Presumably something like this happened when music became recognized as a fine art on its own account rather than merely as an adjunct to dance, drama, a text or liturgy.

But how could a proceduralist theory explain the admission of jazz? It probably was not enlisted by classical musicians, although it interested both Ravel and Stravinsky, among many other composers. Rather, it excited and interested people in much the same way as some classical music had done and, with the development of a tradition of influences and critical commentary, the basic requirements for the status of art music were in place. A mixed functional and historical account seems to explain the emergence of jazz as art music. But, as should be obvious, these historical explanations are fairly speculative. It is difficult to disentangle the various elements and the actual causes of or reasons for a genre becoming "art" probably involve a melange of different factors.

In the case of silent music we find we are pulled in two directions. On the one hand, because Cage had composed proper music we are inclined to follow the usual principle and say that anything a figure of some stature composed must be a work of art, although we may have to add that this particular work is silly, pompous, boring and a waste of time. But then even the prodigiously talented nod. On the other hand, we are inclined to say that this is so different from anything that counts as music that it simply is not music. It has to be at least organized sound to stand a chance of counting as a musical work of art.

What emerges from all this is that there is no single route by which something becomes art. There are many different ways: procedural, functional, historical and recognitional, and, perhaps, others I have not identified. They may function together and it may be very hard to say which is the more important factor in any given case. Some art, too, is art from its very inception. Does it follow from this that no general justification of why an artefact is a work of art is possible? For centuries, philosophers were exercised over the problem of induction. What justifies us in concluding that because all the sheep we have observed are herbivorous, all sheep are herbivorous? The conclusion could be false while the premises are true. After all, generalizations like "All swans are white", which once looked pretty well-founded, turned out to be false. The widely accepted view nowadays is that there is no general justification for induction. What there are are particular justifications in particular cases. I can show why this is a sensible induction given context or subject-matter. In our case, we are considering the application of arthood to something or other and, again, I have yet to be persuaded that a general justification can be given. We might argue that this, that or another item ought to be counted as art. And the reasons will be various.

Understanding and analysis

I began by saying that what philosophers of art have tried to do, on the whole, is provide an analysis; they have attempted to find necessary and sufficient conditions for something being a work of art. Such a programme, if successful, will enable us to rule the hard cases either in or out. I want now to shift the attention from the idea of analysis to the notion of "understanding". For if we think not so much about what it is to be a work of art but what is involved in *understanding* what a work of art is or what it is to have a more or less adequate notion of the concept of art, the question of hard cases can be looked at anew. For to understand the concept of art is to see that cases like silent music are just those cases on the edge of the concept over which no final motivated decision can be made. Our concept of art does not stretch that far. We have grounds for thinking it art and also grounds for refusing that title. In no-man's-land the boundaries are not marked. To mark them entails, as I have said, a decision. Decisions can be well-grounded but even then they are decisions. And it may well be the case that no grounds decisively favour one alternative. The other advantage about thinking in terms of understanding rather than analysis is that understanding can be a greater or lesser, a fuller or more exiguous business. I may have a better grasp of the concept of art than a teenager and my better grasp shows itself, in part, in my realization that the concept has a vague penumbra. As I use the word "concept" it is a product of language use. Our concept of "atom" is acquired as we pick up the context in which the word is used. You don't have the concept unless you have a decent grasp of how the word is used but grasp is not an all-or-nothing affair. I have a better grasp of the concept of an atom than a child but a physicist has a better grasp than me. Likewise, people who are better informed about the arts are likely to have a better grasp of the concept of a work of art than others and, *pari passu*, of the concept of fine art. What remains, even among such experts, is the difficulty of the hard cases.

Some philosophers think that the job of philosophy is to investigate the world at its most general. Metaphysicians, they say, should *inter alia* be studying what art is and that might not be the same thing as the objects that we think of as constituting the range of fine arts. But then the problem is how to delineate the object of study. Unless they mean by "art" what we mean by "art", then, to a greater or lesser extent, we don't know what they are talking about. Since "art" is, in some respects, an unclear concept, we need to become clear about what is central and what is peripheral, what is incontestable and what is controversial about its range, before we say any more. We need first to decide what "art" means, and here lie all the uncertainties. Metaphysicians can be insouciant about this. They will tell you that what they study is not subject to the little incoherencies and frayed edges of what they call "folk" concepts. But then, of course, we ask for the point of this undertaking. Why tempt the raising of questions whose answers are but mere corollaries of the way they define their concepts? One thing is obvious. Unless you deal with demotic concepts you do not deal directly with the concepts which reflect and characterize our culture and our values. The results of this are hugely important for the consequence is that philosophy as cultural criticism is then emasculated. We should be interested in the ideas that are endemic in our culture and whose use reveals what is presumed to be significant; and, if there are inconsistencies within such concepts, what this tells us about the most general features of our culture matters. After all, the problems with the concept of art arise specifically from the hard cases mentioned earlier. Is silent music really music? These cases puzzle the woman in the street and the man on the Clapham omnibus and they should be able to look to the philosopher for help. They won't get it if he insists that how he uses "art" is not subject to the imprecisions that leave us with problem cases.

Look elsewhere for a moment. Concepts of "God" are notoriously problematic. Thinkers have characterized God in a way that cannot easily be made consistent. He is simultaneously omnipotent, omniscient and benevolent. Yet there is evil in the world. Of course, there are countless attempts at making the notion of a deity compatible with the existence of evil. Even if you think, as I do not, that these might be successful, you must allow that it is a possibility that concepts in this arena might not be self-consistent. Even if you deny this, believing that, with the grace of God, a consistent theodicy can be found, you may think that classical Marxism is not so favoured. It cannot be a coherent intellectual enterprise because of, for example, the difficulties in reconciling human freedom and economic determinism. My point is that we allow that broad systems of ideas, ideas that are central in a culture or sub-culture, may not be internally consistent and if we allow this why should we not allow the possibility that the same holds with respect to our ideas about the art of music?

My rejection of metaphysics as a discipline prior to conceptual enquiry is motivated by a feeling that metaphysics has fallen between two stools. On the one hand, it aims at consistency. On the other hand, it also attempts to describe the concepts we have. It cannot be utterly detached from the way we use terms like "fine art". But failure to distinguish these leads to an assumption that ordinary concepts will be consistent and well-defined in the tidy way a philosopher requires.

Those readers familiar with modern philosophy will identify my answer to the question that opened this chapter, "What is art?", as Wittgensteinian, and I will not complain if it is taken that way. But to the Wittgensteinian account there is a traditional objection. Unless you specify the similarity that links different forms of art together, you beg the question. It is no good talking about a loose pattern of disparate arts unless you are prepared to be explicit about the resemblances that lead us to call them all "the arts". Now, I specify some routes whereby things become art but I have not said what general similarities unite the strands. My argument is open to the question: why, on this view, should these diverse phenomena be called art if they have *nothing* at all in common with each other?

We have said something in the preceding pages. Works of art do have some features in common; indeed the concept is paradigmatically what Wittgenstein thought of as a "family concept"; just as there may be no one thing that all games have in common, neither winners nor losers, nor a competitive element, so there may be no one thing that all works of art share. Rather, there are various strands woven into the concept. I have identified four; there may be more. But it is unlikely that we can find any necessary conditions and it seems unlikely that we can find sufficient conditions either. What I would say is that, in addition to what I remarked earlier, to declare that something is a work of art is to suggest that it has two important aspects: expressive content and interpretability. The first implies that it has, in a sense, "meaning"; works of art are the sorts of things that can be ebullient or reserved, as people can. Secondly, they can also comment on our culture and on the times we live in as well as on the more "eternal" themes of human nature; teasing out these "implications" is what we do when we interpret art. What is very much of concern to us in this book is that this expressive content (in the sense of having "meaning") is a feature of music that seems permanently controversial, as might have been concluded from the brief discussion of Hanslick in Chapter 1. In Chapter 3 we shall see how vigorously claims about meaning have been debated. One important preliminary finding is this. You can make a strong case for saying that some music counts as art because it has an expressive face, because it can be followed and because it can be variously inter-preted. But a fuller discussion of what is a complex issue will follow; in as much as there is a gap in my discussion of what it is for something to be a specifically musical work of art, it will be filled retrospectively.

There is, then, a feature that is central to the fine arts such as fiction, poetry, drawing, painting, sculpture and so on, and that is found in music but is either absent or etiolated in the decorative arts such as embroidery or carpet-making. We think of a work of fine art as having "expressive" features. We sometimes ask what a work means, although the locution is perhaps not *le mot juste*. We may describe a work as "sunny" or "tragic", for example. The opening movement, the *Allemande*, of Bach's French Suite No. 5, seems to me to have a frank and open character that needs to be reflected in the way it is played. It is not reticent, nor does it hint at concealed issues. That works of art tend to have expressive characters in this way is, I believe, central to what distinguishes works of art from other things that human beings make and do.

But there are difficulties even for this cautious suggestion. These conditions are neither necessary nor sufficient. There are works of art that present us with a blank face or where we know so little about the background that we cannot "read" them. Interpretation is not a possibility. However, the decision to count something as a work of art means that we search for these features. There may be art for which the search is futile; there is no possibility of interpretation. Much contemporary music seems to lack an expressive character. The music of Iannis Xenakis or Boulez seems to me very hard to describe in expressive terms. (Hanslick thought that some music of the eighteenth century lacked expressive nuances.) Furthermore, we certainly cannot "follow" the music of Anton Webern in the way we can that of Brahms or Mahler.

When I wrote *Contemporary Aesthetics*[12] over 20 years ago, I made two proposals. The first is that "art" is something of a ragbag of various sorts of artefact and the second is that the concept has some distinctive social and political functions. The first point suggests that there is something of contingency about the way that those artefacts that we regard as art count as art and, indeed, I think this is so. It does not seem to me implausible to suppose that embroidery and tapestry, crochet, carved walking sticks, love-spoons, decoupage or scrimshaw may be moved from the category of craft to the category of art. Were this to happen, perhaps we would begin to concern ourselves with meaning, expression and interpretation and the creation of a canon and these would be a matter of critical debate. We would also look for originality. All of this can be a matter of degree, of course. It was brought home to me recently how a skilled carver of love-spoons varies traditional patterns while keeping some of the symbolism.[13] Perhaps, as well, arguments might break out as to whether the unknown Master of some ship had intended a particular piece of scrimshaw, evidently a late work, to have the spiritual transcendence that some commentators have seen in it or whether in fact it expresses a cosmological despair, a sort of oceanic ennui. But although these considerations are signs of arthood, they are not necessary. Primitive art may be created in a context where these considerations are absent and only later may it be classed as art. There is no canon for Benin bronzes and nothing much in the way of interpretative debate, beyond showing how they express certain prevalent ideas in their societies. Arthood is indeed a matter of a melange of cultural, political and historical factors. Among other things, it also marks out the important artefacts whose appreciation requires hard work and preparation and whose understanding demonstrates sophistication, education and cultivation. Once given the status of art, expressive and interpretative features may come to the fore. The function of calling this piece of music a "work of art" is to celebrate its distinction and to cue certain approaches and responses from us. Calling something "art" may then be as much a cue as a description.

Of course, there are works of art that are not worth our consideration. They have an expressive face, perhaps, but they may be sentimental or mawkish. Does their poor quality mean they cannot be interpreted? I think it is more the case that they are not worth interpreting, for to interpret them means spending time in their company and that is hardly worth the effort. Even those who find Wordsworth's poetry moving or thought-provoking will agree that much of his verse is dreadful and does not merit further consideration. Our conception of art is evaluatively centred in the ideal case. But most works of art lie outside this charmed circle. Such bad works of art count as works of art, sometimes by being the noddings of the otherwise great.

Now consider the second point. Understanding the arts is a sort of badge. Some argue that it is a mark that the middle classes place upon what belongs to them and that its function is to mark *them* rather than what they appreciate, a view which was widely advocated in the 1970s. Art simply is an indication of social status, a mark of sophistication. Now there is undoubtedly something in this, regrettable though it is. It was predictable that when the tabloid newspaper the *Sun* sent its music critic to Glyndebourne, he reported that it was an expensive noise. For *Sun* readers to like opera would be nothing less than class betrayal (or possibly betrayal of proprietor Mr Murdoch's tastes or betrayal of his judgement as to what his readers ought to like). The other side of the coin is what James Jolly, the editor of *Gramophone* drew attention to. He exaggerated when he said that the productions at Glyndebourne, generally as fine as any in the world, were presented to an audience half of whom would not be able to tell the difference between what is on offer at Glyndebourne and a run through at a village hall. But he did not exaggerate much. Many in the audience are there to confirm their proprietary rights rather than to enjoy the music. Glyndebourne, like Ascot, is one of the places to be seen.

There is an important lesson to be drawn from the first part of this chapter. To know what a work of art is is to have the concept of a work of art and this is to understand the hard cases for what they are: hard cases. To the extent that you are in the grip of an analysis, you no longer understand the concept of art. Thus the institutional theory, by determining what we should say about silent music (it is art music – or not – because the qualified say so), does what a theory should not do: it imposes an answer. Anybody equipped with the institutional theory can then rule a hard case in or out and any uncertainty he has should disappear. But surely it will not. He cannot get over the discomfort this case produces and, to the extent that he can, he has ceased to understand the demotic concept for what it is. (It is equally true that moral debates and dilemmas are of the essence of the moral life and that a moral theory, such as utilitarianism, that supplied a way of settling them, by that very token fails as a theory.)

To christen a piece of music or recognize it as a "work of art" is, I have said, as much a cue as an identification or a recognition. It sets in train a series of considerations, the music will be seen as offering opportunities and the act of declaring a piece a work of art has implications, none of which are easily captured in the jargon of analytic philosophy. It has something in common with registering with a dating agency or a marriage bureau. The object becomes available for differing sorts of intimate relationships. I intend this analogy to be taken seriously. We live our lives with art. The books, the films and the music that I love are what I continually return to. I want them in the house – on hand. We speak unashamedly of love here, even though, it will be argued, the relationship is single-sided, a claim that will occupy my attention later. The works do not adapt themselves to me as my friends do, it will be said, although I, of course, may adapt myself to them, being prepared to take time, trouble and thought to see what can be seen in them. On this view, perhaps the love of art is more like a love of God than love for friends and family. For on the usual conception of God, my love for Him changes me but not Him, for He is immutable. Similarly, works of art change us but, it is usually thought, we do not change them.

The work of music

Over the years I have heard about half a dozen recordings of Count Basie and his Orchestra playing "Lester Leaps In"; they all vary in the actual notes played, some very considerably. Two versions are very similar in the notes played but one is so evidently the superior that the other sounds like a draft version of it. The former is one of those pieces of music in which every note sounds in place; alter and we would damage it. The ending in particular is so exquisitely managed that it is impossible to suppress a laugh of delight at the elegance with which Basie and Lester Young manage the final bars. Are all of these "performances" of the same work? Or are they performances of different versions of the same work? Asked what Count Basie and his Orchestra are playing in every case we would answer "Lester Leaps In" and we do not think that the same title is being used to cover half a dozen different works. What do we say about Charlie Parker's "She Rote"? The opening is arranged but the rest is pure improvisation on a tune not mentioned in the title – "Beyond the Blue Horizon" – but it isn't the melody of this well-known tune that is used, but only its harmonic base. Is Parker playing "Beyond the Blue Horizon"? Such complicated cases apart, in jazz, generally, it seems as though identity is given by the theme around which musicians improvise or compose. Contrast that with classical music. The notes are very largely predetermined. The failure to play all the right notes in Mahler's Fourth Symphony means that a mistake has been made; but even among accurate versions, those which have been edited by recording engineers, there are differences, but they are differences not in the notes but in the nuances of performance; they differ in tempo, dynamics and in the degree of rubato (the varying of pace within a basic tempo).

In between these two examples, "Lester Leaps In" and Mahler's Fourth Symphony, there are cases where a certain latitude is accorded to the performer in playing ornaments. Earlier music is less fully scored. The eighteenth-century instrumentalist playing a concerto would have been expected to provide a cadenza, perhaps improvised, or a vocalist would have been expected to add ornaments to an aria as she saw fit. Yet the former remains a performance of a Mozart concerto even if at points the notes vary from other performances of the same work. What constitutes a work seems to vary in as much as what the performer "adds" varies in extent. There are conventions that provide a context within which "classical" music is performed. A decent edition of Bach or Couperin shows you how the ornaments should be played and gives you an idea of lower and upper limits as to tempi. Over the centuries the notation of Western classical music has become increasingly specific. This has several explanations. First, the music is no longer played within a sort of guild whose members know the ropes, in the way an eighteenth-century soloist would have known and have been expected to know the conventions of performance. Nowadays music will be played by musicians who will not be in personal contact with the composer, at least after the premiere and the first cluster of performances. Secondly, music is now assumed to outlive its composer and the composer will almost invariably want control over the manner of its performance. Increasingly precise notation enables him to obtain this.[14]

At the other end of the spectrum there are electronic compositions in which every element is decided by the composer and not varied. Each time the music is played it is exactly the same. There are other cases that closely resemble this. A piece of rock music might be created in the recording studio. Vinyl records or CD copies are made from the master recording. A "live performance" of the music may amount to no more than lip-synching. The artists are not really performing at all and the music is the same at each "performance". Incidentally, a pop record producer may stand in relation to the finished product quite unlike that of the sound engineer on a classical recording. The producer may play a creative role in the recordings he supervises through the various techniques of over-dubbing, sampling, adding tracks and all the other means of editing at his disposal. It is tempting to think of the producer as somehow analogous to a film director but the role played by Phil Spector or George Martin is less that of an "auteur" and more that of a *primus inter pares*, it seems. How, then, should we think of such a recording? The rock or pop recording is a sort of prime instance rather like the autograph of a novel or the original of a lithograph. Copies are taken from it by a purely causal process. Indeed, if classical recording came to supplant "live" concert hall performances then it is conceivable that the recording might take on something of the status of the pop or rock recording, as a work of art in its own right. But at present, the Beatles's recording of "A Day in the Life" is very different in its status *vis-à-vis* a work of art from a classical pianist's recording of a performance of a Beethoven sonata.[15]

Although the view that, in rock music, the "work" is the recording is now very widely accepted, in many cases the piece will go on developing through live performances (where the band does not lip-synch to an existing recording). Here what philosophers call the "ontology" is different again. There is a steadily developing conception of a piece of which a recording only offers a snapshot of one particular phase in that development; the situation compares closely with that of the various versions of "Lester Leaps In".

Some jazz musicians may settle into a standard way of doing "Laura" and they play it that way on successive gigs. The notes will be the same each time, more or less; departures from the norm will not count as an "interpretation" of the piece. Performance is closer to playing a recording over and over again. Parenthetically, a great deal of recorded jazz sounds, to the classically trained ear, like hugely competent note-spinning and its interest is limited. Music that seems to have a more lasting appeal, such as Benny Goodman's "AC-DC Current", which I shall discuss at greater length in Chapter 4, has a structural and motivic organization that brings it closer to Western classical music. But this is fairly exceptional in jazz. It is fun to go to a live jazz concert, where the pleasures of watching and listening to a performer, noticing how mistakes are embroidered into the text of the music and used, is rather like watching an experienced lecturer deal with a slip of the tongue by making a joke or weaving it into what he intended to follow. I have heard it suggested that Rachmaninov's Third Piano Concerto ought to be listened to in the frame of mind one listens to Miles Davis and not Brahms. Deep structural unity is lacking in this work, although the constant varying of the melodic motifs, which are drawn from Russian chant, does give it the sort of moment-by-moment logic that Gurney thought was what we mainly require from music. This piece simply celebrates the delights of performance and display. There are other cases again. Some music in the Western classical tradition is nowadays created by the composer improvising at the piano; a microphone in the piano is used to make a recording on a mini-disc, which is then edited on a mixing desk. This might then be notated later on. Which, here, is the work of music? At the other end of the spectrum, there are unrepeated improvisations by musicians trained in jazz, in Indian music or Western European classical music. I have described some of the forms that a "work of music" can take. I have hardly exhausted their variety. Peter Gabriel has produced a CD-Rom, *Xplora I* (1993), which allows his songs to be remixed by the "player".

What, then, is the work of music? It looks fairly evident that there can be no simple answer to this question. The work of music may be a recording engineered and created in a studio. On the other hand, what began as an improvisation becomes more and more rigid in performance until we have merely the illusion of improvisation but not the substance. It may not be written down but, to all intents and purposes, it is as if it was played from a notation that has been memorized, although, while it remains un-notated, the role of interpretation may be more exiguous. Between these two extremes we have the cases in Western classical music on which philosophers have tended to concentrate: a notated music that has to be interpreted by the performer. Thus the criterion of the identity of a piece of music varies according to the sort of music we are dealing with. A discussion of this issue needs to be historically and socially informed. It is no good imagining that the criterion in use for Western classical music for the past two centuries applies universally. As we shall see in a moment, that conception is itself a product of various philosophical and ideological forces and, partly because of this, the debate about what a work of music is has all sorts of implications for its standing as an art and for the relevance of certain ways of listening and performing. These are issues that have considerable importance outside the ivory towers of academe.

Classical music reflects a dichotomy to be found in philosophy at large in a way rarely found in world music, rock or jazz. The sharp distinction between work and performance raises questions about the status of the work itself, questions akin to those that philosophers ask about ideas, properties, mathematical concepts and mathematical and logical proofs. Plato famously thought of "goodness", the Idea or Form of goodness, as something distinct from the goodness of a single act of kindness or generosity. This universal "Good" had an existence that was separate. If you believe that moral values have an existence over and above the morality of individual acts, an existence that can be apprehended in an act of discovery, then you take, in some form or other, a Platonic view. Such values exist independently of what we judge or think and the morality of our actions is to be calculated with reference to them. Likewise many believe that the work of music exists separately from and independently of the individual performance or the score from which the performer works.

Is there any reason to suppose that the status of classical music has been enhanced by its replication of time-honoured philosophical positions? Well, as some have persuasively argued, the notion of a work of music as an object comparable in permanence to a sculpture, a painting or a performance puts it on a par with already established works of art. Performance, by contrast, is evanescent, as evanescent as the flowing stroke play of the Indian batsman Sachin Tendulkar. Although it can be captured on film, seeing it is like hearing a record of a jam session; it preserves an action. There is no work of football performed in an individual game and even though a game capable of aesthetic sublimity, like cricket, is often watched for that quality, it is not and never can be like a work of art. Part of the Platonic inheritance is a belief in the value of what is permanent. How often are works of art described as inexhaustible and their creators as immortals, "not of an age, but for all time" as Ben Jonson wrote of Shakespeare? The distinction between work and performance enables the work of music to claim the same status as works of literature. It has been argued recently that the development of the concept of a "work of music" developed as Western classical music flowered in the late eighteenth century with the first Viennese school. It is, I am sure, significant that the metaphor of the concert hall as an "imaginary museum" developed in the nineteenth century.[16]

In some form or other, realism, at least about classical music, is not to be gainsaid. The "alternative" is to "reduce", as philosophers would say, the work to the performance. Reduction programmes in philosophy are traditional. You "reduce" a physical object if you show that it is no more than a possibility of sensation and not something with an existence independent of perception. More perniciously, a reduction of the mind to the brain shows that thoughts and emotions are "really" only electro-chemical patterns in the brain. Reduction programmes are no more successful in the case of music than they are elsewhere in philosophy. You cannot "reduce" a work either to the class of its performances or to the possibility of a performance. The work is not the same as a performance. Let's begin with a few truisms. A work can exist unperformed, as long as the music has been written out and preserved in a library or a study. It might, as well, be remembered accurately by somebody even if no notated copy exists. While it is remembered, it exists. If the last copy is destroyed then it continues to exist as long as the last person to remember it can do so. After that the work is lost. (Whether it is right to say that it no longer exists is something we shall consider shortly.) So if the work could be performed but is not, there is no set of performances; but nobody would conclude that the work does not then exist. Indeed, if the work is the set of its performances, the more performances there are, the larger the number in the set. But a work does not grow bigger the more often it is performed. As far as the idea that the work is the set of performances is concerned, in order to allow for the possibility that a work exists without ever being performed we would have to treat the set of performances as a class that may be a null class (i.e. a class with no members, but a class none the less). But even if this escapes the present difficulty, a further trap remains. The notion of a work embodies certain normative requirements. It brings with it the possibility of errors in performance.

A second consideration, then, is this. Certainly, two performances might be of the same notes but differ in respect of tempo and dynamics, all those subtle little variations that make it interesting to hear different performances of the same work. Both performances, we can agree, are accurate, but since the notation is not specific with respect to the small nuances that are the difference between a notable performance and a boring one, it is possible for the two performances to differ. There may, as well, be mistakes. Probably no live performance is perfect. But how can we have the concept of "an interpretation" or of a mistake without having some prior notion of what the work is such that this performance diverges from it or interprets it? The problem, then, is that both these definitions of a work (as either performance or as a set of performances) leave us with

59

no way of making the important judgements about accuracy and interpretation we need in our everyday musical life. To be able to make these we need the concept of a work distinct from its performance.

For these reasons we cannot rest content with a description of the work as the possibility of a performance or as a set of performances. If you say either then you need to say more for there is a normative element in the notion of a work of music. It prescribes how a performance should go and departures from that prescription are what define mistakes. If it was just the possibility of a performance that constituted the work there would be no room for the idea of an error. We could be rough and ready about what counted as performing the work. You might argue that our ability to identify it as the work in question would suffice for the preliminary task of picking out the work. But we want more from the concept of a work; we need the element of normativity.

We also describe the work and the performance in different ways. A work can be good but a performance of it bad. Perhaps, too, it is possible to give a good performance of a rather mediocre work, making the best of it. Sir Thomas Beecham was sometimes said to make second-rate music, such as that of André Grétry, sound better than it is. Now I don't know whether this is a fault in Beecham. If it is, it is venal. The worst one can say is that he misled us about the work's stature. Again, a performance can be faithful to the character of the work. There is no possible parallel construction relating the fidelity of the work to the performance. There is no symmetry.

There are further complications for the thesis that a work is a possible performance; it will not cover most improvisations that exist, it seems, only as long as the performance. There is no possibility of a second performance. Here the notion of a possible performance seems to collapse into a singularity. If the improvisation is neither written down nor remembered note for note by the player or hearer nor recorded, it ceases to exist after the performance. (The improvisations of Beethoven and Bach are in that category.)

If the improvisation is recorded, of course, the situation becomes different, although not in a way that saves the thesis. Then, each copy of the record will be an instance of the piece in a way we shall shortly define, and it will be possible to play the work by playing the recording. The situation is, as we have seen, close to that of the multiple printings of a novel or a poem. Barring accidents, each copy is identical with each other in the edition and nothing is gained or lost by listening to one copy rather than another. It is unlike the performance of a sonata, which may be more or less revealing, more or less successful and more or less artistically praiseworthy.

So the idea of a work as a possible performance or as a set of performances does not apply to those works that exist as tapes, or as CDs. These can be played but not performed. More significantly, perhaps, it will not cover cases where a work cannot be performed because we don't know how to do it. Perhaps we don't know what instruments it requires or perhaps the instruments no longer exist or perhaps nobody can play them any longer or perhaps we do not know what the performing conventions of the time were. In the limiting case, a work might be physically impossible to play. But in such cases we would not deny that the work exists.

Could we, then, identify the music with the notated score, the copy that enables the pianist to produce a performance of the sonata? Again, this cannot be right. A score could be inaccurate. Scores sometimes contain contradictory instructions for tempo and dynamics; we then have to choose which characterizes the "real work". Sometimes they are crucially vague. In the last movement of Beethoven's Piano Sonata op. 110, at bars 166–7, Beethoven writes "*nach und nach weider geschwinder*" ("*poco a poco più moto*", or little by little faster again). Now, is the tempo supposed merely to accelerate to the opening tempo of the movement by bar 172? Tovey says it would be "unthinkable" to accelerate beyond that.[17] Or would it be right to go on steadily accelerating to the *fortissimo* close of the movement at bar 207? Myra Hess did, although one runs the risk of creating a merely superficial thrill in this majestic movement. But although a score may be vague, we do not, I think, say of a work of art that it is vague, at least not in any sense relevant here. Furthermore, as in the case of identifying work with performance, if we identify work and score we immediately run into the difficulty that the score might be lost and yet a pianist who has memorized the music may still be able to play it; and if it can be played it must exist.

At this point we need to introduce a little technical terminology from philosophy. The great nineteenth-century American philosopher C. S. Peirce distinguishes between type and token. The type can be roughly understood as an abstract object with which a particular, the token, "complies" (for want of a better word). This paragraph began with the word "At"; this is a token of a type; the type of the word "at" is located nowhere in particular but one token appears here. Among its many tokens are occurrences elsewhere in this book and, of course, in the newspaper I read, in books in the library and so on. Types and their tokens can be complex. The Welsh dragon is a more complicated type with which individual token flags comply. Proust's *À la recherche du temps perdu* is an exceedingly complicated type containing millions of words with which individual printed copies comply. Of course they may contain misprints;

there is no precise answer to the question: how many misprints may it contain before it ceases to be a token of that type?

Let us then regard the work of music as a type with which an individual performance, or a manuscript copy complies. The type is Beethoven's Piano Sonata op. 101. The performance I give, with lots of mistakes, is a token of that type because the mistakes are not sufficient to disqualify it as a performance. (The peerless Beethoven pianist, Solomon, gives a performance in which there are, as far as I can judge, very few errors). Now, I have mentioned "mistakes". In the notion of a type there is a certain "normativity" involved. The type prescribes how a token should go and a departure from what is prescribed means a mistake has been made.

A printed copy of the score is also a token of a type. Should we think of the printed copy as a token of the work? Certainly the type–token contrast seems to be applied in two ways, something that can occur when we apply the contrast elsewhere. My utterance of "At" is a token of a type just as the printed "At" is a token of a type. Does it matter too much whether we decide that the printed or written score and the performance are different tokens of two different types or different tokens of the same type? We need to pay attention to the difference between a score and a work. Notation gradually developed over centuries from an *aide-mémoire* for performers to a notated recipe for performance that was increasingly prescriptive, although without ever removing the need for interpretation by the performer. Perhaps the closest parallel today to earlier notated music is the printed version of a pop song; this is far more of a memory aid than a set of instructions to produce a performance. In a jazz standard with a subtle harmonic structure, like "Laura", it is the harmonic sequence that the notation helps you to keep in mind. The tune can be altered as the spirit moves you. This is leagues away from the latest "ur-text"[18] edition of Bach's Partitas, from which I depart at the peril of my teacher's indignation. One would, I think, need to be very relaxed about how a token complies with the type to allow that various renderings of the standard "Sweet Georgia Brown" on different occasions by different bands are all tokens of the same type. However, from what I said earlier, it is clear that each LP or CD including the Beatles's "A Day in the Life" includes a token of a type, of which the master recording is not the piece of music itself but merely the first token. In some ways, the master recording is comparable to the autograph copy of Proust's novel. Neither is privileged as far as the reader or listener is concerned. If either were lost, the "work" would not be lost. It is very different from a painting. A copy of this is a "mere copy" and if the original is lost we generally regard the work as lost.

My own predilection is for calling music copy not a token of the work but only a token of that type which is the score. The music copy is, after all, obtained from another copy or from the composer's autograph by a causal process and there should not be any mistakes in transmission. Of course, an editor may make alterations but this is in an attempt to repair what looks like a mistake in the process of transmission or a slip on the part of the composer. The relation between work and performance differs. Many musicians work out how a piece should go; once such an interpretation has been formulated, they play that interpretation each time they perform it (give or take a little); but it would be a mistake to think of this as a causal process of the kind that holds between a notated piece and a photocopy of it or between a score that has been proofread and corrected by a composer and the printing of that piece. The intentions of the performer are far too closely bound up with what goes on. The interpretation, too, should be pervaded by the musician's knowledge of the style and of the context in which the work was produced and even the acoustics of the building in which he happens to be performing. All this feeds in to the interpretation. It is as far from a mechanical reproduction as could be imagined.

I have laboured the point that notation has never become so precise as to rule out the need for decisions by the pianist or conductor. Indeed, if you listen to performers of even the most precisely notated twentieth-century music you may be surprised by the way they vary, even while the interpreters are assiduous in respecting what is written.

Realism: for and against

As I have suggested, I think we are bound to accept some form of realism respecting classical music. The work of music exists in between performances. It exists at least as long as there remains the possibility of its being performed (without it being identical with that possibility). But is its existence even less circumscribed? Might it not exist eternally? This question revolves around how we view the notion of a type. Should we think of the type as "created" or "initiated" at some time by some individual? Did Beethoven create or initiate the type of his "Archduke" Trio or was it there from eternity just waiting for Beethoven to identify it? What would lead somebody to adopt the extreme realist view that musical works exist eternally? I think that the motivation is to do with the notion of music being essentially some sort of pattern of notes, or structure of sounds, and there are, obviously, many such possible patterns and structures much as there

63

are many possible geometrical shapes, ranging from the triangle up to shapes of a thousand sides, some with curved sides, some with straight and so on. Platonists think that these exist prior to their being "discovered" by geometricians; if you agree, then you will be tempted to think the same way about musical shapes and structures.

A musical shape is thus something like the philosophical notion of an "abstract particular". It is not a universal like "greenness", because that correlates with a single property whereas a musical shape may be extremely complex, running to many bars and many, many notes. Neither could it be a "kind" in the way tigers form a kind. For, again, the musical work is normative; it prescribes how an instantiation or a token should go. The concept of a "tiger" is not currently normative in prescribing how people should create an instance of it. It is not so much that the notion of a kind is never normative. After all, in the case of an animal there may be a biological norm as to how many teeth it should have and a tiger who has lost teeth does not come up to the norm.[19] But the notion of a biological kind is not prescriptive. Now the idea of a work of music as a set of instructions for producing a performance brings such prescriptive features to the fore. But this, again, cannot be the whole truth. A work is not just a set of instructions; it has a character that needs to be reflected in performance. It is hard to think of a set of instructions as being epic or tragic, for example. Finally, one consideration militating against extreme or Platonic realism is that the notion of "discovering" something normative is itself rather puzzling. Did Samuel Johnson or William Wilberforce "discover" slavery to be wrong? What sort of "facts" are discovered in this way? (The problem will arise again in Chapter 4.)

Furthermore, a kind is a class of entities. But we have seen that a work is not a class; it is a particular thing. For roughly similar reasons we do not usually speak of the composer as "inventing" his music; fairly central in the notion of "invention" is the idea of a pattern that can be repeated. The diesel engine was invented and its construction repeated over and over again. But performances of a piece of music are not separate works of music. They are just that: performances *of* a work. Perhaps somebody invented the fugue, thereby inventing a form in which many different works of music can be composed, but that is about the extent to which we can make sense of the notion of invention in music. Significantly, Arnold Schoenberg was rather foolishly proprietorial about the twelve-tone system. He thought he had invented it and, about this, he was either right or wrong; it may have been simultaneously invented by another musician. But he did not need to be proprietorial about his String Trio.

The implied analogy with mathematics that lies behind the idea of musical works as eternal Platonic patterns of notes or sound structures has deep historical roots and it is highly significant. Clearly Platonists about music are inclined to think that musical works are not so much created as discovered. So the suggestion we are considering is that just as Évariste Galois made a mathematical discovery so Beethoven made a musical discovery;[20] he discovered the series of notes that make up the "Archduke" Trio. The possibility of combining these notes certainly existed before in the way that possibilities are generally thought to exist. It only fell to Beethoven to make the discovery. Now advocates of this view do not have to think the discovery could be made at any time. They could take the view that the culture of music had to be in a certain state, that of late classicism verging on romanticism, for somebody to discover that work. It is also the case that not just anybody could have discovered that work. It needed a musical genius like Beethoven. The situation is thought analogous to that in science. It took a man of Darwin's genius to discover the principles of natural selection and such a discovery could not have been made much earlier than it was. It needed the work of Charles Lyell and others to set the scene.

Platonists think of the eternal existence of musical works as the existence of possibilities that are then made actual by the discoverer. Now you may feel uncomfortable about the idea that possibilities exist and, I think, you would be right to be so. Certainly one objection is that this theory plays fast and loose with our notion of possibility. Possibilities may be said to "exist" in some etiolated sense but it is a robust part of our concept of a possibility that it does not exist in the usual sense until it is brought into existence. Treat possibilities as though they exist in any fuller sense than as "mere" possibilities and you collapse a useful distinction. Indeed to say that the "Archduke" Trio was a possibility before 1811 is precisely to imply that it did not exist before Beethoven composed it.

Furthermore, there is a perfectly respectable sense of "possible" in which we might say that this work was not possible before Beethoven came along. First of all it has the fingerprints of Beethoven and not his precursors. It is hard to see either how Bach could have conceived the opening page or what he would have made of it had he produced those notes while idling at the keyboard. Equally, had the famous Tristan chord occurred to Mozart, it would have been thought of as a progression that required resolution. He could not have thought of writing it as Wagner did. Indeed, the greater the composer and the greater the music, the less likely it is that anybody else could have written it. A banal tune might occur to anybody. "Fairest Isle" is unlikely to occur to anybody short of a

Purcell. The better the music, the more identifiable it is as the work of the master who produced it.

Think again about the case in science. In science more than one man may make a discovery. It is a familiar fact that both Darwin and Wallace fell upon the notion of natural selection at about the same time. A more striking instance is the periodic table. In the 1860s there were six independent classifications of the elements, all pointing to the periodic table we now associate with Mendeleyev. His account was superior but any of the other scientists could have made the final breakthrough. But it is unthinkable that, had Beethoven not existed, somebody else would have composed the "Archduke" Trio. Composers really do not worry about precedence. They are not perturbed by the prospect of somebody else publishing their "discovery" before they do. For what they do expresses something deeply individual. (I argue later that this is profoundly involved with the way we value art). It is true that had Beethoven not existed music would almost certainly have changed over that period of thirty years when he was the greatest living composer. But it is unlikely that it would have changed precisely in the way it did.

But not only does the notion that musical works exist from eternity to eternity in the way some mathematicians think the natural numbers exist collapse notions of possibility and existence, the notion that these works are "discovered" plays fast and loose with our idea of "discovery". Think again about Galois's work in mathematics. The mathematical theorems Galois discovered count as discoveries because the expressions are true. If the expressions were wrong or there were mistakes in his proofs, these do not count as discoveries. Change the proofs and they will, almost certainly, no longer be proofs. But if we were to alter Beethoven's "Archduke" Trio, as an editor might, we have neither another work of music nor have we turned something that is true into something that is false. The "Archduke" Trio is still the "Archduke" Trio; depending on the number of alterations we have made, we might think we have a new "version". It is important to see that notions of truth and falsity, central in mathematics, do not apply to music. The mathematical and musical cases are, crucially, not analogous.

Consider another disanalogy. A proof in mathematics can be lost but cannot go out of existence. A musical work might be lost and found again. But it is not "lost" if the score is destroyed by the composer. Brahms tore up many of his scores shortly before his death. These works are not lost. They were destroyed. They no longer exist.

Certainly a discovery may be made by accident. Digging in my garden, I might discover a Roman coin. If I am searching for it, I already know something about what I am looking for and shall be able to identify it when I find it. I may come across a coin and think that it is Roman whereas it is in fact of later date. But these cases are very different from the cases in mathematics that seem to provide the closest analogy to music. For one thing, although I can quite properly say that I "discovered" a Roman coin in the garden, here I can replace "discovered" with "found". But we cannot say that Beethoven "found" the "Archduke" Trio (except in the entirely irrelevant sense of finding a mislaid manuscript copy). Indeed, Beethoven could hardly have discovered the Trio by accident. That is not a possibility. We can make no sense of the idea that Beethoven might come across the "Archduchess" Trio and mistake it for the "Archduke" Trio.

This is not to say that there might not be some room for serendipity in the composing of music. Suppose that a composer "comes across" a tune in the rather haphazard way that Elgar seems to have hit on the "Enigma" theme. After a tiring day teaching the violin he was sitting at the piano with a cigar "doodling" towards a tune that his wife immediately liked; he entertained her by turning it into a character sketch of a friend. Might we call this a discovery? We might well, but such a tune is not a 35-minute set of variations; it required time, technique and imagination to work it up into a substantial orchestral piece. The tune might have been discovered but *Enigma Variations* was not.

What I am inclined to say is not that the notion of discovery has no place at all in thinking about music but rather that its role is very minor indeed. Most of what a composer does is very unlike normal cases of discovery. The sceptic about Platonism will point out that Elgar's theme is very Elgarian in its step-wise motion. It is the sort of tune that Elgar would have hit on just as the sort of passage work with which Charlie Parker makes something of a banal standard ballad is not the sort of passage work that another alto sax player would produce, except in mimicry. Of course, this sort of objection can be dealt with by the realist. Discovery requires a prepared mind. What Albert Einstein discovered required something of his genius; it did not occur to William Kelvin. Their backgrounds, their particular skills and their interests differed. It is no different with music; it is not surprising that the sort of material "discovered" by Elgar differs from the sort of material "discovered" by Richard Strauss. So much is common ground with the realist.

Should we think of the composer as "selecting" the notes of the melody he composes? Again, in most cases, the usage seems a bit off-centre. A serial composer might "select" the tone row on which he composes a piece. But normally we will say that a melody "occurs" to a composer.

Again, however, there are cases and cases. Consider Beethoven's note-books. What he is doing is working laboriously towards a theme that has the right properties. He doesn't "find" the theme, he doesn't "select" it and it doesn't "occur to him" in its final form. An analogy, although it is evidently an imperfect one, is to think of a mathematician as working towards a proof of a theorem. It is imperfect because the mathematician's criteria for a satisfactory ending point are the truth of the theorem and its valid deduction from his starting point, neither of which have any parallel in music. Interestingly, and it confirms my suspicions about Platonism in music, we don't say that Christian Goldbach "discovered" his conjecture that every positive even number is the sum of two primes (a prime number being a number divisible without remainder only by 1 and itself), but, if somebody were to prove it, we would say the proof had been discovered. Truth matters.

I have made some concessions towards Platonism. What the composer does seems sometimes like a discovery, sometimes like selection. A com-poser might quite properly be said to have "discovered" the theme that is just right for the last movement of his work. In this case, what he is doing is quite close to the solution of a puzzle; the manner and thematic content of his work up to some point imposes constraints within which he has to work to find an appropriate ending. This may be difficult. Some works have remained uncompleted and some have even been performed incomplete while the composer worked on the finale. William Walton's First Symphony is an example. We may allow that some other features of what a musician does might be akin to discovery; one might even allow that a performer could say that he had discovered that a passage makes sense played this way. But we ought not to rush to the conclusion that an entire work could be "discovered". Even if we grant these restricted roles to discovery, it does not imply that a theme pre-exists its composition or that its composition is merely the discovery of a pre-existing order of notes. There are all sorts of nuances here in the differing locutions that philosophers rather typically overlook in their pursuit of metaphysics.

The question that is begged in this discussion is the question of what the identity of a piece of music consists in. Platonists tend to think of it as a structure of sounds, although such a view would have to allow for the possibility that it may be transposed up or down a tone and remain the same piece (or even be transposed to frequencies too high for the human ear to hear). There is debate as to whether the instrumentation is part of the music or not. Is it the same work if it is arranged for another instru-ment? We allow that a lute suite is the same music if arranged for guitar. Do we allow Ferruccio Busoni's transcription for piano of Bach's *ciaconna* for solo violin as the same work? If I arrange Beethoven's Fifth Symphony for steel band is it the same work? Whether we answer these questions in the affirmative or negative depends to some extent on what we think is lost or added. There really isn't a clear answer. The further we go back in the history of Western music, the less it seems that composers had specific instrumentation in view. Then the less we are inclined to haver as to whether a particular instrumental version is an arrangement or not. The notion of an "arrangement" or transcription applies to music after, say, 1700, for, by that date, instrumentation is usually specified. You might, I suppose, insist that a performance of Ravel's *Daphnis et Chloé* on massed piano-accordions was a pukka performance of the work since the notes are all there, but all this does is to reveal your assumption that it is the notes that prescribe the identity of a work. I don't know whether this is so. Indeed, I don't think that our usage of "musical work" is that sharply defined.

If we permit the identity of a work of music to involve its instrumentation, why stop there? We might also include its expressive character, its gravity or jollity and once we do that further complications enter: difficulties that raise the question of what philosophers call "constructivism" (of which more in a moment). For on these matters there can be disputes among qualified musicians as to what the expressive features are. I don't mean the individual markings given by the composer, such as *teneramente* or *giocoso*, although these can be puzzling; it is more the overall expressive character of the work that I have in mind here. Is it ironic or do we take it at face value? A decision about such matters is often critical when playing Shostakovich, for example. Is the imitation of Tchaikovsky in the Adagio of the Second Ballet Suite, affectionate irony or parody, for example? The question is to what extent the identity of a work involves its interpretation and this in turn raises questions about its expressive nature, its meaning and how that is realized in interpretation. That Shostakovich's symphonic style involves both a measure of agitprop and a distancing from such crudity gives it an ambivalence that is very distinctive and poses problems for the interpreter. It also marks the way in which the critical discussion of music, its interpretation in that "literary" sense, bears on the way it is interpreted in performance. The question of meaning is a large one and occupies Chapter 3; it cannot, unfortunately, be briefly but adequately dealt with here. But the question of constructivism is pressing and it is to that I shall turn.

Realism and constructivism

We have seen that a natural way to describe the work–performance distinction is to think of the work as a type but one that has a point of origin. The type was created by its composer. But we have not yet finished with the complexities. In classical music a work is interpreted, and this adds further complications. Before we consider this, I want to make a distinction between two forms that realism can take, for a second conception of realism, one that we have not yet considered, is germane to the question of the interpretation of music.

What is this second form of realism? So far we have considered realism as what might be described as "ontological independence": specifically, the idea of a work having an existence distinct from its performance. But another form in which realism appears is in the supposition that there is an answer to a question we may put prior to the raising of that question. The issue arises in a very clear way in the philosophy of mathematics. For centuries, Fermat's Last Theorem awaited a proof. Now, a realist will say that Fermat's theorem is either true or false prior to any investigation and, of course, prior to Fermat's formulation. If we find a proof we shall discover the truth of this theorem. A non-realist will argue that, since mathematical truth depends upon the existence of proofs of a given theorem, until such a proof is established, the theorem is conjecture and is neither true nor false. I have, of course, over-simplified a complex matter. Is proof something itself to be discovered, as a realist might say, or is proof a concept that essentially involves showing to somebody that something is the case? Does it involve a psychological element?

I want to look at a partial, although only partial, parallel to these questions that arises in the domain of artistic performance. As soon as a performer considers playing a work, she has questions to ask and decisions to make. Look at the opening page of Beethoven's late Piano Sonata in A flat, op. 110. It is marked "Moderato". Now, bearing in mind that it is followed by a scherzo-like movement marked "Allegro molto", and that the ensuing slow movement is brief, (a recitative-like opening followed by a short arioso, would it be best to consider this the slow movement and take *moderato* as close to *andante*, thus balancing fast and slow movements in the work as a whole? This is what some great pianists have done. The marking "*con amabilita (sanft)*" means "with tender affection (easily or gently)". How long is the pause in bar 4? Should the *leggieramente* passage from bar 12 onwards be played a bit faster?

All these decisions may be thought out in advance. I remember a distinguished pianist saying that most of his decisions about interpretation came when he was away from the keyboard, perhaps taking a walk. If he decides on the best way to play a movement he might stick to that decision in successive performances. We say that he has thought out an interpretation and that he repeats the interpretation in various performances. In the philosophical jargon, the interpretation itself becomes a type of which the performances are tokens.

I have not suggested that the way it is played is integral to the work itself. The work is one thing; its interpretation in performance is another. The notes are all being played and given their proper values. But it is true to say that they underdetermine the performance. Especially with a work like this, we can imagine it being played in different but equally valid ways. But we need not think of the directions as vague. They are sufficient unto the day.

But suppose now that we identify the work with the work interpreted so that each interpretation of a work in fact individuates a new work. To put it crudely, the work comes into existence with the interpretation much as a mathematical truth comes into existence as it is proved. This view is known as "constructivism".[21] It can be formulated in different ways. Thus we could, indeed, identify the work with the performance so that different performances would be identical where their interpretation is concerned but count as different works. But this is not a popular option. For reasons I shall explain, and that derive from broader features of modern culture, it has been usual for constructivists to identify the work as "the work-as-interpreted". So the Beethoven sonata becomes "the sonata-as-interpreted-by-Brendel", for example, and Alfred Brendel may repeat this interpretation in different performances. As recorded performances have made it possible to compare interpretations to a degree not possible before, the discussion of varying interpretations has become of considerable interest outside the world of professional musicians. Ordinary music lovers have become interested; this, after all, is the way we experience music. We experience it through the minds, hands and voices of interpreters. So constructivism, it might be argued, actually brings to the fore a significant feature of our life with the art. Music is always experienced through the interpretation of somebody or other. (Of course, it is a view that applies primarily to Western classical music; I hardly need to reiterate the point that the requisite distinction between work and performance is not always found elsewhere. We have seen the differences between jazz, improvised music and rock music on the one hand and Western classical music on the other). More broadly, constructivists have been given succour by the strong tendency in our culture to press the thesis that we see and hear everything under an interpretation; as it is sometimes said, "interpretation goes all the way down". There are no naked historical facts, for example, that it is the historian's job to reach. The historian is both the proponent and the victim of narratives and worldviews. This widely accepted thesis has unquestionably influenced thinking about the arts, although it is open to very obvious objections in disciplines like history.

A question that has much exercised philosophers is whether an interpretation can be true or false. Is a certain interpretation of *King Lear*, as a play about blindness, say, true? There are parallels, although not quite exact parallels, in music. Is there only one right way of playing Beethoven's Piano Sonata op. 110, and is it then proper to say that this interpretation is the correct one and that the statement "This is the correct interpretation" is true? A corollary is the question of whether an interpretation is correct prior to its being considered by the player (and here there is a close parallel with the issues in the philosophy of mathematics). On the whole, the consensus is that musical interpretations, much like literary interpretations, are multifarious, and that no single one is *the* valid interpretation, although it is fair to say that not all philosophers agree about this. Since constructivists allow no independent uninterpreted work, it is hard to see how the question of correctness or validity in interpretation can arise for them.

There are, as I said, various forms of constructivism. You might identify a work with the class of its interpretations, a view that seems a particularly counterintuitive form of constructivism since it, inevitably, makes the work of art inconsistent; for of many works there are interpretations that are mutually incompatible. This is particularly evident in performing arts like music; you cannot play a movement at two different speeds simultaneously nor, at a certain point, both make and not make a pause. You may narrow the class that constitutes the work to include only defensible interpretations, thereby excluding eccentric judgements about tempi or dynamics (a jazzed-up version of Bach's *Goldberg Variations* is then, arguably, not a viable interpretation). If you are a singularist and believe that one correct interpretation exists, then you reach the vanishing point of constructivism. The correct interpretation is then true of the work of art in much the same way as a description of its other properties, such as its length, instrumentation and so on. Again, you may want a distinction between the idea that interpretations change their objects and the idea that a new "object-of-interpretation" is created in interpretation (a distinction that I do not find clear). Or you may think of interpretations as "completing the work". What constructivists have in common is the idea that a work of art is the part-product of an interpretation. Thus Beethoven's

"Moonlight" Sonata is not just the score nor the note structure but it is the sonata under an interpretation and the interpretation gives the possibility of a performance. Non-constructivism maintains that the work is separate from its interpretation.

The principal objection to constructivism is that since interpretations are the stuff of critical debate, we need a distinction between the work and the interpretations it bears. Without this we do not have the wherewithal of a debate. If we identify the work as the work plus interpretation, different interpretations merely individuate different works and a critical debate becomes merely a confrontation between different works. But surely there must be a difference between preferring Brendel's interpretation of Beethoven's op. 109 to Daniel Barenboim's and preferring the op. 109 to the op. 110. In any case, we can say that some interpretations are not viable; you may not play the opening movement of Beethoven's Fifth Symphony as slowly as Boulez did in a notorious 1970s' recording.

Let me describe a second objection before I continue. I said that some constructivists think of a work as being completed by an interpretation. The idea that works need to be "completed" by interpretation suggests that they are half-formed before. But we do not think this. In the greatest cases, we feel both that the creator has got things absolutely right, and at the same time, because the greatest works are the most multiply interpretable, we think they are open to many ways of seeing, reading or listening. The great works of art are both utterly distinctive and open to various ways of understanding. Their distinctiveness, or uniqueness, is connected with the way that we think that the creators got it right because we think that cuts or alterations would be damaging. Mozart's mature string quartets seem to me among the most perfect of human creations but there is no doubt that they can be played in different ways. This might look like a conflict. But it isn't, not as long as we remember the distinction between work and interpretation. It might be worth remarking *en passant* that different ways of playing a work may not amount to different interpretations; there are many different ways of playing Monteverdi but they do not, I think, constitute different interpretations. The idea of "interpretation" really becomes appropriate with Bach or, possibly, Purcell and thereafter. This is, of course, all a matter of degree. As scholars and performers converge on decisions about the correct vocal style and instrumentation, it may become evident that there are different interpretations abroad. Against this, we need to remember the far greater range of expressive predicates that can be properly used to characterize post-baroque music; it can be bitter, ironic, kitsch, sardonic and so on, and, as I shall argue later, the variety of these expressive descriptions relates to the variety of ways in which the music can be understood. Interpretation comes to the fore once we have to decide whether this passage is to be taken at face value or not.

A change of locution offers us another way of making a distinction and thereby suggests a third objection. Let us replace "convincing" here by "true to the work" (which does not mean that I want to say that interpretations can be "true" *simpliciter*). An interpretation can be true to the work but the work cannot be true to an interpretation; therefore the work and its interpretation cannot be identical. Symmetry fails.

Fourthly, there is a powerful argument against constructivism that derives from the complicated relationship that exists between the value of the work and the value of an interpretation. If you are tempted by the thought that the work of art is either completed by an interpretation or, stronger still, comprises a class of interpretations, consider the following. A work of art can be good and an interpretation of it bad. Examples abound. Could a work of art be bad and an interpretation good? I do not see why not. Bellini's *Norma* is an opera of conspicuously poor invention but it is performed because there are a couple of splendid arias in it; we might do our best for it. So the constructivist does have problems; because he excludes the existence of the work of art uninterpreted, he cannot make the distinction which I have just referred to, between a good work of art and a bad interpretation of it.

Finally, the possibility of a multitude of stimulating interpretations all of which are grounded in the work is one thing that confers value on the work itself. That is another possibility lost to the constructivist. He cannot rate Beethoven or Mahler as greater composers than Delius on the grounds, among other things, that Beethoven and Mahler can be played in many more convincing ways than can Delius.

The major and distinctive problem for the constructivist who wants also to retain a concept of the work as the locus of interpretations is one I have adumbrated: the problem of consistency. On the one hand, if we argue that the work is completed by the interpretation we multiply works, and then have no means of comparing and contrasting interpretations. But if we allow that interpretations can really conflict but want to retain the identity of the work as currently conceived, then the more we draw the interpretation into the work of art, the more we render the work of art internally inconsistent. A work of music cannot possess contradictory properties. There cannot be inconsistencies within it. (If we find inconsistent metronome markings, we assume a slip in transcription.) Some interpretations may, of course, be compatible and thus jointly sustainable. But it is a point of enormous importance about the arts that they can be understood in different ways that may not be mutually compatible and yet may be equally plausible. The common-sense realist assumption has always been that while there are questions as to the properties a work of art has that are "matters of fact" and to which there are pre-existing answers, these will be questions such as whether *Hamlet* has five acts or whether Mozart's *Eine Kleine Nachtmusik* is in sonata form, but not interpretative questions such as "Does Mahler's Sixth Symphony express his reaction to his own life crises or is it 'about' the collapse of bourgeois society?" The answer to the latter is neither yes nor no, although reasons can be given for one answer or the other. We shall see, in Chapter 3, what considerations make one such interpretation plausible and another unacceptable.

Is there a truth in constructivism?

Now the arguments against constructivism, as we have seen, look over-whelming. Yet might there be a truth in constructivism? Picasso's studies of *Las Meninas* might alter the way Velasquez's original is understood and hence change its meaning. On one understanding, of course, this is uncontroversial. A writer, painter or composer might not understand all that might be encompassed within the work he has created since there may be unconscious factors in the creative process. The hard cases are where the work of art picks up features neither consciously intended, uncon-sciously intended nor available to the creator in the culture in which the work originated. Now, I think there are at least some cases where a work changes in that an interpretation of it becomes so much part of the way of understanding it that the interpretation becomes the starting-point for an engagement with it; and although these are often cases where the creator seems to have an inexplicit intent, not all are. So sometimes constructiv-ism seems to give an accurate description of the engagement with art. Some features of an interpretation become part of a tradition. Later in this book, I shall discuss the performing tradition for Beethoven's "Moon-light" Sonata, a tradition in which it has become customary to give the first movement peculiar weight. It is partly connected with a romantic interpretation of the "meaning" of this movement, with tales about Beet-hoven's romantic attachments and with the view of it as a sort of nocturne; no evidence for any of this can be found in the score nor in *obiter dicta*. But a tradition has built up which is pretty nigh inescapable. There is an element of constructivism about all this. The work has been endowed with features that it did not originally possess. Decisions as to where to place the climax of a single movement may also come into this category. Different interpretations of Rachmaninov's Second Symphony may well place the salient moment at differing points. But for many works, there is an agreed tradition and, in many cases, there will not be much intelligent argument as to where the climax should be; the structure makes it plain. For many works, interpretative questions can be given clear answers. But some of the greatest music raises questions to which there are no very clear answers. In saying that sometimes a work seems to "acquire" a meaning, a way of interpretation, during its history of performance, I am not saying just that it has come to be viewed differently. That would be a triviality that nobody would deny. It is also a matter of the work's identity that is at stake here. This comes out in the way in which a failure to give the first movement of the "Moonlight" Sonata its accustomed weight will be taken to be an error in performance or, at least, an eccentric interpretation that needs defending, possibly by a recasting of the later movements.

Reflections on this may suggest a stronger form of constructivism. Consider this analogy. What I see in my friend is how she reacts to me and I to her. Does it follow that she has, as a matter of fact, those characteristics? Yes. Then is this how she really is? Well, what significance do you give to the word "really"? Sometimes it may be said in extenuation "She isn't really like that"; she was rude but it was an aberration – she was upset at the time. What is undeniable and easily observable is that other people bring out different characteristics in us. With some people you may be reticent, and with others outgoing. Of course, other features may remain constant. You are not simply the creation of context. Why should not art be likewise? It takes on a different character as different people encounter it. Some characteristics, expressive and interpretative, are permanent. They will not change. But others do.

For to deny that a work of art really possesses features that attract and move us, if those features are not seen by others, is no more plausible then for a mother to agree that her son is not really kind just because others do not see that quality in him. The non-constructivist might say "we see meaning in music" or "we project meaning on to the music" but we do not, I suggest, think of art as something we invest with meaning and, were we to think of it in that way, it would be a very different business. And yet, puzzled, we acknowledge that others see in art features that we do not see. (The very considerable implications of this for the way we value art will become a little clearer, I trust, in Chapter 4.)

It is true that our experience of music is characteristically to be thought of in expressive terms. We may immediately categorize it as plaintive or spirited. If you wish to categorize such judgements as interpretative, then interpretation does indeed, as they say, "go all the way down". But, I suspect, to do this transmutes interpreting into something else, something still "intentional" in character, as philosophers would put it, but more inclusive. So although the initial impact of a work may be exciting, awe-inspiring or moving, I think of these as basically causal judgements, albeit causal judgements that lead to expressive judgements about the nature of the work. They are not properly interpretative because the role they play in any debate about the nature of the work is distinct. Interpretations are, of their nature, contestable and a good deal of debate may be needed before we cancel our initial judgement. I do not have a choice as to whether or not to hear the opening of Mozart's Symphony in G minor as grief-laden. This is a reaction and this distinguishes it from interpretation proper, which may be largely within my power, in as much as I can call upon the relevant considerations. Of course, we can imagine listening to a great interpreta-tion, like that of Beecham, and find the music more uneasy than grieving: neurotic and anxious rather than tragic. After this, we might find it difficult to characterize the music in other ways and feel that other interpretations, by comparison, are rather superficial. Then the interpretation moulds our reaction. We subsequently hear the music as unsettled and if the character of another interpretation is different we may feel the interpretation is inadequate to the nature of the work. Nor should we ignore the fact that there can be uncertainty about the initial reaction. In some cases there may be no initial reaction at all; perhaps another hearing will enable us to form an impression or perhaps reaction has to be guided by somebody leading us to hear what can be heard. In which case, we might well have a case where interpretation is at the foundation. It does "go all the way down". But quite commonly it will not be like that. There will be some sort of ur-reaction and when that reaction is very strong we may be reluctant to have it countermanded by someone else, even when he or she is more experienced.

To summarize, then, sometimes music does acquire features that are a product of an interpretative history. Sometimes, too, we describe it in ways that others would dispute, but that we cannot retract. To this extent constructivism holds. But, then, it is quite common for a great interpreter to strip away the accumulation of tradition and show a work in a new light. This introduces questions about performance, and I now turn to these.

Authenticity

What would it be to be a realist about performances, as opposed to works? Well, in one way, of course, we are bound to be realists about perform-ances. The performance has the features it has and we, the listeners, grasp that or fail to. We do not, as listeners, do any interpreting. We simply

77

recognize or fail to recognize the way the pianist plays it. We don't endow it with features that we contribute to the occasion. If we think that it is a somewhat detached performance then we are either right or wrong about this. Like tables and chairs, the features of a performance are independent of us. Constructivism about performances is not much of an option. We are not tempted by the thought that, as listeners, we add something to the performance so that the performance becomes the "performance-as-heard". Still, we might wish to raise another question. Can performances be correct or incorrect? From what has been said about the multiplicity of interpretations, the answer will seem to be negative, although we may always raise the question as to whether a performance is true to the interpretation conceived by the performer. After all, a performer could fail to produce the interpretation she planned through technical inadequacies or a loss of concentration.

For those who favour the idea that a performance can be correct, a natural unreflective assumption is that the correct interpretation is the one the composer intended or would have endorsed had he settled down to work out an interpretation. (The latter proviso is important because there is no reason to suppose that a composer can encompass all the varying ways in which his piece might be played; it might well be that he would endorse a number of these, in which case there would, on this "intentionalist" thesis, be no single correct interpretation.) The matter of the creator's intention has been most widely debated with respect to literary interpretation; what a poem means, intentionalists propose, is what the poet intended by it. The opposition argues that the poet is merely the first reader of his poem. What it means is up for grabs; the reader brings her own background to the reading. Now Western classical music is different from poetry in one crucial respect: performance is essential if people are to encounter the work of music. We can read a poem to ourselves but, in music, we need the work of the performer before we encounter the music. Admittedly, some have argued that reading the score is better than listening to the limitations of a live performance but it is hard to believe that music heard in the mind's ear is equivalent to the experience of hearing the music played. Brahms famously claimed that reading the score of *Don Giovanni* was preferable to hearing the music in the theatre; I don't believe him and, even if he was telling the truth about his own experience, for very few musicians or music-lovers could this be so. If performance is essential, then intentionalists will claim that the correct performance is not only accurate to the score but is interpreted in accordance with the way the composer intended on the instruments he chose. It will sound as he intended. Such a performance will be "authentic".

There is an alternative. This second approach is less concerned about the business of getting the music to sound as the composer intended. It stresses the importance of a performing tradition. Pianist after pianist has played Bach and Beethoven and modern players can draw on their accumulated wisdom. Interpretative ideas are passed down from teacher to pupil. Certain technical problems are solved and the newcomer learns how. This might lead us to prize the inherited musicianship of a modern player above historical re-enactment. Why relinquish the wisdom of the ages? There are two things to be said about this. First, there need be no conflict with the first approach; there is no reason why at least many of the interpretative insights that Clifford Curzon, say, brought to Mozart cannot be reproduced when Mozart is played on an "authentic" instrument such as the fortepiano. Secondly, and sceptically, I suspect that the performing tradition is not really cumulative. Indeed, Mahler called it *Schlamperei* (sloppiness). On this view the tradition looks more like a gradual accumulation of performing habits until there is a sudden reversion to a fresh approach based on an examination of the original score, studied with fewer preconceptions. This is how conductors like Arturo Toscanini and, to some extent, Beecham, were seen by their contemporaries. Like the restorers of great paintings, they strip away decades of varnish. The tale is much more like Kuhn's account of the history of science, with scientific revolutions establishing new paradigms at various points in its history. Indeed the history of performance is probably a good deal more like what Kuhn imagined science to be than science is.[22]

Why are modern musicians so interested in what is called the "authentic" performance of music between 1700 and 1900? The term has been much bandied about and readers of this book will probably be familiar with the "authenticity" movement in the playing of pre-classical music and in the idea of the "historically informed" performance. It is, of course, a modern interest with an historical explanation. Generally, musicians prior to the latter half of the twentieth century did not think they were in any way obligated to perform music other than how it sounded best to them. The nineteenth-century development of an historical understanding of old texts and what they mean was extended in the twentieth century to the study of old music. It seemed equally important that we should treat old music in the same way as historical documents. We want to ask questions that, as far as possible, parallel the questions asked by historians: for instance, what could this text have meant to contemporary readers? The two questions that need to be separated are "How did it sound?" and "How did people hear it?" These are evidently different. We might, by reconstructing the eighteenth-century oboe, produce the sound Handel would have heard. It is then, of course, an additional question as to what tempo, dynamics and ornamentation are in order. Suppose we can settle this so that we do have the sound that these musicians and their publics heard. It is also a fact that, at that time, the sound would still have had the pastoral connotation of the shepherd's pipe, something that we need to learn and internalize. And then the whole idea of "the pastoral", a concept that played such a large part in Classical and Renaissance literature, is relevant and has to be reconstructed. This is something we can learn, although it will not be second nature to us because we are not children of that culture. Still, we can learn it sufficiently well so that it no longer requires a laborious act of imagination to enter that world. These things are not impossible; but they may require painstaking work from us while the original listeners acquired it simply through growing up in that society.

If we reconstruct the original sound and pin the correct interpretation to that which the composer intended or might have allowed at the time of composition, then we identify an interpretation or a class of interpretations as "authentic", or "historically informed", as they now say. Since this is often put forward as an ideal towards which the performer should strive, we should consider what arguments might be offered in its defence.

First, it might be argued, the music is the creation of the composer and we owe it to him to present his work as he conceived it. This prompts one important question: can we find out how he expected it to be heard? Let us assume, as seems plausible, that we can get half decent ideas about how he conceived the music from scholars working on instruments of the period, from reading contemporary manuals on performing practice or descriptions by contemporary listeners and travellers, and from looking at contemporary pictures of musicians. Thus the musculature of the face might show how vocalists produced their sounds and the pictures of players show how they held the instruments. So the first difficulty is not insuperable. We can go some way towards meeting it. Of course, the earlier the music the more difficult this is. But that it is difficult is no reason for not trying it and there seems no reason to deny that we can be partially successful at least.

Some argue that since the composers in question are dead, they no longer have rights over how their music should be played. I don't countenance this argument at all. The death of my mother did not cancel my duty to respect her wishes about the disposal of her remains. An author cares as well, that if his books are read after his death they should not be distorted. For me this argument may trump any consideration that the music might be improved by a later hand, though it depends somewhat on the stature of the music. In one of the works I quoted earlier and which appears in the discography at the end, I suspect that an Italian original from the seventeenth century has been heavily arranged in such a way as to make it attractive to a modern ear. The result enchants me but I don't approve. No more do I approve of some of the performances of the *Domine Deus* from Bach's Mass in B minor where the conductor has been unable to resist making prominent a particularly luscious string melody with the effect of unbalancing the whole. Such an expressive treatment may tickle the ear but its stylistic inappropriateness damages the whole. Some, convinced that the point of music is to give pleasure, are impatient with the whole authenticity business. If you like it what does it matter? The answer to that depends upon a more responsible and, I argue, morally informed view of what the business is all about.

Thus I am uneasy about an interpretation that "improves" a work in what may, at first sight, seem a more defensible way. Suppose a performer plays the music in a way that the composer did not and would not have endorsed and yet can be justified in terms of the score, the composer's cultural background and influences and so on. What then? Suppose you play the bombast in some of Richard Strauss's tone poems as self-mocking or ironic. Would this be impermissible? Suppose you treat the triumphalism in Elgar's First Symphony as hollow, something to which the later Elgar might well have consented. In such a context, Elgar seems a greater figure but it is not obvious that such were his intentions at the time of composing. In both cases we no longer see the work in its true light and that is a reason for misgivings.

And these considerations raise the question of the way the piece hangs together. I have heard a Mahler specialist new to Elgar attempt to play Elgar as though it is Mahler, that is by treating the music as essentially contrapuntal, displaying lines of approximately equal weight. Played this way Elgar's music does not add up. The line is melodic and the inner parts supporting. Where music is primarily contrapuntal, it is important not to "bring out a tune" in such a way as to obliterate the other lines. Bach is, and this is elementary, not to be played on the organ as though the organist was playing Messiaen.

Why should we care? Suppose we like the grand sound of a Cavaillé-Coll or "Father" Henry Willis organ and don't care about the authenticity of the Bach as long as a thrilling sound is being produced? Well, anybody interested in the arts will be aware of the way the very great astonish us. The notion of "genius" is not a Romantic invention.[23] The ridiculous argument that Shakespeare's plays are intrinsically no better than those of his Elizabethan contemporaries and that only the "Shakespeare industry" ensured his pre-eminence evaporates, for all save the cloth-eared, by comparing a half-decent performance of any mature Shakespeare play with a very good production of anything by Ben Jonson. What Bach, Purcell, Mozart and so on achieved is rarely something on which we can improve. So we need to hear what they composed and not something factitious. Their pieces hang together. Indeed it is noteworthy that very few arrangements survive in the repertoire. How often are Leopold Stokowski's Bach transcriptions played? A few are. Ravel's orchestration of Musorgsky is the most prominent example of a successful arrangement of a piano piece by another hand and some transcriptions of Bach chorales for piano are regularly played. Liszt's transcriptions of Schubert songs are played but perhaps ought not to be for they are more show-cases for the virtuoso than pieces of genuine musical worth.

It may take time for the virtues of an historically informed performance to become apparent to us. We may need to learn new habits of listening; we may need to pay attention to what we overlooked before. Perhaps the music will not appeal to us in its new guise, even after careful and knowledgeable listening. The conclusion we should draw is not that we have regrettably lost a pleasure in the music that we once enjoyed. Rather, we should be glad that the scales have been lifted from our eyes and that we are no longer under an illusion as to its real value. After all, there is nothing virtuous in false pleasure; we should not take pleasure in music that does not have the qualities that we thought it had, music that is being falsely presented to us as other than it really is.

So there is both a moral and an evaluative reason for playing the music the way the composer's contemporaries would have heard it. We owe it to the composer to play it in the way he conceived it and it normally sounds better that way. Admittedly, unlike moral considerations elsewhere, these vary with the stature of the music. The first argument has far less purchase with composers who are not of the first rank. It seems less of a crime, if a crime at all, to mess with Sir Henry Bishop than it does with Bach, although a few misgivings show a basic decency. The "moral" argument is less significant than assumptions about the stature of the music for, in the matchless, every individual element is part of the total effect. We cannot revise Mozart's finest works without damage and this extends to the mode of performance as well. Great works were conceived to be played in a certain way. Undoubtedly, within these constraints there will be more than one way of doing it. Bach might not have worried as to whether his keyboard music was played on the harpsichord, clavichord or early piano. He might have had preferences but any of these instruments would do. But I suspect that ornaments would have mattered as intensely to him as they did to Rameau, and we know Rameau cared, given his instructions on the matter. If you iron out the *notes inégales* in Rameau you ruin the effect. *Notes inégales* require what is notated as of equal value to be played as a sequence of alternate long and short notes – or vice versa – producing a skipping effect. Styles of playing cannot be disjunct from notation. The two complement each other and when the first is known and expected, it will not be notated. The more widely the conventions of performance were known among the anticipated performers, who were, after all, the composer's contemporaries, the less needed to be written down, and the more incumbent it is for our scholars to discover what they were.

It has been suggested that authenticity is achieved when the music produces the result in the audience that the composer intended it to achieve. Authenticity then becomes a matter of the effect the music has. This has been called "second-level intention". So Haydn, wanting to shock his audience by the sudden *fortissimos* in the "Surprise" Symphony, may need to have his orchestration beefed up in order to produce the same effect in a modern audience in a larger hall. The problem then is that other elements in the music are lost, for the precise timbre of a smaller ensemble disappears when forces are increased. Besides, this example is somewhat exceptional. For most music, no such specific effect has been calculated. The composer is concerned to get a piece right. The reactions of the audience and their characterization of the piece may surprise but not bother him. If they find "spirituality" in his work and he is an agnostic, he may not be too concerned. Members of an audience may, in any case, react differently. I do not think there is any good reason to suppose that the composer composes with an ideal audience reaction as his goal and so I don't think such a conception can play the role in authenticity that this theory suggests.

For some Western music the question of authenticity does not arise. It can only arise when we have a notation without a recorded legacy. It will never arise for the music of Britten and Stravinsky who recorded all their major works. We know how they expected their music to sound and future generations will know how contemporaries interpreted it. The only question is how much variation from that is permissible. The question is a question about the limits of interpretative licence and not about how the music should sound – and, although these questions may not always be easy to separate, nevertheless they are distinct.

Still, in the end I don't wish to rule out entirely an appeal to "what sounds best". How do we choose between the various versions of the Bruckner symphonies? Bruckner was persuaded by some of his friends to make alterations. Should we take these changes into account when performing these works or assume that he was too easily led? The authenticity movement has led to a prejudice that first thoughts are best thoughts. There may even be an element of expressionism in this with the unspoken assumption that the music will be best if it is closest to its original inspiration, as though the composer was trying to communicate a mental state immediately prior to the creation of the music, a mental state from which he is increasingly separated by the passage of time. But surely we ought not rob the composer of the capacity to revise. Since the 1960s, Leoš Janáček's *Jenůfa* has been played without the orchestral revisions of the conductor and composer, Karel Kovařovic. These alterations are particularly striking in the closing pages of the score. Yet Janáček intially approved Kovařovic's revisions in letters to his wife, praising them very highly. Later on, in correspondence in the 1920s, he objected strongly, although how much of his animosity was due to a dispute over royalties is hard to gauge.[24] I much prefer Kovařovic's version. In other ways I think we need to be less than purist. Another example or two will help. When conducting Verdi's *Otello* with the NBC Symphony Orchestra, Toscanini replaced a *pianissimo* with a *piano*, explaining that in Verdi's day Italian orchestras played everything *mezzo forte* and that the only way to get any variation at all was by exaggerating the markings. Erich Leinsdorf said that the six horns required in Prokofiev's *Romeo and Juliet* reflected the weakness of Russian players and that in an English or American orchestra, four would do. Surely in such cases changes are justified.[25]

Still, when all is said and done, I find the arguments of those who espouse "authentic" or "historically informed" performance very difficult to resist. All this relates closely to those questions of value that are discussed in Chapter 4.

Chapter 3

Meaning

Aunt Lily sat down ... breaking off every now and then to say, "It's the thought I appreciate, she's such a thoughtful kiddy", ... It did not escape us that there was a certain falsity, a greasy and posing self-consciousness, about these expressions. We had very often been sharply warned against sentimentality, and though we might have been able to define it only vaguely as the way one should not play Bach, we recognised it.   Rebecca West, *The Fountain Overflows*

Music and language

What can music mean? The question arises most directly with respect to instrumental music; indeed, it seems to have occurred to thinkers after music emancipated itself from text and dance, so becoming a fully-fledged art in its own right (what is described as "pure" or "absolute" music). When music accompanies words, its significance customarily lies in underlining or counterpointing the meaning of the text. In such cases the question of meaning does not arise in the same way.

So the problem comes to our attention when we think, say, of Beethoven's late quartets or Bach's *Goldberg Variations*. These sublime works seem to say nothing for which we could find verbal expression, at least in the sense that we cannot say after hearing them what we know that we did not know before. Indeed the fact that music cannot make statements explains, in part, why it was so tardily embraced as one of the fine arts. While the arts were expected to serve a moral purpose, to teach and instruct, it was hard to see music as one of them. Nor can music issue commands or question although it may, as we shall see, have a commanding manner or a

questioning tone. The questioning manner of the opening of the last movement of Beethoven's last quartet, op. 135, is, in fact underlined by his
writing *"Muss es sein* [Must it be]?" in the score. However, the music itself
asks no question that could be put into words. But to conclude from that
that the music is meaningless seems dismissive. Certainly we can describe
it in expressive terms. The music has a character and the character may be
noble, charming, thrilling or whatever. So much we can say, properly, of the
music in verbal terms. But in characterizing it in this way we are certainly
not saying that these are statements that it makes. Of course, we might find
it equally hard to say what we know now that we did not know before
reading Wilfred Owen's "Dulce et Decorum Est" – have we discovered that
war is a waste of precious human life? We knew that before. We might say
that a great poet "brings these things home to us", and that is so. But
although we may find examples of cases where he tells us what we did not
know before, these can be quite hard to find. What we won't deny is that
statements may be made within a literary work of art – statements that may
themselves be true or false – and that it may be possible to put what a poem
says into other words, although if the poem is any good it would be
destructive to do so. But the *Goldberg Variations* does not contain a message, for a message that is not communicable in words cannot be a message;
any attempt to persuade us that there is one will involve some distortion of
the word "message". "Message" certainly will not be taken in its usual
sense. However I shall suggest that you may be able to say what it means,
though in saying what it means you won't be saying anything true of the
piece of music. In this respect the case is not so different from making a
non-banal claim about "Dulce et Decorum Est". This sounds paradoxical.
I shall explain, but before I do there is some preparatory work to do.

One of the first things that strikes us when we begin to think about
music is its power over us. Why does it affect us so deeply? It is not hard
to see that our natural sympathy for others makes us feel pity for people
who suffer and, the closer they are to us, the more we share their misery.
Although it is certainly puzzling that we should feel sadness for the fate of
Mercutio in *Romeo and Juliet* when we hardly have to think to remind
ourselves that he does not exist, it is surely not such an apparently
insoluble problem as our being moved by music. After all, Mercutio is a
character, albeit fictional, with cares and worries. We find it more
puzzling that, when Vaughan Williams's *Serenade to Music* was first performed at a Prom in 1939, the composer's wife turned to Rachmaninov,
who was sitting in the same box, to find him in tears, saying it was the
most beautiful music he had ever heard. Mighty sounds can make us
tremble.

I am not sure we can do very much to explain this effect. The effect of music in opera, where the dramatic situation is underlined, is easier to see. I am very moved by the end of Janáček's opera *Jenůfa* because the spectacle of forgiveness and reconciliation moves me. The modulation of the music into a major key breaks the dam and it is hard not to weep. Equally a text will determine the expressive function of the music. When Billie Holiday sang "Strange Fruit", the words and the voice spoke of the sufferings of black people and the music underlines that. Sometimes quite unprepossessing music tugs at us. The little string phrases in the opening of Act II of *Jenůfa* express a domestic tranquillity; Jenůfa and her stepmother sit quietly at home. Of course, their poignancy depends on our knowing that Jenůfa is pregnant by a worthless fellow. But music also moves us when it is not underpinning a text or action.

Perhaps it is worth mentioning, as well, in case anybody is troubled by it, that we need to distinguish associations from meaning. Some music is irrevocably bound up with a particular time in one's life. In particular pop music, just because it is evanescent, and because it is something that especially appeals to the young, becomes, in later life, suffused with nostalgia and as potent in releasing the past as the taste of madeleines dipped in tea was for Proust. But such idiosyncrasies, which typify the "power of cheap music", as Noel Coward characterized it, have little or nothing to do with its meaning. They are private; meaning is public. They vary from listener to listener, but the expressive character of music, its lightness or gravity, its stealth or laconic stride, is something open to any competent listener to identify.

To the other question that is likely to strike the layman who begins to think about music, there is an answer, or more properly, a set of answers. This question is very familiar to philosophers who reflect on music. It is the problem of how we can apply what have been called "expressive predicates" to music. Examples of these have already surfaced in the discussion. Philosophical writers have tended to concentrate on the application of the word "sad" to music. But there are many others; how do we justify calling music "exuberant", "exhilarating", "exotic", "gentle", "grave", "funereal", "detached", "distant", "grandiose", "grandiloquent", "resigned", "comic", "ironic", "sentimental" or "dispassionate"? Purely instrumental music can be any of these without our being able to identify anything that it "says" in the way that a piece of ordinary prose says something. Yet we may find this form of description apt.

Lurking in the background is one salient feature of our relation to music. We seem to have a need to capture its character in words. Consider this passage from Beethoven's Piano Sonata op. 109, variation IV from the final movement.

The temptation is to think that because we cannot describe exactly the expressive nature of this passage, it must be saying something too deep – or too precise – for words. What it communicates is ineffable. Certainly some writers have said this. Very famously, Mendelssohn said that what music expresses is too precise for words. We can say that the bars following bar 8, remote from the main key of E major yet constantly leaning towards it, express yearning. But there is also something curiously oblique about the passage – the music seems to look at us askance – and there is a consequent air of detachment, which links with the otherworldliness supposed to characterize late Beethoven. We want to characterize it more exactly, to capture the *je ne sais quoi*, but it somehow escapes us; we feel uncomfortable and uneasy at being defeated, as though we have not quite got there.

But should we feel thus? At one level the music is deeply satisfying. If we listen to the recorded performance by, say, Solomon, we will feel that at last a great pianist has the measure of this very difficult and elusive work and that nothing needs to be said. No qualifications or reservations are required. But then our urge to describe insinuates itself and we are frustrated once again. But music might be no different in this respect from the ambience of an evening spent in beautiful surroundings with somebody you love or the perfection of a fine wine.

Might we say that some music, at least, refers and its meaning is a matter of its reference? Some writers have been prepared to say that sad music refers to sadness. Such music then becomes rather like a string of proper names. A cheerful passage refers to cheerfulness, it is followed by a passage that refers to sobriety and so on. But as soon as we spell this idea out in such detail it looks highly implausible. Normally I refer to something or somebody in the course of saying something about it or her. I refer to the Queen in the course of saying that she has celebrated her Golden Jubilee. The mere uttering of nouns one after another sounds like a form of linguistic insanity. There are only a few occasions where such an activity would have any sense; at a reception, a man at the door may call out "Colonel and Mrs Blimp", "The Right Honourable James Golightly" and so on. In these cases the giving of names in sequence does, I think, constitute acts of referring. But normally, even where lists are made, the entries do not refer. Beachcomber's *Directory of Huntingdonshire Cabmen* did not refer to these fictional individuals any more than the *dramatis personae* at the beginning of the text of *Macbeth* refer. My late father-in-law used to discipline his children when they used vulgar language by insisting that they read sections of the London Telephone Directory, inserting the offending word after each entry. But, in this witless attempt at reforming their usage via boredom, the children were not referring. (Of course, it reduced them to fits of helpless giggling.)

Offhand, I cannot think of any context that would entitle us to suppose that the solemnity of a piece of music refers to solemnity. Neither does Beethoven, in imitating the sound of a cuckoo in his "Pastoral" Symphony, refer to an individual cuckoo he might have heard in the Vienna woods or to cuckoos as a species; no more do I refer to a bear in particular or in general when I amuse my grandchildren by pretending to be a bear or by imitating a bear. A conductor once observed that in the slow movement of Haydn's Symphony No. 93, the bassoon imitates a fart. But we don't say that Haydn or his music referred to a fart. To imitate is not to refer. When an impressionist imitates the halting speech and confused syntax and semantics of George W. Bush, he does not refer to him. Apart from the way music can imitate bird song or the sound of trains, particular instruments have long established conventional associations: the oboe with the pastoral, the horn with both hunting and with cuckoldry. But none of these constitute anything like a referring function. Most significantly in music, because it does not make assertions, there is no space for placing referring within an act of communication.

So if music was, in fact, a list of names following each other in sequence, it would be hard to see that this constituted the music having meaning. We might equally well call the music meaningless just as we would call the gibbering of a madman who endlessly repeated names meaningless. What we might do, of course, is to ascribe meaning to music by interpreting the sequence of characters that the music possesses in terms of some overarching narrative. When we describe Beethoven's Fifth Symphony as the triumph of man's spirit over fate, we do just that. Perhaps this is not a very insightful or interesting interpretation, but it does show how music might have a meaning via the process of interpretation. But a full discussion of this must await later developments in this chapter.

Perhaps, you will say, this is all a very big mistake. Perhaps those who think that music has no meaning at all are correct. This is what, in a different area of philosophy, is sometimes called an "error" theory. On this view it is an illusion that music has meaning. Unsurprisingly, of course, this depends upon what we understand by "meaning". As I hinted earlier in this chapter, if "meaning" is construed with the meaning of sentences or statements as the paradigm, then it is pretty clear that music does not have any meaning. But music does not have to be construed that way alone. We also speak of what somebody meant by a certain gesture or a certain tone of voice. We speak of what a certain action meant. In all these cases, there is a supposition that the speaker or the agent intended her words or her action to have that meaning, although whether she intended or expected "uptake" by the listener or onlooker is another matter. An ironic tone of voice signals that one's words are not to be taken at face value and it is quite proper to speak of what somebody "meant" by using that tone of voice.

So talk of the meaning of music might be premised on the latter sense (or senses) of meaning. "That was a gesture of consolation", I say, "and you misinterpreted it when you took it as ironic." Equally a musical passage might be consoling. It is a short step to saying "it expresses consolation" and a somewhat longer step to saying that it has that meaning. Perhaps the latter is acceptable if marginally unidiomatic. But it is certainly idiomatic to say that a passage by Schubert is meant to be consoling and that, if we miss this, we misinterpret or misperform the piece. I shall have more to say about this sort of meaning later. All in all, though, I think talk of the meaning of music here uses "meaning" in a somewhat vestigial way. We can find locutions where it is proper to talk about the expressive features of music as a matter of what the music means or what the composer meant by the music but even here there is a slight feeling of discomfort, a sense that language is being stretched to accommodate a figure on which it is not a comfortable fit.

Famously, Stravinsky denied that music expressed anything at all, either a mood or a state of mind, and this, *a fortiori*, would prevent it having a meaning even in this somewhat attenuated sense.[1] Stravinsky's is what I take to be an error theory. It is not plausible. It flies in the face of what we do say about music; later on, he modified it considerably, stressing the conventional connections with extra-musical phenomena. If the connections are conventional then of course, you might argue that there is a parallel with the way in which the meaning of words is established. In one sense the meaning of "cat" is conventional in as much as other languages have different words for "cat" and we can introduce technical terms into a language simply by specifying what they are to mean. But it is seriously misleading to suggest that the expressive significance of music is conventional. That music that seems to rage is expressive of tempestuousness is not unconnected with the fact that someone in a tempestuous mood shouts and is voluble, their voice rises and falls, and they wave their arms about in animated gestures. This does not seem to be a matter of conventions that might or might not be found in a particular society. As will by now be clear, I reject an error theory. However, we have yet to determine in what sense we use the word "meaning" when we say that music has meaning. We still await an answer.

Set aside, then, the question of whether music "means" in the way that language "means". For the expressive descriptions that we make of music we may use in characterizing people independently of anything they say. Their exuberance may show as much in the way they move, their gestures or in their faces as in what they say. The gist of the problem is this. To be sad or to be happy, to be bold or to be fearful is not just a matter of having a certain private feeling that we may, or may not, betray to others by our actions and behaviour and by what we say. It is widely agreed among philosophers that there is what is often called a "cognitive component" to our feelings. To be angry with somebody normally implies that you think he has injured you or somebody else in an avoidable way. He is guilty of a misdeed. You have beliefs about the situation. When I call somebody "angry" I imply that he is likely to behave in certain ways. I imply, as well, that he is angry about something, which in turn implies that he has certain beliefs about the situation and so on. But music seems to lack the requisite cognitive elements; it has no beliefs and no propensities to behave.

Before I go on to discuss the various ways philosophers have tried to account for the difficulties in applying these descriptions to music, let me recapitulate. What is the significance of all this? Because of these ways in which we characterize instrumental music, it is not a decorative art but one of the fine arts. It is, we might say, a "humanist art", much like the representational arts: literature, drama, film and painting. It is not like the patterning of a wallpaper or of the arcading of a great building. Certainly these can be described expressively but in a much more limited vocabulary. A pattern might be frenzied or calm, possibly, but not ironic, nor sad tinged with sentimentality, which music can be. Indeed it is highly probable that it was the great expansion of the ways in which music can be characterized that led to its being embraced as one of the fine arts towards the end of the eighteenth century (although the terms in which the matter was being debated suggested that music was then being thought of as expressive or representative of mental states). To describe a mere pattern such as the architectural arcading of a blind-storey as melancholy would be to place an onus upon the speaker to defend this claim. As it stands it looks a bit like a metaphor and needs some teasing out. She will need to point to some detail that justifies the claim. But in the case of music such talk is unproblematic, save to philosophers, and it is not thought of as especially figurative.

Now it is not just the range of expressive predicates that makes music unequivocally one of the fine arts. Like the arts whose medium is language, we can follow music. We usually have some expectation, not necessarily consciously formulated, as to how a phrase will end. At the simplest possible level, we expect the phrase

A   D   E

to end

A

I give the letters of the notes for those who cannot read staff notation but know the names of the notes on the piano. The figure is contained within a single octave. It is the ground bass in an anonymous southern Italian seventeenth-century "*Passacaglia della Vita*", the text of which is in Italian but bears the Latin title "*Homo Fugit velut Umbra* [Man Flees like a Shadow]". (Details of the recording are in the discography.)

As has been well understood for half a century or more, this mirrors an important feature of language. If I leave a phrase uncompleted, you may well be able to complete it for me. With clichés and proverbs this is easy: "In this day and ... [age]"; "Too many cooks spoil the ... [broth]". Our ability to fill in this way helps us to combat distortion or interference when we are listening to public announcements in an airport or on the railway. This feature of language is partly a matter of grammar or syntax (grammar may call for a noun at a particular juncture) and partly semantics. We don't have too much trouble filling in the missing words, although, of course, we can make mistakes. A famous pub sketch from the television series *The Two Ronnies* makes use of the latter. Ronnie Corbett has a propensity for getting lost at the end of his sentences and Ronnie Barker offers suggestions as to the word or phrase on the tip of Corbett's tongue.

RC: I always used to work with ...
RB: With pride?
RC: No.
RB: Within reason?
RC: No.
RB: With an overcoat on?
RC: No. With Harry Hawkins.[2]

But with music it is the syntactic features alone that enable us to supply what is missing, for there is no semantic element. Different notes and chords do not approximate to nouns, adjectives, prepositions or pronouns. If we attempt a glossary of music, we will take either whole phrases and whole harmonic sequences or notes in relation to the tonic and give them a character of the sort I have described above. Thus we may think of a rising major sequence as optimistic or a chromatic descending passage as sad.[3] But the syntactic element that enables music to be followed is crucial to the way we value it. Music that is merely a concatenation of agreeable sounds does not have the same appeal. The very memorability of music connects with this capacity to be followed. The recognition of this feature has led some to think that the debate over the meaning of music should be formulated in terms of a contrast between those who think that the meaning of music is internal to the music itself and those who think that it is external, in the sense that music can mean what is extrinsic to the music itself. In fact there is some truth in both positions, although the second needs careful formulation.

I shall not spend too much time on a theory that was once popular. It is the idea that a piece of music is impassioned because the composer was impassioned when he wrote it; the objections to this are fairly obvious and have been around for as long as the theory has been around. First, empirical evidence suggests that it is false. From what we know of composers, they do not necessarily have to get themselves in a certain mood in order to write impassioned music. It is a familiar point that a composer can write a triumphal march for a state occasion to order. Secondly, a more philosophical objection is that we establish the character of the music independently of anything we know about the composer's mental condition. We do not need to consult him or his biographies in order to find out what the music is like. This, of course, does not preclude the possibility that his mental state causes him to write the sort of music he does; but, as I have just said, there seems evidence against such a causal connection being general. The idea that music has to be an outpouring of the soul in which the composer works out his own emotional turmoil is a romantic one. It is the product of a culture that encourages people to look inwards and in which narcissistic self-concern goes unquestioned. It underplays the element of craftsmanship of artists, the sheer pleasure to be taken in making something and getting it right, so that the transitions are inventive and neat, that the harmonic structure and design maintain our interest, that it is not merely a collection of clichés and that the various parts fit together. To get it right is to produce something that holds and interests the listener. This aside, my main point here is that it is a mistake to suppose that you could either deduce the character of the composer from the character of the music or find out what the character of the music is by initially finding out how the composer felt. You cannot. From learning that a composer was depressed over a period of months you cannot reliably deduce that the music he produced over that period was sad nor from the tragic nature of a funeral march can you deduce that the composer was downcast when writing it. Any auto-biographical account of how music has the expressive significance it has must come to terms with the fact that most of the major settings of the Requiem and Mass after Beethoven have come from unbelievers.

This is not to deny that we may be particularly moved by a work which strikes us as "authentic" or "sincere", or as the raw portrayal of a real human being's emotions – it is hard to dissociate the music of Shostakovich from the life of the composer, for example – and we may love music for the power it has to bend us to its mood. The point is rather that not all the music we love and value is either autobiographical or causally active in this way. Expressionists tend to over generalize about this and, I think, hidden here in some forms of expressionism is the thought that Hanslick rejected: that the value of music lies in its power to move us to the emotions it expresses. I shall argue, to the contrary, that while the value of music lies, in part, in its power to move us, this is not to say that what it moves us to are the states that it expresses.

Perhaps, you might think, a more pallid version of expressionism might fit the bill. When we listen to music that is uneasy or disturbed, do we imagine a person who suffers these mental states that we ascribe to the music? Is there a sort of musical equivalent to the narrator of a tale, a narrator who may or may not be identical with the author?[4] Perhaps we may listen to music, aware that the composer probably did not suffer the angst that we ascribe to the music, but listening to the music "as if" there was such an individual. Behind the music is an imaginary persona suffering these states. But for many of us, music is not listened to in this way; there is just the music, which may be wonderful in itself and requires no props or make-believe. Indeed much music resists this imaginary exploration. It needs an effort to listen to Bach's *Forty-Eight Preludes and Fugues* or some of Stravinsky's late music in this way. We might imagine an austere and rather neutral persona. Even if we do, the familiar difficulty re-emerges. The persona has to be calculated from the character of the music. As an explanation of the expressive features of the music, this is question-begging. We already have to recognize that character in order to invest the imaginary persona with the relevant qualities.

The expressionist theory I discarded earlier often goes with a belief that the composer recreates his feelings in the listener via the music. This is an element in what has been called the "infection theory of art" and it is often associated with Tolstoy.[5] Detach the second part of this theory, the theory that the music recreates its own character in the hearer and you have a view that I have just adumbrated, which is commonly described as "arousalism'. On this view, a view that has become popular in the past decade, what character the music has it has in virtue of its effect on the listener. Such a theory owes us some investigation of the nature of our responses to music, and I shall categorize it as "phenomenological" in line with the philosophical movement that tried to investigate the character of human experience of the world. We may contrast this with what is called "cognitivism"; cognitivists claim that it is the music itself that is grave or exuberant and not the composer or the listener (or the performer for that matter).

Arousalism

We are now, then, in a position to make a preliminary distinction. Contemporary answers to the question "What is it for a piece of music to be sad?" fall into two groups. Either they ask what is characteristic of our experience such that we should call music sad, that is, they look for a phenomenological answer, or else they ask what is it that entitles us to call music sad, and this leads into an investigation of metaphor and enquiries as to what extent "this music is sad" is metaphorical. Some of the answers I shall consider are answers that belong to the phenomenological category and some to the "metaphorical". My main contention will be that no one account does for the entire range of these predicates; we need different answers for different contexts.

So one way in which we might explain the grimness of certain music, such as the opening of Shostakovich's Eighth Symphony or the reflectiveness of the Jimmy Giuffre Trio's *The Train and the River* is that it makes the listener grim or reflective on listening to it.[6] Now, as I have said, we can hardly deny that sometimes music has this effect upon us. Indeed, it might be a testimony to the power of great music that it affects us in just this way. We are overpowered by the mood it expresses. It arouses our feelings. You might describe the effect of Purcell's "Hear My Prayer, Oh Lord" as a kind of twisting in the vitals. But arousalism is not a very interesting or controversial thesis if it merely maintains that sometimes music moves us to the moods it expresses. It then is merely a causal claim and one that is not even universal; sometimes music moves us to the corresponding states and sometimes not. In order to be a thesis of philosophical interest, it needs to claim more: to propose that in general we describe music in these terms because of the effects it has on us. It needs to give priority to the response over the music's initial character. Some of the arguments I shall assemble are knock-down arguments and I shall end by rejecting arousalism; nevertheless, as I have just remarked, there is something deeply plausible about arousalism simply because its emphasis on the effects music has on us relates to the value music has for us. For no philosophy of art can afford to stray too far from issues of value. What we prize in music may connect with its power to move us to a particular mood; this gives us a close link between expressive power and value in music. So if it seems curious, a sort of corollary of my initial remarks in this chapter, that we should place such a high value on such an abstract art, then the fact that music should be so imperious in its ability to move us may help us to find a connection. We admire and acknowledge such a power, although I suspect we admire and value this power more than we value the states it puts us in.

A few caveats are required here; we may be ambivalent about this power. I might admire the power of a particular piece of music but feel uncomfortable about that very power. I may even dislike the effect it has on me. Some of us feel uncomfortable about the effect of Wagner's music – not because of his anti-Semitism and the unpleasant and foolish ideas he frequently tried to propagate in his music dramas – but just because he overwhelms. We feel we have no private domain left. We do not go out to meet Wagner's music as we do that of Mozart or Bach or Miles Davis. He envelops us. Just because of this I may value it in one way but not in another. I think it is great music but I don't want too much of it in my life. There is too much egoism involved in this demand for our submission. This is the manner of the demagogue or the evangelist.

Now the form of the phenomenological account with which I am concerned is the arousalist thesis and I have conceded that some music arouses passions in us that match the music. Reflective music may make us reflective or grim music grim. There are two questions:

• How widely does this apply?
• Is such a response a necessary feature of an adequate response to the music?

Before we examine these issues, I should warn the reader new to the topic that in no area of the subject is she more likely to encounter very approximate philosophizing than on the topic of music and the emotions. Anxious that music that they love should not be seen as trivial, otherwise good thinkers make claims that are hard to understand and, once understood, are seen to be patently false. A very distinguished philosopher claimed recently that music has profound connections to our emotional life and is ultimately experienced by the listeners as about them and their emotional life.[7] On any understanding of what "our emotional life" means, it is preposterous to suggest that music is connected with it save superficially. The sequence of rages, infatuations, jealousies and the rest is barely affected by listening to music and cannot be represented in it. What emotions we experience in listening to music are invariably evanescent and even the very self-absorbed could hardly imagine that the music is "about them".

Let us turn to the difficulties with arousalism. First of all there is a great deal of music that has an expressive face that simply could not be mirrored in the listener. Music may be sad or happy, detached, grave, impassive, reflective or exhilarating. But it can also be ironic, bombastic, grandiloquent or fey. I can see that Charles Mingus's "Thrice Upon a Theme" is grave and thoughtful in character and I could become grave and thoughtful in response. Exhilarating music exhilarates me, given that I am in a receptive state of mind, though at least part of my delight lies in appreciating the fact that such music exists. But I appreciate the wit and economy of Benny Goodman's "AC-DC Current" without being made "witty" myself. I can even appreciate the growing sense of tragedy in the first movement of Mahler's Tenth Symphony, his last, without being made "tragic", whatever that could possibly mean. How could the irony of Mahler and Shostakovich make me ironic? What am I to be ironic about? And if some of Elgar's music is bombastic, how could that make me bombastic? Bombast is something displayed in my speech and manner. But I listen quietly and silently. It is not very plausible to suppose that my character is temporally changed to being bombastic whereas before it was shy and retiring. It is certainly implausible to suppose it could be permanently changed. Since classical times, few thinkers have made that sort of claim for music and it is certainly not part of the arousalist thesis. They make a claim about the mental effect of music for the duration of the music and, perhaps at most, for a short time after. Indeed, I can admire and want to return to a work that does not move me to any particular state just as much as I may to a work that regularly moves me to tears. As I shall argue elsewhere, there just is no general pattern.

Let us consider some parallels. You might find the flat lands of the Netherlands on a wet winter's day a glum prospect and be inclined to call it a glum landscape. Does it make you glum? After a while it can get you down, but if you are on your way to a winter break in the Bahamas it may be registered as glum without making you glum. In normal circumstances probably it will make you feel glum principally because nobody much likes cold rain. Should we then say that subdued music has a tendency to make you subdued unless there are contrary features of the situation? This is a natural move. But should we take it? After all, the assumption is that the proper response to music is to move with its mood. But why should your appreciation of the composer's craft, your pleasure at the way he handles the form, be any less important, and if it neutralizes the effect of the music's sadness on your state of mind, why should we dismiss that as an improper reaction? In such circumstances, we ought not to be prescriptive about reactions. Music appeals in many ways. A good listener combines alertness to the technical skill with an appreciation of its expressive character.

Should we perhaps say that we "hear the bombast" in the Pomp and Circumstance marches or "hear the wit" in "Lester Leaps In" rather in the way that we might say "I heard his misery in his voice"? This, however, suggests a way of construing the bombast or the wit of the music in a way that rapidly misleads. If I hear the bombast then the suggestion is that I might fail to hear the bombast if I am inattentive. That is certainly the case. So to ask "Can you hear the bombast in the music?" is to draw attention to what might be overlooked. But, aside from such cases, why would I want to say "I hear the bombast in the music" rather than simply that the music is bombastic. What is achieved by drawing back to a consideration of *my* response rather than the qualities of the music? After all, in most cases hearing the bombast in the music is tantamount to recognizing that the bombast is there and the cognitivist position is conceded thereby. It is the music itself that is bombastic. Further, to say "I hear the music as bombastic" carries the suggestion that it can be heard in other ways and it further suggests that I am making no strong claim that the music really is bombastic. The locution is only appropriate in a restricted range of cases; namely, those where the music has an ambiguous character that is a bit difficult to settle.

In the end, however, there are even more compelling reasons to reject arousalism. The vast majority of pieces of music have an expressive face but they have no effect upon us. They are dull and incompetent. Listen to half an hour or so of current pop music. The music alternates between the frenetic and the maudlin. The harmonic structure and melodies are crude and banal, the music moves from cliché to cliché and the level of invention is desperately low. We can give the music an expressive face while at the same time being bored or repelled by it. The character it has does not depend upon that character being reflected in us.

Now the arousalist might reply that the fact that we grasp the expressive nature of the music independently does not show that the character of the music is not determined by its effect upon us. After all, this is basically an epistemological matter; we all agree that we discover its character by listening to it. But that may be compatible with our grasping it in virtue of an unconscious registering of the music through its effect, an effect that may not rise to the level of conscious awareness. The problem now is that we seem to have rendered the theory uncheckable and, in many, if not most cases, unmanifestable. If we describe a piece as "tumultuous" in virtue of it making us tumultuous without our being aware of it, all that we have is an *ad hoc* move to preserve a theory under threat. We would need very strong arguments in favour of arousalism for this to be a defensible strategy. It would need to be the case either that other arguments yet to be provided or the intuitive plausibility of arousalism or both have a force so great that the price of making it unfalsifiable is worth paying. I do not think that is so.

So, to recapitulate, the character of the music is independent of its effects upon us. We do not inspect our feelings to find out what expressive features it has. Any form of arousalism that claims that there is a "proper response" to sad music and that is for the listener to be sad (all things being equal) faces a further difficulty. If the arousalist needs a notion of "an appropriate response", the upshot will be that an inattentive listener, or a listener who is not properly prepared, or one who is weighed down and distracted by cares outside the music, may respond wrongly or fail to respond at all to the character of the music. But the normative element introduced requires the notion of a match between the descriptions of the music and the description of its effect upon us. *That* requires that the character of the music be something independent of and prior to the response. We have to know what the expressive character of the music is independently of our experience of it in order to know that our reaction is appropriate or inappropriate. It might be that we see this by seeing how others react but this is neither necessary nor usual. Indeed, we might criticize the reactions of all our fellow concert-goers as wrong-headed.

On other occasions and in other circumstances, of course, arousalism gives the right answer. If music is exhilarating or amusing, it exhilarates or amuses the receptive listener. If it is disturbing, it disturbs her. Some sections of our expressive vocabulary are arousalist because they mark the power of the music to affect us. We cannot deny that there are occasions when music does move us to the expressive states that we detect in it and there is a group of expressive descriptions that attribute to the music a causal power to bring about in us just those states. But it is worth remarking that what we do matches the music as often as what we feel. Listening to Sviatoslav Richter and Britten playing Schubert's great

"Duet Fantasie" in F minor, I cannot resist a raised eyebrow, a shrugged shoulder and a half smile at the knowing way Richter (I think) phrases a rising figure in the bass. Wittgenstein famously remarked on the relevance of gesture to understanding music.[8]

The plausibility of arousalism must, in the end, depend on claiming that these cases are central to our relationship to the arts, even if they are not universal. The art would be very different, perhaps an art of decoration only, if it were not the case that sometimes music moves us to states that it expresses. The music is properly described as grief-filled and it produces a response in the listener that, if not exactly grief-filled, is nevertheless sombre. Perhaps it makes your heart "feel full". This is music that we particularly value. If this is so, and I can't think of a philosopher who has argued this thesis, it would perhaps be "the truth in arousalism", as strong a case for arousalism as could be reasonably made.

Even if this is true, we still have to decide how we justify many, perhaps most, expressive descriptions of the music independently both of composer and listener and this leads us to the second family of explanations: those that treat these descriptions of music as posing a problem about the development of ways of talking about music, about their justification and their point.

The basis for expressive descriptions

Whatever causal relations exist between the composer, the music and the listener, or performer, music and listener for that matter, they do not answer the general question: what is it for music to be sad? Many thinkers have come to the conclusion that the gravity of such music is something in the music itself. As has been said, it is like the redness to the apple and not the burp to the cider.[9] But this suggests that the sadness is "heard". We cannot, however, be very comfortable with the suggestion that the sadness is a heard property of the music in the way the redness of the apple can be seen. If we hear the sadness in the music it is more like the way we see that a friend is sad. The nuances are important.

However we describe this, we already know from Hanslick what difficulties it produces. How can music be grief-laden? I may be made grief-laden by the death of a friend and the death of my friend is what strikes me with grief. There is both a cause and an object here. Something causes my grief and there is something to grieve about. The cause and the object are the same in this case, although in other cases of moods or emotions the two may be distinct. (A frequently cited case is that I may fear death but *ex hypothesi* my death has not occurred so, in this case, the object of my fear cannot be the cause of my fear since a cause cannot post-date its effect.) But the music cannot have an object of grief nor is the grief caused by some loss. Music simply does not make judgements nor possess beliefs. Furthermore, someone who grieves feels something; she is in what psychologists call an "affective state". But the music feels nothing.

Certainly there are many expressive descriptions of music for which the corresponding mental states normally lack objects; these apply to the music without raising this difficulty. I might be sad without being sad at something in particular or without some particular event making me sad. There is a case, then, where music might possess sadness in a relatively unproblematic way. No object is required.

But for many such expressions there is no objectless usage and for many of these it is the beliefs about the object that give a precision and determinacy as to precisely what the mental state is. It is the differing beliefs about the nature of the object that distinguish anger, fear, hope and jealousy more than the nature of the "internal feelings" of the person concerned. If music did have objects for its expressive states, then there would be a precision and determination about its description. But such an object is almost always missing. In the case of human emotions, the objects of those emotions together with the beliefs that the holder of the emotion has about those objects introduce a degree of determinateness about the emotion that has no parallel in music.

Perhaps we should try another approach. Many writers, faced with the difficulties of expressionist or arousalist theories and with the difficulties of taking descriptions of music literally, have assumed that they must be metaphorical. Think of the mewing of a European buzzard. This does seem melancholy (although nobody is inclined to deduce that the buzzard spends its life in fits of depression while the skylark is a generally happy bird). Perhaps, then, the relation of sadness to music is like the relation of sadness to the crying of a buzzard. When we say that the mew of the buzzard is melancholy, do we mean it metaphorically? I don't think so. So when we say that music is grave, do we mean it metaphorically? Again, I would say not. Part of the problem is that thinkers about the topic of metaphor have been too ready to assume that a sharp distinction can be drawn between the literal and the metaphorical. There isn't one. When Macbeth says, "My way of life is fallen into the sear, the yellow leaf", we have a clearly metaphorical phrase on which we may reflect. "Sear" means "dried-up" here, and we might think about what is meant. There are no new currents of life coursing through Macbeth. His life is drawing to its conclusion just as leaves turn yellow in autumn. But when metaphors are dead, their use in a remark may be straightforwardly true or false. If I say that Bertrand Russell had an incisive mind, the notion of "cutting" that once belonged with the adjective "incisive" has long become inactive. The statement is simply true. Indeed, we may well question whether there is the vestige of a metaphor here any longer. "Incisive" simply has an extra usage. But a sensitive reader of Thomas Hardy's much-loved poem "Afterwards" will reflect on how the line "When the Present has latched its postern behind my tremulous stay" works. She may, after such reflection, decide that the word "tremulous" is peculiarly apt to describe the fragility of life. Such reflective consideration is or is akin to interpretation and its product is less a judgement of truth or falsity and more a judgement of aptness. Would we say that "life is tremulous" is either true or false? This is a metaphor in full fig and if, when pressed for an answer one way or the other, we say that it is true, we are merely registering its insight.

Let's return to music. When I describe music as grave, do I speak metaphorically? Well, as much or as little as when I call a mind probing or incisive, I would say. We need to think of language as occupying a spectrum that runs from the evidently literal such as "George W. Bush is the current President of the USA" to the clearly metaphorical as when I say "This rain is icicle-sharp". But our use of language, particularly the usage of those who use language well in speech and writing, is immensely flexible and capable of doing very different things in different contexts. Vary the context and an ordinarily literal utterance may be clearly metaphorical. To say that somebody is dogging my footsteps is normally a dead metaphor with a single literal sense. But if I described somebody whom I had asked to follow behind me on all fours looking for a lost contact lens, as "dogging my footsteps", the weak joke would play on a similarity between being on all fours and moving like a dog and would then carry a metaphorical overtone. If his or her face had any overtly canine features, the joke might be a bit better, although it would then be in questionable taste. We move away from the literal in all sorts of contexts, in punning and word-play, in jokes that turn on ambiguities and on the occasions when we find something difficult to describe but make an attempt nonetheless.

Often our description of music *is* clearly metaphorical, of course. Here is Tovey on the first movement of Brahm's Double Concerto:

Soon the syncopated theme reappears in a pathetic calm in the orchestra, while the solo instruments weave around it a network of trills. Before long the calm becomes a stiff breeze, and the breeze a storm, through which the first theme cries out angrily in the woodwind. [10]

Sometimes description is not metaphorical at all. Quite often it is hard to say. One listener or reader might take it as metaphorical and another as not metaphorical but straight. The speaker's intentions are not going to help here. How often do we knowingly and deliberately speak metaphorically? In any case, on many occasions it will be a matter of decision to take it one way or the other and there will be no prior fact of the matter about speaker's intentions as to which way it should be understood.

So perhaps we should set aside the matter of metaphor as rather unhelpful and consider rather what might make somebody decide to call music "grave". Such ways of talking about music do have a history and the history is of a widening range of epithets from the medieval "*dulce*" to the much wider range of descriptions to be found in writing on nineteenth- and twentieth-century music. Many of these will not be true or false of the music so much as opening gambits in a process of interpretation. Such interpretations are of their nature debatable and may well be challenged by the reader or hearer. But more of this later.

Suppose we stick to relatively uncontroversial descriptions, describing a slow movement by Schubert as "sad" for example (they usually are). What makes us accept such a description? In calling it uncontroversial, I commit myself to its being true. (Perhaps we should remind ourselves once more that mood-words and emotion-words are only a sub-class of the words we use to describe music, although philosophers have fastened upon them to the virtual exclusion of others.) So what can we say to explain calling such music "sad"? Such a question has a fairly standard answer and I am not going to depart from it save by means of a few provisos. I should, by now, have said enough to make it clear that the problems are less severe than philosophers have sometimes supposed. Language does "spread itself" in such a way that a command of it requires knowing both central and peripheral applications of words as well as a readiness to use a word in a novel context. (We saw that this was so with the phrase "work of art"). What we need is some explanation of how such expressive descriptions have come to be applied to music with such regularity and such acceptance. Certainly, they are not quite central applications of expressive terms. Music is not made sad by the contingencies of life, the news, bad luck, domestic problems or mental instability. But I may describe a ruined cottage as a sad sight without anybody feeling sad and my hearers have no trouble in understanding me. As I have said we should be wary about calling these metaphorical usages.

If they are metaphorical they are on their way to becoming dead metaphors. The metaphorical content is certainly not obvious. The descriptions look, for one thing, clearly true or false and this rather tells against their being fully-fledged metaphors.

So much of all this depends on the context in which the speaker makes her observation and how we read it. In poetry we look for locutions that we interpret; in everyday speech we may expect more often to be informed. Let's return once again to music. Why should I describe a piece as sad? Think about setting words to music or choosing or writing music to accompany a dance. If you want to produce music to accompany a funeral, what music would you produce? Something slow and stately. In our culture, wild expressions of grief are not quite the thing at funerals, so the melody would be subdued rather than angular and likely to move step-wise from one note to the next; the rhythm will not be jagged or syncopated. (How hard it is to avoid metaphors even in this attempt at explication!) Again if you are setting a lively text, then a faster tempo, an energetic and more agitated line will be appropriate. This is largely to do with the vocal manner we think appropriate for delivering sad news or its opposite. On such slender foundations, our expressive vocabulary is extended to music. We do not have extensive points of similarity between the manner of sad or lively people or the manner of sad or lively music. But we have enough. I recently heard a violin sound described as "sweet", too sweet for the piece the reviewer thought; what does "sweetness" here, which we readily understand, have in common with the sweetness of tiramisu or the sweetness of Shirley Temple or the sweetness of some-body's temper or the sweetness of a kitten? Not much, I imagine. But no one of these usages is clearly literal and the others clearly metaphorical. No one is paradigmatic. What these cases have in common, arguably, is that in all of them there is a quality of being ingratiating but this explana-tion only helps a little. Somebody might refuse tiramisu on the grounds that it is sweet but hardly refuse a kitten on the grounds that it was sweet. Now the sweetness of the violin tone is more like the sweetness of tiramisu than the sweetness of the kitten. But again the reviewer did not object to the sweetness of the violin tone because of its sweetness *per se*, but because it was too sweet, cloying in fact. The complexity of all this does not prevent a child from picking up the word "sweet", possibly by hearing and using it for one or two of these cases and then extending it effortlessly to new cases.

Parenthetically, I think the way in which we speak of pitch as "high" or "low" and of a theme as rising or falling has the same sort of explanation. Philosophers have found this somewhat puzzling. A flight of stairs ascends (if we are at the bottom) and a scale ascends if we start on the lowest note. Language might spread itself from the first group of cases to the second because effort is required to reach higher notes, or because the "head voice" is required. Even if the precise origins of these shifts is a matter of speculation, I am sure that the explanation is to be found in such factors.

Now it may well be that "sad" does have an established central use and that usage is that it is people who are, primarily, "sad". Possibly this is a paradigm case of sadness. But it is an easy extension to describing news as sad, a face as sad, a wreck as sad, and, further, to music as sad and land-scapes as sad. The procedure isn't different. We certainly do not think that we speak metaphorically when we say that Schubert's "Death and the Maiden" Quartet is sad.

So some expressive descriptions of music are straightforwardly true. We cannot deny that much music has a character that is determinate and uncontroversial. *En passant*, it is worth noting that this expressive vocabulary is itself culture bound. We cannot describe music of the seventeenth century as bourgeois, neurotic, kitsch, sanctimonious, maudlin or sentimental. Or, perhaps more accurately, were we to do so we would have to defend such claims in the ways we defend metaphorical descriptions. We would have to show why one or other of these is *le mot juste* and we can imagine debate as to whether such a description is or is not anachronistic. In the same way when some critics argue that the final speech of *Othello* is sentimental, we may feel that sentimentality is not in the repertoire of Shakespeare or his characters and that this criticism cannot be fair. However it seems right to describe Richard Strauss's *Symphonia Domestica* as bourgeois, Schoenberg's first *Kammersinfonie* as neurotic, Saint-Saëns's "Organ" Symphony as kitsch, Charles Gounod's *Messe Solennelle de Ste Cécile* as sanctimonious, parts of Tchaikovsky's Sixth Symphony "Pathétique", as maudlin and Schumann's *Liederkreis* as sentimental. We do not always appreciate how much information we introduce into our assessment of this music. We have some common understanding of the history of our culture that remains unformulated but which determines the range of descriptions we think apt for a particular piece of music. Certain expressive possibilities exist at a particular time and place. Thus Richard Strauss's settings of poems about classical Greece have an extraordinary mixture of wildness and opulence that must, I imagine, owe something to Nietzsche's revisionist views about the classical world. (I am thinking especially of the *Gesang der Apollopriesterin* op. 33 no. 2, although the style is more apt for *Elektra*). We judge a piece of music according to our knowledge of its historical setting and if we stray beyond this range, what we say will look "more metaphor-ical", more a case to be mulled over.

In attempting to show how expressive descriptions become attached to music I have made much of the fact that what we may call "concert music for instruments only" is comparatively recent and comparatively restrict-ed to Western and Indian cultures. Music has been and still largely is a mixed media affair. Apart from its use in setting words, the other main connection with extra-musical features is, of course, the relation of music to dance. With some music it is difficult to keep still and dance can exhilarate. The sound track of the cult movie *The Blues Brothers* is infectious and the dancing hilarious and liberating but the exquisite music that Rameau wrote for *Les Fêtes d'Hébé* also demands movement, albeit movement of a more sedate form. Recall the adage that the farther that music is from dance, the more it is moribund. For most of its history, music either set texts or was an accompaniment for dance and it may well be that purely instrumental music would not have the effect it has if we were not brought up in a culture where our first experience of music is likely to be through singing and being sung to and moving in time to music. Perhaps this is where we should look here for the primitive basis for our expressive descriptions of music.

This rather familiar idea of music as evolving into the purely instrumental has tended to involve a rather controversial idea of progress, stigmatized by English-speaking philosophers as Hegelian; it is some-thing we should resist. We ought not to assume, as was assumed quite widely in the nineteenth century, that music marches onwards and up-wards towards pure or absolute music rather like the notion, contemporary with this, of evolution as the ascent of man. For one thing, if we think of music as making progress towards a greater independence from words and movement, we may think of pre-Renaissance music in the wrong way. The sacred music of Ockeghem and others certainly owed little to the constraints of the text. These composers were not illustrating or matching the words in any way. To all intents and purposes the elaborate and intertwining vocal parts where many notes were devoted to a single syllable was an instrumental music in which the instruments happened to be human voices. Be that as it may, the assumption that instrumental music is superior is no more than a prejudice.

To summarize, then, I suggest that the application of words like "grave" or "lively" to music is a modest extension of the way we describe human beings and animals in a way that is neither unusual nor particularly puzzling. Although the sadness of music is not very much like human sadness, the points of contact are sufficient to make such an extension easily acceptable. Sometimes it is pretty obviously metaphorical; more often, not. In the end the "problem of expression" comes, like so much else in philosophy, from a faulty view of language.

The limits of musical description

If we can solve this problem of "expression", albeit in this rather messy and non-generalizable way, then we are left with another issue to which philosophers have not devoted much attention at all. Just how far can we go in describing music in either expressive or non-expressive ways? For example, one writer says of Sibelius's Fourth Symphony that the tritone destroys the music of this work and leaves it bereft of melody; in this he sees Sibelius's comment on the destructive force of Schoenberg's atonalism.[11] Consider another example. A correspondent wrote to Sibelius shortly before the composer's death, asking whether his symphonic work related in some specific way to landscape and the geology that underlies it. Sibelius confirmed this very abruptly in a reply. It is difficult to make this claim precise but the use of metaphors like "large-scale contours" or "slabs of material" does seem peculiarly apposite to, say, the finale of the Fifth Symphony, where the great horn theme is mirrored at a much slower speed in the bass. Some listeners to Mahler, noticing his penchant for little fanfares on horns or trumpets that seem to come from the distance, find themselves imagining a landscape with distant hunting calls. The Scherzo from the Fifth Symphony comes to mind. Indeed, it is a rather striking feature of some of Mahler's music, and some of Dvořák's as well, that it possesses a sort of three-dimensionality. In some of Dvořák's *Slavonic Dances*, one theme seems to disappear behind another only to reappear later, like dancers circling. The Trio of *Slavonic Dances* op. 46 no. 5 is an excellent example of this. These are examples taken from non-programmatic music that does not set a text. Are these reflections justified? What sort of illumination is being offered?

This is a problem of practical import. Some analysts of music regard such reflections as self-indulgent and irrelevant. Whether we are dealing with Western classical music, jazz or world music they will sternly point us in the direction of formal analysis and key structure as what is crucial to music's quality. But this puritanism robs us of something significant about music: that it is open to interpretation in a sense other than that in which it is usually employed. When we talk about the interpretation of music we usually refer to the decisions a performer has to make about tempo, dynamics or phrasing. A performer of classical music, unlike an improviser, has to decide how to play the notated music. When the composer writes a hairpin showing that he wants a crescendo at this point, just how much louder are we to make the music? The notation does not prescribe in such detail. This is what "interpretation" in music currently means, and because the term has been commandeered to apply to performance in this way, we have been lulled into thinking that verbal accounts are no more than descriptions of it, metaphorical or literal.

But one form of musical interpretation is different. We may be concerned with the significance of the music and that significance may be a matter that takes us outside the individual notes to broader issues connected with the culture of the time. Holst's *Hymns from the Rig Veda* are not well known, perhaps because they are difficult to programme. The second series contains a funeral chant for women's voices and orchestra. The text, translated by Holst himself, ends:

To those whose souls are born of fire,
The poets of a thousand songs,
The Holy Ones who guard the Sun, unto the Fathers,
May he go forth!

By a gradual overlapping of entries in closer and closer imitation, combined with a gradual diminuendo and a move to remoter keys, Holst creates an astonishing sense of a multitude of voices welcoming the spirit in regions of greater and greater space. It is music that succeeds in capturing something of what mystics are supposed to experience. We could understand the music in this way even if we set aside, if we can, the clues the text offers.

Is this a justified interpretation of the significance of the music? Of course, it goes beyond the notes and this would be enough for some theorists to call a halt. Music cannot have this sort of significance, they would claim. It is a formal and abstract art. Certainly, unlike one of the interpretations of Sibelius's symphonies that I mentioned, I know of no *obiter dicta* to support my reading, although Holst was composing at a time when there was some interest in Eastern religion. But then, I also know of no extra-textual observations that legitimize reading *King Lear* as a reflection on the various ways in which blindness may be literal or metaphorical and how blindness damages love. Nor do I know of any remarks by Shakespeare that show it to be a reworking of a folk tale or a reflection on the old adage "Love is blind". But the absence of clues does not prevent us from interpreting. That is the job of critics. They are licensed to go beyond the text and the great body of critical writing about painting, sculpture, literature and drama is precisely this: a defence of certain interpretations that can be made of the works in question. When we are told that *King Lear* is about blindness, we see how we can see, read or produce the play in the light of that claim. We highlight or foreground certain passages. We don't for a moment think that this rules out other approaches and other interpretations and, in the end, it may be a testimony to the greatness of the play that it can be understood in different ways. Music is not different. Operas, of course, can also be understood variously; but so can purely instrumental music, at least since the dawn of the Viennese classical era. Given that Western classical music has been composed with a serious intent for three or more centuries, why should not the business of interpretation be equally permissible?

It is, of course, and once we see this we should see that the two forms of interpretation are linked. Decide on the general character of a piece, a movement or an episode and you see that certain decisions are required from the performer to bring that character out. As I intimated, performers sometimes say that the crucial thinking about a work takes place away from the practice room when you see the overall character of the work and the phrasing or structural characteristics that display this.

The more basic expressive description is primitive in a sense; it is this that leads us into the interpretative maze. Lower-level expressive description of the music as "yearning" or "opulent" are the precondition of interpretation in the sense we are now considering. What an interpretation will typically try to capture are those moments that initially move, delight or impress us. I said earlier that I may not have a choice as to whether or not I hear the opening of Mozart's Symphony in G minor as grief-laden. These are reactions and it is this that distinguishes them from interpretation proper, which is something that may lie more within my power. A particular passage may deeply affect me and become, for me, the centre of the work. The rest of the work I see as leading up to that moment or leading away from it. For most listeners and most interpreters there is a moment in Sibelius's great Fourth Symphony when the theme of the slow movement, assembled very gradually, eventually emerges in all its majesty. (In the end it is cut short in a way that leaves you feeling short-changed at one level but not at another.) I find it hard to imagine a satisfactory interpretation that does not make that passage central. Still, it may very well be that what somebody proposes as an interpretation will "foreground" a different section of the work; I might be swayed by this and then the interpretation has moulded my reaction. I now have a different view of the work. Furthermore, we might subsequently revise a view not because we were persuaded that our reaction was in some way deficient but rather because subsequent experiences did not highlight those lines. Then we will foreground these other features and capture them in a revised interpretation. Or we may consider that any of the these interpretations is satisfactory. Again, the original view may prove resistant to persuasion or subsequent experience.

I shall assume that you will allow me all this and reject, as I do, the critics who think that music should only be analysed as a form of mathematical set theory. To the question as to what limits can we place upon such interpretation, I give the same sort of answer as I would give for literary texts. In general, we should not venture beyond the culture of origin of the symphony, quartet or opera. Thus one reason why a link with geological mapping is apposite in the case of Sibelius's later symphonies but not Beethoven's "Eroica" Symphony is that knowledge of geology was sparse and certainly not general in Beethoven's day. In the case of Sibelius, it provides a connection with the stark landscape of Finland that is part of the aura of associations that may legitimately surround a hearing of the work. The unique feature of music is that it can be afforded a "meaning" in this way without there being any "lower level" of statements or representations from which the interpretation begins.

Meaning

All this has directed us towards an answer to the question: what is the meaning of music? What people are thinking when they ask whether music has a meaning is not at all clear. Do they expect music to express some "spiritual truths", whatever they may be? Sometimes they do. Messiaen evidently thought that his music stood in some intimate relation to Roman Catholic doctrine. But if Messiaen thought that music can express Catholic dogma in the sense of stating it, he was egregiously mistaken. To say that music expresses "spiritual falsity" would be to denigrate the music *qua* music. It would be an indirect way of saying that it is sentimental or sanctimonious. I have never heard this charge made but I can well imagine some might think it a justified charge against Wagner, Liszt, Elgar or perhaps Mendelssohn. It is a way, and perhaps not much more than that, of objecting to an overblown idiom. In the case of Elgar it might be more precise as a criticism of *The Dream of Gerontius*. I know that for some listeners the work produces a distaste, an almost palpable feeling of disgust. The text airs what they think should be private – the death of an individual – and is embarrassingly mawkish. To say that Elgar's idiom, which sounds to them like John Stainer's *The*

Crucifixion overhauled by a student of Wagner, matches this is hardly to praise it.

I doubt whether people who ask whether music has a meaning have a very clear understanding of what the question might mean. They certainly do not usually have an understanding of what would make it an intelligible and, indeed, intelligent question. For music under-determines the meaning that people ascribe to it. It was long ago observed that the same music can illustrate a tempestuous love affair or a storm at sea. In *The Dagenham Dialogues*,[12] Pete and Dud, mistaking the title of Debussy's *La Mer* for *La Mère*, declare that you can almost hear the tea being poured by Debussy's silver-haired old mother, followed by the adding of the cream.

My reference to under-determination provides a clue. If the question of what music can mean (as opposed to what expressive properties it has) is a question about interpretation, then music clearly can have a meaning and the meaning is suggested by the context in which it was produced and by its history in very much the way that "the meaning" of *King Lear* is determined by history and context. The meaning of a Beethoven "Symphony" is like the meaning of *Hamlet* and not like the meaning of "O, What a Rogue and Peasant Slave am I".

Robert Graves can be a difficult poet. In "The Challenge", the following lines occur:

The Moon's the crown of no high-walled domain
Conquerable by angry stretch of pride:
Her icy lands welcome no soldiery.[13]

His biographer suggests that these lines mythologize his lover at the time, Laura Riding, describing how a young prince flies his hawk at the moon, only to lose both bird and kingdom.[14] Graves apostrophizes Laura's intellectual authority and supremacy but in chilling images of coldness and icy remoteness, and in ultimately destructive terms. You will not find this explicitly in the poem. You might well be able to spot the ambivalence of the poem, but this cannot be read off the page directly. The critic has to think what the poem might mean and, with a writer like Graves, link the poem to his preoccupations at the time of writing. Edward Cone[15] connects Schubert's "Moment Musical" in A flat D.780 with Schubert's realization that he is suffering from syphilis; his letter of the same year as the piece, 1824, expresses his despair at the loss of his health. An insidious foreign element creeps into the music, much as a disquieting thought to an easy-going nature. Eventually this element takes over. As in the case of the interpretation of the poem by Graves, the critic steps outside what can be directly read off from the poem or the music. He or she uses biographical information to construct a meaning that goes beyond the obvious and this information is extraneous to both poem and music. Knowing it you see how the work has that character. If you were ignorant of it, you might still be able to see something of that character but without the degree of specificity the interpretation allows.

But an influential critic may stamp his authority on one particular interpretation making it part of the meaning such that later interpreters start from there. I doubt whether any informed reader of *Oedipus Rex* can ignore the Freudian interpretation that is now commonplace. That has entered the text, so to speak. Beethoven's "Moonlight" Sonata offers a musical parallel.[16] What is called its "history of reception" recounts how the nickname became attached to it and how it picked up various significances over the first century of its existence. (Liszt played it, in the presence of Berlioz, in complete darkness, not even in moonlight.) The opening Adagio was given increased weight as the focal point of the work. It came to be associated with love and, in particular, with renounced love. It was thought to relate to Guilietta Guicciardi, with whom Beethoven was romantically involved during its composition. Tolstoy made it central in his novella *Family Happiness*. It is no longer easy for us to hear it with the opening Adagio simply as a first movement. Indeed, perhaps it is now impossible for us to "foreground" the two following movements.

It is always open to a hostile critic to accuse the interpreter of anachronism, of course, and of "reading in" what is not there rather than of drawing out what is latent. There is a divide between those who think that art of significance is open to constant reinterpretation so as to make it "relevant" – to use the catchphrase of a decade or so ago – and those who think that great art tells us, *inter alia*, about the culture in which it originates, a culture that may be very different from our own, and speaks to us today only because human nature varies between fairly circumscribed limits. The *rapprochement* between the two will come through the claim that the intentions of the artist may be unconscious. An artist of the past may write of Oedipal themes without being aware that he is doing so, and what he writes may be decoded into a Freudian vocabulary that he does not possess. Certainly Freud believed this. In this respect, music does not differ from poetry, or from film, drama and painting for that matter. It is worth remarking here, although it comes up elsewhere in this book, that it is a mistake to contrast too sharply performance and writing and talking about music. For the character that a good critic finds in a work may well

directly affect the way it will be played.[17] Characteristically, great interpretative performers also think deeply about what they play.

Interpretation does not have to be so keenly dependent on biographical
information as my musical examples might suggest. Poets and musicians
may create works that have much less to do with their own personal
preoccupations. Sometimes, too, a work can display features that it is very
unlikely the creator would have intended. It might come over as a parody
when this was not intended; it may seem to support a cause contrary to the
one she favours. If it is ironic, of course, then we assume that this is an
attitude that is adopted by the creative mind. Failure to notice irony can
mean that a quite contrary meaning is given to what is said. But if a work
is ironic it is intended as such. (You cannot make much of a case for
unconscious irony.)

So when we are asked what music means, we would be advised to
invite our interlocutors to say what piece of music they have in mind. We
then engage in the same process of interpretation familiar to us from the
other arts. To repeat, asking what the "Eroica" Symphony means is like
asking what *Hamlet* means. You might question whether those who ask
what music means are likely to be satisfied with this answer. I don't know,
mainly because different people will have different ideas as to the significance of the question, as is obvious from our previous discussion. Suffice
to say that relatively few people have a sufficiently clear idea of what they
are asking for it to be correspondingly clear what answer is required. The
arguments of this chapter rule out some answers to the question. The
answer I give here is an answer to a question that can reasonably be construed in such a way that the answer I give is a plausible one. It is about the
best construction I can place on the question "What does music mean?":
the construction least likely to lead to philosophical difficulties. In this
context people sometimes speak of "significance" rather than "meaning"
in order to maintain a distinction, a distinction that can be obliterated by
using "meaning" to cover both the meaning of an everyday statement or
instruction such as "Pass the salt" and the "meaning" of *Hamlet*. The
motive is laudable but the word "significance" is not without baggage. It
tends to import thoughts about value for a significant work is one which is
important. Consequently I prefer to use the word "meaning".

But a problem remains. Somehow we have to find a way of permitting
some interpretations while rejecting others. It may be all right to see
Schubert's mixture of guilt and terror at the onset of syphilis in one of
his piano pieces. Is it equally permissible to see Beethoven's Fifth
Symphony as a celebration of phallic power and its climax as a paean to
the male orgasm? Such licence in interpretations is characteristic of what

is called the "new musicology" and it raises the question of how we draw the lines between "interpreting", "reading into" and "using" a work.[18] Parallel questions arise, notoriously, with respect to opera production. Opera production is not commonly in the hands of musicians. Possibly as a result, producers seem to have a very considerable degree of licence. But when a producer sets Berlioz's *Les Troyens* in 1960s' America, and has the Trojan horse drawn by a procession dressed as cowboys and native Americans, is he any longer even reading into the work? He is using it to press upon the audience some banal thoughts about imperialism that have nothing to do with a nineteenth-century French composer's understanding of the classical world. There are, I think, two questions to be asked. First, what does an interpretation offer us apart from a means of whiling away half an hour or so? Secondly, what does it contribute to our understanding of the music? One way in which an interpretation can help is that it might direct us to certain details in the music. Cone's interpretation of Schubert does this and the pianist who is persuaded by Cone may then accentuate certain details so that a particular structure becomes more apparent. He may play a certain section with anguish rather than mere melancholy. The listener who accepts Cone's interpretation understands the work anew; she will look for a reflection of this understanding in the pianist's characterization and judge the performance more or less harshly if it fails to make the nature of the piece plain. (Of course, the pianist could be instructed to play the piece this way without being told why but, in a sense, it would be a hollow interpretation, akin to an actor mouthing the words without understanding their significance.) Could the interpretation of Beethoven's Fifth Symphony as phallic have a parallel effect? Could it lead to a difference in the way the piece is played? I doubt it.

Some writers assume that the point of all this is to help us to see the work in a better light. But, of course, the consequence of an interpretation may be that we judge the work more harshly. At least one critic finds Elgar's First Symphony so objectionable that he cannot listen to it. He sees in it an unintelligent and uncritical celebration of British imperialism; it is not easy to exclude this interpretation partly because of the idiom the symphony shares with the *Pomp and Circumstance* marches. The Second Symphony is rather ambivalent. The quiet, reflective close may anticipate the dissolution of the imperialist dream or it might represent the ideal of a *pax Brittanica*. Similarly some find Strauss's *Metamorphosen* objectionable because it dwells on the death of the German cultural heritage at a time when something far worse than the destruction of the Munich opera house was happening in Germany.

We are, to an extent, retreading paths trod in the discussion of constructivism so the next point should not come as much of a surprise. A way in which interpretations might be kept on the straight and narrow is to restrict acceptable interpretations to those that the composer intended to be possible interpretations. Faced with a sexual interpretation of Beethoven's Fifth Symphony, we might point out that nothing in Beethoven's letters or conversations suggests such a view. Judging from his attitude to Mozart's *Don Giovanni*, Beethoven seems to have been something of a prude.[19] This cuts little ice with its advocates, who will insist that such elements can enter unconsciously into the compositional process. Suppose we are liberal enough to allow unconscious intentions, what limits should we place upon these? Suppose an interpretation allows something alien to a composer's outlook. It might be anachronistic or it might reveal something of the composer that he would, had he known, have preferred to keep quiet. Had Renoir appreciated that his female nudes, through combining the facial features of a pre-pubescent child with the voluptuousness of a young woman, suggest a perverted sexuality, would he have painted them? More controversially, had Wagner realized that the anti-Semitism of *The Mastersingers* or the *Ring* might pass some twentieth-century listeners by, would he have made it more overt?

There is, then, the possibility of an interpretation revealing something that the music might plausibly be thought to represent, something that the composer might not have intended and, in one sense, could not have intended since, had he known it would be taken that way, he would have composed differently. For this reason, it is not even feasible to restrict interpretations to those the composer *could* have intended. In some cases, of course, the interpretation is dependent on the composer having specific intentions. If it is a correct interpretation of Schumann to "read" the encoding of certain names in his music, it is because Schumann intentionally encoded them. If they were an accident then any interpretation that revolves around the occurrence of these names is illicit.

The situation is, indeed, complex. It is natural to want to rest our interpretation in the culture that provided a seed-bed. We are right to be anxious about the viability of an interpretation of a Beethoven sonata that owes so much to a high romanticism obsessed with sexual love. Unless we relate the work to its culture we risk creating an artefact that merely reflects back our own preoccupations and never can show us different ways of seeing our world. But neither can an interpretation merely reflect what the composer intended to put in. Not only may he have unconscious motives, but he may also be unaware of currents in society that surface in his art. Interpretations cannot be circumscribed by what the composer could have intended to be understood by it.

You can deduce from all this that I am not very sympathetic to formalism ("no longer" would be *le mot juste.*) Always latent, even when listening to instrumental music, are images, a biographical or cultural environment, and associations that make the music capable of a more specific meaning. In so far as we are dealing with pieces of music as works of art, the task of investigating the meaning is always in the offing. For this reason, I do not think the sharp distinction between instrumental or pure music and opera, ballet, programme music and music for film (what are called "mixed media" or "mixed arts") is tenable.[20] This is not to say that what I have represented as fairly general interpretations of music is the same as giving music a programme. From time to time, and particularly in the nineteenth century, the composer might provide a narrative that the listener is expected to bear in mind while the music is played. Among the more elaborate of these is the story that Berlioz provided for his *Symphonie Fantastique*, recounting the artist wandering in the country and his opium-fuelled dreams and nightmares. In the case of some programme music, the transitions do not make much sense without the story. The structure of Berlioz's *Roméo et Juliette* only seems ineluctable in the light of Shakespeare's play. Where a programme is more important then, trivially, the understanding of the music is weakened by ignorance of it. In opera, of course, the importance of knowing the dramatic situation is obvious. The music may have its own logic but a fuller understanding requires seeing how the music underpins and comments on the drama and text. It might be more accurate to say that the dramatic persona is created by a combination of words, action and music. Notice how the Count in the finale of the second act of *The Marriage of Figaro*, adopts a deliberately plebeian manner when quizzing Figaro about the letter of assignation. The music is blunt and commonplace, although commonplace music in Mozart's hands still delights us.

You might say that instrumental music can be understood and enjoyed knowing nothing of all this. But that does not show that our understanding cannot be enriched by hearing the music with a knowledge of its setting and the interpretative possibilities this may set off. If, like some poetry, it has to be interpreted in the sense discussed in this section in order to be followed at all, then that is for the worse. The very greatest music, like great literature and drama, can often be appreciated in many ways, "at different levels", as they say. Indeed, we can even identify music as profound without knowing what interpretative conceptions cast light on it just as we can judge a performance as profound without knowing the conception that led the performer to play it that way. But "profundity" is a puzzling phenomenon in music, and it is one we need to address next.

Profundity in music

So, as I draw to the end of this chapter, I want to concentrate on one particular difficulty that has occasioned a good deal of comment from philosophers in the past decade. We sometimes speak of music as "profound'. What could this mean? We have already decided that music contains no propositions and therefore cannot express thoughts. But it is surely thoughts that we think of as "profound" and thoughts we express as propositions. If we want instances of profound thoughts we look to literature. Typically it is remarks that strike us as wise that we will most often think of as profound. When Samuel Johnson remarks that there is very little hypocrisy in the world but rather an abundance of self-deception in its various forms, he displays wisdom and insight. He helps us to be more charitable in our judgement of others. In "imaginative literature", perhaps such nuggets of wisdom are rarer. Indeed, in a novel they can come over as self-conscious. It is rather striking that when one of Shakespeare's characters gives a list of such injunctions, the author is clearly satirical. Polonius is a bumbling, officious and rather pretentious old fool whose attempts at wise advice to his son fall flat.

But to suppose that literature is always profound through the sentiments directly expressed is a mistake. After all, Lear's closing lines are so moving that many of us feel that they are too much to bear. When Lear, with Cordelia dead, asks "Why should a dog, a horse, a rat have life, And thou no breath at all?", the sentiments are commonplace. Yet if anything in literature is profound, it is *King Lear*. Now, perhaps you would point to something other than the fact that these lines move us as the locus of profundity. After all, to be profound is not the same as to be profoundly moving. And that is true. It is when *King Lear* forces us to reflect upon love, on the chilling effect on relationships of demanding proofs of love, on blindness both literal and figurative, that the profundity of the play is brought home to us. If this is right then profundity has much to do with the possibility of interpretation and the possibility of certain sorts of interpretation; namely, interpretation in terms of the major preoccupations of human life, love and death. Where music does offer this it does so through opera, of course, and we immediately think of *The Valkyrie*, of Brunnhilde's recognition of human love between Siegmund and Sieglinde, of Siegmund's decision to choose earthly life and inevitable ageing and death with the woman he loves rather than immortality as a hero in Valhalla; we think, too, of Wotan's farewell to his daughter and wonder whether fatherly love has ever been more precisely captured.

But what about "pure music", as it used to be called (with the illicit implication that it was somehow superior to other forms)? What about instrumental music? Some of it is certainly described as profound. Talking to a pupil about the opening of the slow movement of Beethoven's *"Hammerklavier"* Sonata, Dvořák said "if anything is profound in music, it is this" and Tovey describes Bach's *The Well-Tempered Clavier*, Book 1, no. 18 as "one of the profoundest in the whole Forty-Eight". From another branch of music, let me cite Charlie Mingus's "Thrice Upon a Theme".

It might seem as though the standard account of the expressiveness of music does the job here. Profound music has the features that profound utterance has, albeit without the content that profound utterance has. The manner of a profound utterance is slow and weighty with a sense of the importance of the matter. Should we then conclude that if that is all there is to profundity in music, then the profound in music cannot be distinguished from pseudo-profundity? It is merely portentous to utter platitudes with the manner of speaking deep truths. Much wisdom literature does this, in fact. (Skim through the Old Testament's Book of Proverbs again). The essays of Francis Bacon often say the obvious with an air of self-importance and it may be this that led an early critic to complain that he wrote like a Lord Chancellor; he would have been an apt prototype for Polonius. If music utters no propositions but merely has the manner of depth, then its profundity is merely show. As Samuel Johnson remarked, "To be grave of mien and slow of utterance; to look with solicitude and speak with hesitation, is attainable at will; but the show of wisdom is ridiculous."[21]

Yet this cannot be an accurate picture of the business, not simply because we resist the thought that music never is profound but only pretentious, but because we can make a distinction within music between the profound and the pseudo-profound. I am afraid that much of the music of the holy minimalists strikes me as exhibiting pseudo-profundity; the music of Henryk Górecki and Taverner is slow and weighty, and the texts are "spiritual" but there is nothing very much there. It would need music of greater melodic and contrapuntal interest to underpin these pretensions. And here lies a clue. Music that seems too easily achieved cannot make any claims to profundity anymore than the mouthing of mere clichés displays wisdom. Furthermore Beethoven's late piano sonatas and quartets, like Shostakovich's late works, are the products of a composer we know to have suffered terribly and, in addition, the product of a composer whose technique is not in question.

In the end, however, the profundity of music connects closely with the question of its meaning. As we have seen, there is a sense in which music has meaning without it having any propositional content. Profound music is music that makes demands upon the interpreter and listener. The word "profound" can suggest that which is deep or concealed. In literature and the other arts, what is concealed is brought out through interpretation. Interpretation is the means by which we can give a meaning to something that can be understood in many ways, and I suggest that there is a connection between depth and the possibility of a multiplicity of interpretations (something that we may recognize without identifying the varying possible interpretations). This applies also to the more usual sense given to "interpretation" in music: the decisions required of a performer. Thus a pianist, faced with one of Beethoven's late sonatas, has decisions to make. It can be paralysing for all but the very good or the foolhardy. How do I voice the opening of the slow movement of the "*Hammer-klavier*" Sonata? There seem to be so many ways of playing it. How do I manage the way the movement gradually takes flight? Every decision I take has implications for the playing of other passages in the work. By comparison, playing a piece by Emmanuel Chabrier only poses minor problems, mainly of a technical sort to be solved by deciding on fingering and hand position.

There is no denying that music is valued by us in part as a consequence of its power to express. It would be a different art, an art of ornament merely, if it could not be optimistic, pessimistic, grandiose, sentimental, exhilarating or tragic. The peculiar appropriateness of certain music for certain texts, dramatic situations or public occasions and its power to move us, sometimes, to the states it expresses are important elements in our love for the art. Hanslick's thesis that it is false that beauty in music depends upon the accurate expression of emotions looks like a half-truth. (Again let us substitute "value" for "beauty".) Of course, the precise expressive state of some music matters little, but it is one reason why we think of some other music as good. The expressive state of yet other music usually substantiates a negative judgement, as when we declare that a piece is sentimental or cold or faceless. But once again this depends upon the context. Chilliness may be right for this passage at this juncture. And once again there is no general pattern.

All this has to do with the value of music and this is perhaps the right place to turn to that complex and difficult matter.

Chapter 4

Value

"In the field of the arts, impartiality is what reason is in the field of love; it is the property of hearts which are cold, or only minimally enamoured." Stendhal, *Life of Rossini* (1824)

Many of the questions I shall attempt to answer in this final chapter are quite general questions about the value of works of art and how we attribute that value, although some of the questions arise in a more acute and pressing form for music. But before we consider these perhaps there is an even more general question we should consider. Why, you might ask, do we need to make judgements of the relative value of pieces of music at all? After all, doesn't the whole thing smack of university league tables, of Sir John Lubbock's hundred best books and so on? (The question, of course, arises for the other arts as well.)

There is a short answer but perhaps it ought to be prefaced with the observation that talk of "value" is a little odd here. Its use is, I suspect, just one of the many ways in which a materialist culture infiltrates areas where it is manifestly inappropriate. For outside philosophy, it is used mainly to indicate monetary value. It is largely used to signal the price that a sculpture or a painting might get in the auction room. In the world of music, nobody much says that this or that symphony is a work of great value. Instead we talk in terms that suggest a less precise business of comparing stature. Some pieces of music are great, some mediocre, some engaging but transient and some poor and so on.

Now for the short answer. Without some comparative judgements, it is hard to manage in as complex a society as ours where so much in the arts is available. We do not need to determine whether Mozart's "*Hoffmeister*" string quartet K.499 is the equal of Beethoven's "Razumovsky" string quartets, but we do need the sort of judgement that Hume thought obvious, that Milton is a greater poet than Ogilby or, in the case of music, that Purcell is a greater master than Jean-Baptiste Lully or that Charlie Parker is a more significant figure than Ornette Coleman or, in the case of individual works, that Purcell's "Hear My Prayer, Oh Lord" is finer than Samuel Wesley's "In Exitu Israel". We need comparative judgements because so much is available and it is necessary to ration our time so that we afford time only to those works that are likely to reward. If we had only the handful of books available in the early fifteenth century or even the relatively small recorded repertoire available when I was a teenager half a century ago, matters would be different. But we need guidance when so much is available and the more that is available the more we need guidance.

There is another point about all this. Composers learn from other composers. Often they study with them as Beethoven studied with Haydn. But they learn also from models. Mozart was explicit about his debts to Haydn. Haydn's *The Creation* was stimulated by the model of Handel's oratorios and so on. In particular, jazz musicians generally acquire their art by listening to and copying recordings of older musicians. Now, of course, part of what the listener needs to understand music is a knowledge of these debts and the way the debts are repaid; sometimes we only understand the music properly when we see this. So to understand a musician it is sometimes necessary to know his models and good composers often, although not invariably, use the best available. So in the very intelligibility of music itself there is a dependence on prior judgements of value. Of course, great musicians often leave their models behind, as Purcell did with the French school of the late seventeenth century, or Bach did with Vivaldi. Sometimes, too, the influences are no longer figures of any great musical interest. Bach was influenced by a number of minor north German composers whose music is now rarely played; any airings given tend to show that their neglect is entirely justified. Nevertheless some music is homage to justifiably admired masters, from Stravinsky to Tchaikovsky, Ravel to Mozart, Fauré and Couperin and so on.

Generally speaking, musicians get it right about other musicians, in particular those who are not their contemporaries. But, like the rest of us, composers have their blind spots and these blind spots quite often illuminate their own characteristics. Britten said that he played Brahms once a year so as to remind himself how bad it is and it was the unfortunate Brahms whom Tchaikovsky called "that talentless bastard". Stravinsky's contempt for some of his contemporaries may be put down sometimes to a quite unnecessary jealousy but some of those he disliked are musicians of a very different stamp whom, perhaps, he could not have been expected to admire. Performing musicians, in the nature of the case, have to have a more embracing and catholic taste. They often have to perform music they do not like.

This mixture of history and model becomes formalized in time. In most areas of music, a recognized lineage has formed. Read any history of classical music and you will find a concentration of major figures who are strung together in patterns of influence and debt. They form a canon. A history of eighteenth-century classical music cites Bach, Handel, Scarlatti, Haydn and Mozart as the major figures. Histories of jazz pick out Louis Armstrong, Benny Goodman, Count Basie, Lester Young, Charlie Parker, Dizzy Gillespie, John Coltrane and Miles Davis as central. A canon is less in evidence with popular song but if we were to look at cover versions of other writers' songs we would find that Cole Porter and George Gershwin and, latterly, John Lennon, Paul McCartney and George Harrison wrote music that is still used. More to the point, if some recent writers are to be believed, a rock canon is beginning to form through the selective reissue on CD of albums of the 1960s and 1970s. The best are transferred to CD and remain available. In the past few decades, alternative canons are emerging and the suzerainty of the classical canon, itself largely German and Austrian, has come under fire. To pursue the pun, what we have, in effect, is an assemblage of loose canons.

In saying all this I have used a number of locutions that prompt the most important questions about artistic value. I have spoken of "getting it right", of "blind spots" and of a "canon". We speak as well of "likes and dislikes" on the one hand and a "consensus" on the other, of having a "catholic taste" and of "the test of time". But what do we mean by these and how would we explain and defend judgements in these terms? The implication of "getting it right" is that there is a true and accurate assessment of the merits of the work that can be obtained. Is this to say that there is a way in which the goodness or badness of this sonata is something independent of our judging it to be so, as realists about value maintain? Or does it merely mean that any judgement I make is open to qualification by somebody more experienced in music or more in tune with this piece of music and no more than that? On this latter view, the value of a piece of music is not independent of human judgement.

This is where the question of value in music debouches into broader questions in the philosophy of value, as it is called. As I said at the outset, many of these questions are of quite general significance; their practical import lies in our need to make a distinction between what the work's value really is and how any individual listener judges it. But although the questions are, as I said, general, the divide between work and performance makes the situation more complicated in music, for here we do characteristically judge the performance of a work to an extent independently from the judgement of the work itself.

This all leads us to a perennially fascinating question, probably the fundamental philosophical question about the arts: is value to be equated with individual taste or is there any sense in which the greatness of, say, Bach's Mass in B minor is independent of human judgement? Are we to be realists or not? We saw earlier that realism can be understood in one of two ways; both of these have some relevance to the discussion. To recapitulate, a realist about quarks or charms believes that quarks or charms exist independently of the researches of the scientist. They are not merely theoretical entities invented to do a job in explanation. But another form of realism, and one that does not coincide with that, is that an answer to questions may exist prior to the questions asked. Thus a realist philosopher of mathematics of this second persuasion might believe that every even number being the sum of two prime numbers is a matter of fact that is independent of our proof procedures but he probably will not believe that there are numbers to be inspected in some Platonic heaven. A realist about artistic value could think that whether Berlioz's Requiem is a masterpiece or not is a matter of fact independently of what any musician thinks but he would not expect to find that proposition lodged in a Platonic inventory or, for that matter, in the mind of God.

Some non-realists about value have tended to construe the question on the first model. Its rejection is then for them a fairly straightforward matter. John Mackie's book, *Ethics: Inventing Right and Wrong*,[1] begins with the assertion "There are no objective values"; his celebrated "argument from queerness" complains that moral values would be strange entities indeed. Where could we observe them? What would it be like to discover them? But this is to construe the debate about value as though it paralleled the debate about whether quarks exist; the question is, then, whether they are objects like viruses or bacteria. But, as I have indicated, the debate about realism in the arts is certainly not primarily a question about the independent Platonic or quasi-Platonic existence of artistic values; that question rarely arises in post-Platonic times. It is first and foremost about whether saying that the "Eroica" Symphony is a great symphony is saying any more than that I admire the "Eroica" Symphony, or, more plausibly, that a conspectus of qualified judges would, yawningly, assent to this judgement. It is not, either, merely a matter of a contrast between my individual judgement that I like the work and the stature of the work independently of my judgement. Realists and non-realists both make that contrast, as they have to if they are to do justice to the life we live with the arts and the way we talk about paintings, literature, music and so on. The question is: what do judgements about the stature of the work amount to? Is the greatness of the music like the redness of a pillar box?

A little tidying up is in order before we continue. Moral values are properties such as courage, fortitude and compassion. If they are our values we admire people who display them, *ceteris paribus*. People who are compassionate are, to that extent, virtuous. Artistic values may be originality, vivacity, elegance and so on. They are our values if we prize works of art that display them.

Those who claim that values are objective (Mackie lists Francis Hutcheson, Richard Price and Plato as objectivists) probably would not deny that some values are also subjective (these are the wrong values as opposed to the right ones). However, I can see no case for values being either objective or subjective. Neither position looks plausible. If I value concision and an elegant argument in music while you look for fascinating textures or, say, very loud music, in what sense are my values objective in a way that yours are not (or vice versa)? We simply value different things in music (and don't think that my reference to decibels is intended as a jibe – very loud music does turn some people on). Coming out of a Bach concert, I heard one man say to another that it was very restful. I don't value music for restfulness *per se* but, although I assume that my taste and judgement in music is superior to anyone who says something so silly, I would not represent that as implying that my values are "objective". The only sense that one could give to this would be some more or less factitious sense dependent on a consensus of the informed about what values to look for in the arts. Perhaps I would say that the concert-goer who looked for restfulness in music had the wrong values just as a newspaper film critic recently implied that anybody who values Nick Roeg's *Walkabout* for the sequence in which the young Jenny Agutter swims in the nude approaches the film with the wrong set of values. In fact, we judge a set of values as inferior just to the extent that they either prevent somebody from seeing what is great in art or to the extent that they lead him to the wrong set of considerations in judging merit. By concentrating on "restfulness", a listener is missing what can be interesting and stimulating in the music. If we assume that taste is to be cashed out as a repertoire of values, then that repertoire is judged by the assessments made of individual works. To take values as fundamental in the arts puts the cart before the horse. The dependency is the other way, as my examples illustrate. Since values are neither objective nor subjective, to make them fundamental and to make the judgement of the individual work parasitic on those values forfeits the capacity to defend the "objectivity" of the individual judgement. Not only can the issues of realism and anti-realism not be raised but the crucial distinction between the independent standing of the work and individual likes and dislikes is lost. As we shall see later, it is the individual judgement that must come first. We work out the values of a listener from the judgements she makes. Those values are to be criticized to the extent that they obstruct her appreciation.

The second form of realism I described earlier is where the answer to a question as to the value of a work is presumed to exist prior to that question being asked and, therefore, prior to any enquiries we make in the course of arriving at an estimate of that value. Now, whether or not he believes in the objectivity of values, a robust realist will say that the object really is beautiful or ugly prior to the question being raised (unrepentant realists go for outmoded concepts like "beauty"). He will argue that where there is a divergence of judgement, one of the parties is simply wrong. Indeed, in the last resort, he could say that we might all be wrong about the value of a work of art, as a realist conceded to me in conversation. Now, although I am not going to argue this in detail here, I cannot make much sense of a notion of value so completely separated from what we love and admire. Such a very strong form of realism I think is difficult to defend. I think it possible that a work might be fine without anybody knowing it to be so but I would want to rule out a work being fine where experienced listeners over a sufficiently long period find against it. If qualified people have listened to the music fairly and decide it is no good then I think that the possibility that it is an unacknowledged masterpiece has been closed off. I would have to add the rider that it is possible that the interests and concerns of a society might change so radically that what was once admired is admired no longer. But by that token, we would conclude to a greater or less extent that they no longer have the same conception of the arts. The test of time is relative to a certain community of interest and concerns. But more of this in a moment. What we need for practical purposes is a means of distinguishing between the real merit of a work of music and the judgement made about it by any one individual listener.

Before we go any further, let me explain the sequence in which I propose to examine these issues. The questions are these:

- Does music have value because there are quite general features about it that make it good, features which can be specified in criteria?

- Could it be the case that a work is good if and only if it meets with the approval of an ideally qualified listener?
- Is the merit of a piece of music a matter of what philosophers call "inter-subjectivity"? Is it dependent on a consensus among the qualified, an agreement within an elite?
- How do we explain differences of opinion, not just within the sphere of casual listeners but within the elite itself?
- Further to this, are there unresolvable disagreements about the merit of a piece even among the qualified? If there are, does this raise fundamental difficulties for the philosopher who insists on some form of realism about judgements of value?
- Should we see the judgement of art as, ultimately, particular? On such a view, single judgements by a qualified listener take precedence; what generalizations there are are mere rules of thumb, restricted in their area of application.[2]

Criteria

Can we have very general reasons as to why a certain piece of music is good? Sometimes we do say things about music that imply that we think it good because of certain features it has. We describe it as lively, or as spirited or moving. Conversely we might describe it as sentimental or boring. In this are we giving general reasons as to why a piece of music is good? Some have thought so. If they are right, then the music is good in virtue of belonging to a certain class of items that meet certain standards. We know that a good knife is a sharp and well-balanced knife and a good knife meets these quite general requirements. To start with, then, when a work of art has value does it have that value in virtue of the work meeting certain criteria? Is it all a matter of the possession of certain features, such that if a work of art possesses these it will pass muster? Most of what I shall say here rules out such a theory. Indeed, the notion that the value of art is criteria-bound finds little support these days; the traditional difficulty is that the proposed criteria either seem so vague that it is unclear what meets them or so precise that it is not too hard to find exceptions. Now criteria have to be reasonably specific to count as criteria. A doctor qualified abroad has to meet certain criteria to be allowed to practise in Britain. There are specific criteria that a car has to meet in order to pass the annual roadworthiness test in Britain and so on. These criteria are not only specific; they do not of themselves incorporate any positive grading. An extra premise about what counts as a roadworthy car or a competent doctor is required for this. But when criteria are rendered specific in the arts, trouble is inevitable. The rule that one should avoid consecutive fifths or octaves in writing harmony used to be part and parcel of the teaching of elementary composition. But it is a rule that, if elevated into a criterion, would be immediately shown to have exceptions. Schoenberg explains the rule in the following way. What the rule prohibits is writing where two parts go from one fifth or octave relation to another by parallel motion. The assumption is that the independence of the two voices is thereby compromised. But Schoenberg points out that sometimes octave doublings are used because they "sound well" or because avoiding them would take the voice or instrument outside its range.[3] Certainly there are many instances of the rule being broken by classical masters. (Parallel fifths are used by Puccini at the beginning of Act III of *La Bohème* to represent winter chill.)

So those philosophers who defend the existence of general reasons for verdicts about merit usually do so in a way that does not commit them to very specific criteria. They will talk broadly about unity and variety, which is hardly precise enough to help. I suppose it might be important to realize that poor works can be immediately damned because they contain elementary mistakes that can be picked up via criteria. The beginner had best learn to avoid consecutive fifths. If the pupil eventually masters compositional technique then he can decide whether to conform or not. The problem is, as is generally the case, that in the philosophy of art our paradigms are the masterly and, in these cases, the satisfaction of general principles is even more remote from what makes them good or bad. The peculiar cases of the paradigmatically classical artists, such as Mozart, really have little to offer in this regard. We don't admire them because they satisfy certain general good-making rules but because they show what an inventive mind can do with clichés.

It might seem that to cite qualities like "vivacity" or "elegance" offers a more promising route to criteria. But, given what we have just said about the nature of criteria, I don't think we would call "elegance" criterial; there is likely to be as much debate about whether the work counts as elegant as there is about the overall verdict. We have not gained enough in precision and we have, of course, lost by prejudging the issue; we have imported a judgement of value into the assessment because "elegance" is normally a positive feature. I say "normally" because we might judge that elegance is inappropriate in a particular context. Elegance would not be a virtue in a craggy work like Bruckner's Ninth Symphony. But elegance might be a description used to call attention to a passage in another piece, a passage of significance that might pass the casual listener by. (Perhaps she might not see that it is elegant because the style is unfamiliar.) But, even here, its merit is hardly likely to depend upon its elegance; calling it elegant anticipates the conclusion for elegance is a merit. To the extent that judges disagree about the merits of a piece they will disagree either about whether it is elegant or whether elegance is a merit in this particular context.

The way I have explained this might suggest that what philosophers call the "fact–value gap" is at the root of all this. How do we get from noting mere matters of fact about the music, such facts being value-neutral, to the conclusion that the piece has merit? But what I want to emphasize here is something different. It is that the judgement of merit is much more concerned with how a device works in, at the minimum, a passage and, at the maximum, a movement or a work. We would never say that the famous Tristan chord has intrinsic merit that would enhance any work into which it might be placed; in a movement by Mozart it would stick out like a sore thumb. But it would be wrong to conclude from that that its intrinsic merits are cancelled out by its inappropriateness to that context. It does not have any intrinsic merit at all. Enlarge the context to several bars either side and now it might well make sense to describe it as having merit. It is a finely composed passage. But inserted in a movement by an earlier composer it would be unintelligible. What works in one place will not work in another. Artistic judgement is essentially holistic and individual.

The basic problem, then, is that criteria either have exceptions or are too vague or they beg the question by importing a judgement of merit into the considerations on which the verdict is made. Now the defender of critical generalizations might argue something like the following. Of course, critical generalizations have exceptions, but in that respect they do not differ from generalizations elsewhere. Laws of science may hold for ideal conditions to which the conditions we meet with in everyday life only approximate. Nobody denies that there are laws relating the temperature and pressure of gases just because, in the empirical case, we are not dealing with ideal gases. Equally, critical generalizations apply to idealized cases; in the rough and tumble of ordinary aesthetic judgements they need to be taken with a pinch of salt.

But the analogy does not hold. Take the examples I have given. In no sense does the prohibition on consecutive octaves apply to the ideal case. If anything, the ideal case, the outstanding music of a period, is the music that is more likely to infringe these rules than not. In any case, the viability of rules depends on context and may require the judgement of the experienced hand. Consider performance and consider the rule that a pianist should not pedal through harmonic changes (because it blurs and renders opaque those very changes). This certainly does not apply if you are playing Debussy. Indeed, even Beethoven often asks you to do just that. But it is a good general rule in eighteenth-century music (unless you think that the use of the pedal, or indeed the use of the pianoforte, in music of this period is a complete solecism, in which case the question does not arise). Yet even here, there can be disagreements between experienced musicians; there may, as well, be a way of playing Bach such that pedalling is not an offence. In Beethoven its use needs to be qualified by a realization of the difference between Beethoven's piano and the modern instrument and this again calls for the judgement of the experienced musician. So one problem is that the *ceteris paribus* cases are not themselves clearly defined. We do not have a clear notion of where the rule applies and where it does not. For, although I have given some indications of its applicability, there will always be central cases as well as borderline cases where instructions on pedalling have to be judged with an ear to the context.

The ideal observer theory

Set aside, then, the possibility that artistic merit can be assessed by virtue of general criteria stating non-evaluative characteristics whose possession automatically makes a piece of music good. What alternatives do we have? The ideal observer theory is fairly familiar in its moral guise, although it has not been particularly mainstream in ethics. In essence, the claim is that to say an act is right entails holding that, if there were an ideal observer, he or she would approve the act. The ideal observer might, of course, be an omniscient deity; then the account gives us a way of connecting religious belief and moral obligation. The ideal observer theory has seemed to some to suggest a plausible parallel account of what it is for a work of art to have value. So the ideal artistic observer, like his, her or its counterparts in ethical theory, offers a way of defining what is artistically valuable or what a work of art means without losing sight of the fact that the way in which art is valuable is deeply connected with what it offers human beings.[4]

The ideal observer (or, rather, listener) in music will be somebody who knows all the relevant facts, experiences the relevant expressive features of the music and understands all the possible relevant approaches to the music. In his essay "Of the Standard of Taste", Hume sometimes seems to be proposing an ideal observer theory, although he does oscillate between that and the consensus theory that we shall be considering next. Any individual critic can attempt to approach the status of an ideal critic by discounting her individual quirks, the likes and dislikes that she knows are personal to her. So she might grade the music of Richard Strauss, which perhaps she dislikes, by setting aside her own predilections and looking at his mastery of the orchestra, by taking into account the views of other qualified but more sympathetic listeners, and so on.

Now there are problems; first, there are disputes about what facts are relevant in the first place. To name only the most obvious, there are disagreements as to whether the composer's intentions are relevant or not in any debate over what a piece of music expresses or what it "means". Some think they are; some think not. Remember our discussion of the differing theories about how close performance should be to what we think the composer intended. Now, disagreements either about what the creator's intentions are or about their relevance need not directly affect our judgement of the work's value. Most works whose interpretation is a matter of debate are works whose stature is beyond question; the consensus has long since determined that these are outstanding and that they have canonical status. What these works mean would not be of any interest if they were not of supreme merit. However, where such disagreements do matter is where they precede the judgements about the merits of the music. For how we judge the music may ultimately depend on our estimate of its character; for example, a failure to see that music is ironic may lead us to arrive at the wrong verdict. The finale of Shostakovich's Fifth Symphony is a *locus classicus* for this. The music was long excoriated as a paean to Stalinist communism; what it really is is a bitter pretence of rejoicing.

What follows from this is a problem of a different sort for the ideal observer theory. Given that an assessment of at least some music depends upon determining an interpretation, the existence of many different interpretations, all of which may be defensible but some of which might not be mutually compatible, means that the deliverances of the ideal observer who takes into account all points of view in an impartialist way cannot be coherently characterized. She has to embrace conflicting interpretations. Just how serious this difficulty is depends upon what "taking into account" involves. It cannot mean "accepting" for the reasons just given. If "taking into account" merely means "registering those interpretations that are viable", then the criticism does not count for much.

We required that the ideal observer be familiar with the expressive, experiential features of a work. Should she also be moved by the music? Well, first, intense emotions can get in the way of judgement. Knowing that this is the last performance of a dying diva might cause her to misjudge the scale of the performance. Of course, the fact that she is moved may be something she allows for or explains away. In other cases, she might see that the features of the music that excite her are superficial and will not survive repeated hearings or even see that this is music that ought not to involve her (although it does) because she can see that it is meretricious. No real problem here. Secondly, suppose she is not moved; we might think that somebody who knows what the expressive features of a piece of very good music are but is not moved by it might not be in the best position to judge. It is not good enough, it might be said, for the critic to know that others are moved but not be herself moved. Furthermore, when a critic, as an experienced listener, sees that it is not the sort of thing that moves or excites her but judges that it *might* move someone else, she ought to be cautious in making a judgement about its value. It might be technically competent but lifeless. These features complicate but do not, I think, fatally damage the ideal observer theory. Its advocate would be entitled to reply that such an individual is not the ideal observer, the perfect critic.

Although at least the last of these criticisms is not particularly telling, it points in the direction of the overwhelming problem with the ideal observer theory. It is that the entire and complex relationship that we have with works of art, generally and not just music, will be affected if we think that the position of the ideal observer is something towards which we should strive, which is how ideal observer theorists see it, even when they acknowledge that the status of an ideal observer is not attainable. Among all the works of art available, there are some for which we have a peculiar affection. Perhaps it is right that we try to broaden our horizons from time to time and try to understand and appreciate works that are initially remote from us. But it is also important for our relationship with the arts that these attempts sometimes fail. For if we were to succeed, the peculiar way that art is entwined with our lives would disappear. Compare. Although it might be praiseworthy to try to care for other people who are remote from me, if this were to be at the cost of the special concerns I have for my wife, my children and my friends, it would not be an outcome to be wished for. Such a person would be unnatural and chilling in his lack of the normal human loyalties and prejudices. And the person whose taste is not, in some ways, idiosyncratic and peremptory is a bit too close to Wilde's auctioneer for comfort: "It is only an auctioneer who can equally and impartially admire all schools of Art."[5] Why should it be preferable to have a completely catholic taste in music rather than, say, having a passion for Dixieland jazz or for Indian music? Somebody who has an impartial concern for everybody, like Dickens's Mrs Jellaby, but who ignores the desire of her children for her special attention does not commend herself to us as particularly admirable. We might, too, think that somebody who liked all music equally – proportionately, of course, to its merits – would be something of a cultural monster.

I have touched here on an analogue to what in ethics is called partialism. In moral philosophy this is the doctrine that we have special obligations to our nearest and dearest, to wife or husband, children and parents and to pets as well. What does being a partialist about art involve? Well, first, you might love a piece for its associations, for the particular place that it has in your history. At the same time you may have no illusions about its merits. Equally, you may share a history with some relative for whom you may care even though you recognize his faults. Uncle Arthur is the black sheep of the family; you love him nonetheless. There are no immediately striking differences between art and morality here. But then, secondly, in the case of the arts you may think, rightly or wrongly, that a particular piece is undervalued and have a mission to convert others to an appreciation of it. Here the differences appear. When you act on behalf of your children you act in order to ensure that their interests are being met but, it will be argued, works of art do not have interests. It is in our interest that they are not damaged, not their own. In this sense the notion of partialism when applied to the arts is certain to be somewhat etiolated. Your desire to get other people to listen to a piece of music you believe to be neglected is more to do with your obligations to other people. You would not like to have missed hearing this so you want others to hear it as well.

Hume said, memorably, "We choose our favourite author as we do our friend, from a conformity of humour and disposition". [6] It is interesting that the partialism that is endorsed here takes, as its model, friendship. It is proverbial, although perhaps false, that we choose our friends and not our relatives, but it is certainly possible to love a relative who you find rather unlikeable. A shared history creates a connection that is not easily dissolved. In a somewhat parallel way, as I say, a loved book or recording or painting being part of my history of taste is often of enormous importance to my attachment for it and that attachment may survive the realization that it is not very good. Probably the ideal observer theory can live with this; the problem is that it does not see an individual relationship of this sort as anything other than something to be overcome.

My final criticism is another serious objection to the ideal observer theory; it does not accurately describe how we arrive at an artistic judgement about the status of a work. Certainly a new work may surprise and absorb my attention and I then may judge that it is of stature, only to be surprised when others do not share my judgement. If I accept the verdict of others, I do not arrive at my assessment by the process of discounting my prejudice. I arrive at it by looking at the consensus. The consensus will embrace readers or listeners or viewers of various persuasions and our assessment of the verdict is not arrived at by discounting their various idiosyncrasies. These remain *in situ*. Indeed, how could I know mine or anybody else's to be idiosyncratic in the first place? Only by looking at how others judge and react to the music. The consensus theory that, I suggest, is presumed by an ideal observer theory embodies all this, as we shall see. But on the ideal observer theory alone, what should I do? It gives me no lead on what I should discount.

There is a further consideration; if the situation is analogous with ethics, as its proponents tend to assume, then *ought* I to appreciate the music of John Coltrane just as, having found out what the ideal ethical observer endorses, I ought to act on the recognition that that is what it is right for me to do? But the notion of a consensus in the arts does not call for common human reactions or progress towards common reactions. Those who make up the consensus themselves differ in taste and preferences and they retain those differences. I can agree on the stature of a composer or a work while feeling no pressure to like it. On any reading of the nature of major divergences in taste, these divergences may remain. The only pressure I might feel is that, in ignoring a work that others praise, I may be missing something. (Setting aside the much discussed issue of moral objections to some art; in music such objections tend to occur mainly in the case of opera.)

In as much as a "realist" or "objectivist" account can be given of judgements of merit, it is a sort of surrogate obtained by something closer to qualified majority rule (where some listeners count for more than others) rather than by any particular procedure that enables us to arrive at the "real truth", independent of particular judgements about the status of a work of art. (The ideal observer theory looks intriguingly like the notion of a "scientific method", which, once found and deployed, guarantees that we shall discover the truth.) We do need the consensus; it is a guide for the novice but, to a large extent, we throw it away as our own taste forms. What interests and involves us in maturity may be a sub-class of the music we enjoyed and admired as we were getting to grips with the art. At that earlier point, our taste converged with that of the consensus. More than one music-lover has remarked to me that he doesn't now listen to the Beethoven symphonies with the same enthusiasm that he did as a teenager.

The consensus among connoisseurs

We cannot give any usefully precise and evaluatively neutral features that, satisfied, make a piece of music meritorious. The ideal observer theory does not help. How, then, do we justify verdicts? Well, we have already anticipated a plausible account in our criticism of the ideal observer theory. Most philosophers who have thought at length about this have concluded that the answer must lie in the operation of a consensus of the qualified. The roots of this approach are to be found in Hume's already mentioned, much discussed essay, "Of the Standard of Taste". Hume sets out the requirements for a good critic. A consensus theory allows for disagreements among well-qualified critics: those who, in Hume's words, have "strong sense, united to delicate sentiment, improved by practice, perfected by comparison, and cleared of all prejudice". Of these, he says, the "joint verdict" is "the true standard of taste". (The phrase "standard of taste" is not helpful here; Hume never says precisely what he means by this obscure term.)

The general idea among defenders of a consensus theory is that, even if a well-qualified listener has an antipathy for early Louis Armstrong, the majority of those who have expended time and trouble on this music and are experienced in the style, agree that it is of surpassing quality. A few dissenting voices among them do not seriously damage the authority of the judgement. Frank Sibley felicitously described it as "more a concentrated scatter than convergence on a point".[7] Thus some good critics think that Armstrong is the *ne plus ultra* whereas others give Jelly Roll Morton the palm. Some think "West End Blues" was Armstrong's finest achievement while others rate "Potato Head Blues" more highly, and so it goes on. But within the elite whose opinion counts, there is a weighted verdict (a majority allowing for blind spots, differing tastes, differing degrees of engagement with the music and so on) that makes Armstrong the major figure in classical Dixieland jazz. This domination of a consensus of connoisseurs was described by the philosopher Samuel Alexander as "a conspiracy of the qualified".[8] We need, too, to remember that people rarely spend hours and years in listening to, comparing, and analysing a body of music unless they find it of very great interest. When we speak of the "test of time" as the examination that outstanding works pass and mediocre works fail, we reflect the way that great works reward many different players and listeners over a long period. That such a consensus forms, that a body of qualified listeners constitutes itself, is already a testimony to the value of the music. Since we cannot specify the features that make a piece of music fine, the consensus gives us the next best thing: the basis for a distinction between the "true verdict" and idiosyncratic likes and dislikes.

Unfortunately, the operation of a consensus of experienced and attentive listeners cannot be the whole story. A consensus theory alone is an anti-realist account. It does not tell us that there are features in the music that bring about a response from the qualified listener. A question remains for anybody with realist inclinations; what is it about fine music that attracts, interests and moves the music-lover? There surely is a causal element as well. We must foreclose the possibility that musical merit is either a delusion of the cognoscenti or, as the philistines of the British tabloid press propose, a pretence concocted to preserve social distinctions, to exclude those who are not of the educated middle class. Those of us who love music know that our response to it is neither a delusion nor a pretence. But enmeshed in the problem of causality is a thorny issue.

The problem of irreconcilable differences of judgement

For both ideal observer theories and for consensus theories, a problem remains and the problem is that of irreconcilable divergences of opinion even among the qualified.[9] In order to locate this question, some background discussion is required. Consider, first, a feature of the arts that many people find worrying; it has certainly worried me on and off for most of my life. Faced with, say, a style or school of painting or an individual artist whose work, in Wittgenstein's phrase "I can't see into", what sort of judgement do I make? In the other arts, I might, for example, be unable to see past the frivolity, as it seems to me, of Fragonard or, like Samuel Johnson, find the metaphysical style of the poetry of Donne and his successors strained and artificial. The problem has been particularly pressing for me in music; by most people's standards, I have a very catholic taste but there is music I have been unable to make much of, ranging from Pérotin and Guillaume de Machaut on the one hand to the second Viennese school on the other, and also including Miles Davis and John Coltrane, Harrison Birtwistle, Pierre Boulez and Massive Attack. A good example that has struck some other writers on this topic is Tchaikovsky's "Pathétique" Symphony, which is variously viewed as maudlin or powerful. Most of you will have similar gaps in your personal taste that worry you to a greater or lesser extent. As a young man, I was told that familiarity with the music of Schoenberg, Alban Berg and Anton Webern was required in order to appreciate the cutting edge of new music. Not wanting to convict myself of a provincial or conservative taste, I duly bought vinyl records of the *Variations for Orchestra* and *Pierrot Lunaire*, taped the string quartets and listened to them over and over again. But the penny never dropped. I grew to love Stravinsky but I never cared whether I heard anything by Schoenberg again. As he himself remarked with anguish, we do not go to sleep with his music echoing through our minds and wake up longing to hear it again. Or at least I don't, and apparently Schoenberg himself did not. I was highly motivated to find memorable themes, entrancing textures, moments of climax and all that excitement that made a life without Bach, Haydn or Schubert unthinkable. I just didn't find them. What could account for this misfortune? There are, of course, other examples. There is still dissent over the status of Berlioz and many find the operas of Handel bland.

There are various explanations of my failure to appreciate the music of these composers.

- I have not done enough work on the music. Some of this music is not for the lazy listener. I need to listen more carefully, perhaps with a score. But then, you ask, how much work is needed? If a couple of concentrated hearings do not produce a passage of interest, then mightn't we as well give up? The fact is that very few works offer rewards to you only after you have given them a decent try. The adage "try and try again" is of limited applicability in the arts.
- Connected with the first explanation, I am listening to the music in the wrong way. My expectations are not the proper ones for this sort of music. I need to approach it with a different gestalt. It's no good listening to later Tippett in the expectation of the sort of linear development we find in classical music or listening to Handel with ears attuned to the virtues of Mozart.
- It is simply not to my taste. We all have blind spots. This is no more problematic than the fact that many people don't much like the operas of Wagner or that they have idiosyncratic likes and dislikes in the other arts.
- The music really is not all it is cracked up to be. This might be a tenable view even if many experts judge the music to be of high quality. For their putative misjudgements can be accounted for by pointing out that they deceive themselves; after all, there is some kudos in being members of the cognoscenti and, particularly, in being the first to recognize a major new figure. Critics thus have a motive for liking certain music and this can distort judgement. Of course, we would expect that the negative judgement on the music would be borne out by the way the consensus develops over time. Eventually

one realizes, as perhaps people now realize, that Schoenberg is not a major composer. He is rather what Tovey used to call an "IHF": an interesting historical figure. Perhaps, too, they confuse the interest of technical proficiency with the more general appeal of expressive power. A developing consensus would enable us to distinguish between music of real power and stature and music that is merely technically accomplished.

Note that the first three of these are cases where we shall consider discounting our initial adverse reaction to a work of art; we discount where we set aside our response as grounds for valuing or disvaluing the work. In these cases we might grant that the work has stature even though it does not appeal to us, for we know that competent judges rate the music highly. This is a familiar scenario in the philosophy of art, although not in aesthetics more generally. (I am not sure whether "I don't like this landscape although I acknowledge that it is really beautiful" is a possible judgement, although there will be argument about this, I suspect.)

Consider the third explanation. It is just a difference of taste. How significant are such differences of taste? Now the first two explanations are explicable in terms of an epistemological failing. This can be put in various ways but each way we put it assumes a connection between understanding and valuing. I do not find these works interesting, I do not enjoy them or I do not follow them because of various interfering factors. This connection between understanding and valuing is, of course, one of the features that separates the arts from other cases where our aesthetic sensitivities are involved. It might be argued, although there may be exceptions, that generally there is nothing to be understood about a landscape that is relevant to its aesthetic appreciation. Only if you agree with those who have recently made a case for aesthetic appreciation being enhanced or dimmed by knowledge of the geology or history of the area could that sort of understanding be relevant. Equally, your enjoyment of a ripe peach seems to owe nothing to understanding, although perhaps the situation would be different in a Michelin starred restaurant where your gustatory experience might be enhanced by an understanding of the art of the chef. But, in various ways, understanding is relevant to artistic appreciation, and this underlies the centrality of interpretation for the arts. The Orson Welles film *Touch of Evil* is generally regarded as a masterpiece. You might find it hammy and cliché-ridden. Now this might be a case of the second explanation. For what seem clichés can be a consequence of foregrounding the wrong sorts of things in a work. For the film-goer who does not find these to be clichés somehow sees them as part of the quotidian style and sees the way they are used creatively. A superficial listener might see clichés in Mozart's music; the informed listener sees other things. Re-education may help us to see what is there.

Such a case may be described as one where lack of the relevant knowledge stands in the way of my appreciation, of my seeing what is there to be valued. A listener may lack an adequate awareness of the conventions of the *galant* style and thus fail to notice how Mozart uses them in a rather different way. A way of bringing out the epistemological undertow here would be to put it this way. If every case of a difference of taste were epistemologically based, then where two of us differ in our responses to a work of art, those differences could be reconciled by an appropriate re-education process for one or other of us. This is a line of argument that naturally appeals to realists about artistic verdicts. Of course, and this is important in the arts, one of us can certainly allow that something is masterly while not liking it. If I allow that, then there is no pressing need for resolution; we might consign the differences to broad differences in values and not be concerned enough to do anything about it. The only reason why we should bring our responses into line is because one of us is missing something important and valuable and this, of course, is the predominant reason why the matter worried us in the first place. We want to appreciate what we are told has merit (when we are told on good authority) and the importance of that ought not to be underestimated.

Suppose, though, that no re-education works. I try but fail to respond to Schoenberg's *Variations for Orchestra*. There might be a deeper basis for this. It might be that we have here a genuine case of the third explanation. It is not that I need to work harder at the music or acquire more information, nor that the music is of poor quality. I simply have a blind spot as far as Schoenberg is concerned. One explanation of this might be that my dislike of Schoenberg connects with broader aspects of my taste and to like this work would require such seismic changes in my taste that I cannot contemplate it. My dislike of Schoenberg might relate to a sense of a certain academic stuffiness, a lack of rhythmical verve and a dislike of that somewhat opaque orchestral sound. (Of course, I may be wrong about all this. Then make allowances for my deficiencies of taste and find another example to suit. Remember that the argument at this point requires a major figure over whom there is dispute.) On the other hand, I admire Schoenberg's capacity to build huge structures that, despite their size, are coherent. In all these matters, to an extent, one's acceptance or rejection of these as grounds for valuing may come and go. We must allow both that our tastes change over time and that they sometimes oscillate in a disconcerting way. You may find yourself admiring a musician you have not previously cared for. Then the temptation to put down your absorption in the music to a temporary lack of critical nous or even to deny that you are really fascinated by it may be quite strong.

What I have been concentrating on is a case where values differ between listeners and where the difference in values determines a difference in the judgement of individual works. In as much as you can explain why you don't like a piece, then differences of assessment will fall into this category. So my dislike of Schoenberg connects with my dislike of some aspects of the German musical tradition and that is a fairly broad feature of my taste in music. (It is important to bear in mind what I said earlier: we may be dealing here with judgements about the merits of the work, mere personal likes or dislikes or any one of the many complex ways in which we relate to art.) A case that I find much more puzzling is the case of Berlioz, because I cannot fathom why others do not love his music as I do. How can anybody fail to acknowledge that Act IV of *Les Troyens* is one of the most astonishing things in all opera? Berlioz does divide listeners. There are many, including the thousands who made it difficult to get tickets for the Berlioz Odyssey in London in 2000, for whom he is unambiguously one of the greatest of masters. There are others for whom his music is eccentric, over-the-top, self-indulgent and harmonically bizarre. In some cases the latter judgements can be explained in the ways previously described as cases of the first and second explanations. A solidly German background in music might make it hard to accept some of his harmonic progressions, which are, uniquely in a great composer, not based on competence as a keyboard player. The seemingly strange fact that he is relatively unappreciated in France might be explained by his passion for Shakespeare, which led, in turn, to an unacceptably unclassical handling of form.

If our tastes are idiosyncratic in these fairly general ways, then divergences are to be expected; we simply cannot love everything equally and some things we cannot love at all. We are not Wildean auctioneers who admire everything equally, proportionate to its merits. We can link this with the way we might, as we sometimes do, try to offer reasons why we like or dislike a work. Then to take a feature or features as a reason for appreciating one work might render problematic the appreciating of another that lacks it. The idea here is that tastes differ where one or other of us has a stock of features, a repertoire of considerations that we value and look for in the arts. It applies quite generally. There are poets, novelists, dramatists, film-makers and painters who exhibit these. There are some who do not. A catholic taste may well admire some of the latter or, more often, some works of the latter. Thus Vaughan Williams did not much like the music of Beethoven but he did admire the Ninth Symphony and I have heard *The Valkyrie* described as "the Wagner for people who dislike Wagner". But even a fairly catholic palate won't embrace all the works of a creator who is, by these tokens, marginal to its taste. If a visual model helps here, think of tastes as an arrangement of overlapping circles. Values, as Isaiah Berlin impressed on us, may not be commensurable.[10] Tastes, I suggest, may differ and there may be no common measure on the basis of which some can be judged deficient and others not.

It is worth pointing out that individual judgements of value may agree while judgements of their basis may differ. We might be puzzled by Schumann's judgement that Mozart's Fortieth Symphony is the epitome of Grecian lightness and grace, yet he agrees with us about its pre-eminence. Many will concur in thinking that the expressive judgement is wrong. There is an atavistic element of *Sturm und Drang*[11] in Mozart's mature G minor works that passed Schumann by, although he said different things about Mozart at different times, but we all agree with him on its stature. Such differences may be replicated in performance. Most conductors treat Haydn's "Military" Symphony as genial and high-spirited; the soldiers are toy soldiers. But turn to Nikolaus Harnoncourt and you find the symphony treated as expressing menace and disquiet; it then becomes natural to take it as a protest against the horrors of war. Defending such judgements turns one towards those issues of authenticity that we discussed in a previous chapter; you may claim that there is a proper mode of performance and, at the same time, an informed stance from which the work is properly assessed. My point here is that diver-gence in judgements may not only involve the evaluative; they may involve expressive predicates as well. There may be agreement about evaluation but irreconcilable difference of opinion about the expressive nature. I can easily imagine Beecham and Harnoncourt agreeing on the superlative quality of the "Military" Symphony but disagreeing about the expressive features and I can imagine that such a disagreement might not be settled even if a newly discovered letter from Haydn made it clear which side he belonged to. For it is open to a performer to insist that the composer's *obiter dictum* is not the last word.

Recognizing differences of taste often neutralizes differences of opinion, of course. Once we see that our tastes differ we are inclined not to argue further. One reason for this may be that argument is no longer thought very worthwhile, although where I am still under the thrall of a film seen, a novel read or a piece of music heard, I may not be so easily satisfied with the nostrum "It's just a matter of taste". To the extent that it matters to me and to the extent that I believe that the judgement I have made is not merely a consequence of my particular biography, my defence of the work may be robust and I shall regret the inability of my interlocutor to appreciate it.

Here we touch on the "residual cases": those cases where a divergence of taste persists despite our best endeavours to come to some agreement over the stature of a writer, painter or composer. The strongest of these residual cases is where a discrepancy of judgement is not explicable in terms of varying repertoires of values in the arts. I don't like this, you do, and there's an end to it. Our tastes do not differ but our judgements about this case do. It is these cases that I find most interesting and puzzling. There are disputes about a work's status that do not seem to be explicable in any of the ways I have described, where not only is there no reason to suspect that there exists such an epistemological explanation of how the differences arise but also the difference is not necessarily grounded in the repertoire of values. Typically these cases, and there may not be many such, occur where one person has an overwhelming sense of the power of the work, a power that allows no denial, while another simply does not respond in this way.

Equally, of course, I may be struck by the ineptness of a work where others admire it and where I admire other works by the same creator. Thus, recently, I have had occasion to listen carefully to several different recordings and a live performance of Vaughan Williams's *A London Symphony*. I have come to the conclusion that, a few episodes apart, it is a terrible work and I cannot credit how it comes to be programmed and recorded so often. Obviously others disagree; some readers will; but my initial judgement of its poverty and crudeness bears in upon me just as strongly as my reactive judgement to Berlioz's Requiem is that this is awe-inspiring stuff. This coexists with my belief that some of Vaughan Williams's works are as near perfect as we are likely to encounter this side of Mozart. Of course, I might acknowledge that my judgement that *A London Symphony* is a poor work is idiosyncratic and that the consensual view that it is a masterpiece is right; but in this case, I am very reluctant to do what I do elsewhere and set aside my own judgement. This is not a case where the various features I admire in his music happen to be absent in this particular case. It is rather that this particular *work* offends me.

So the really problematic case comes where, while two people agree in taste, they diverge over the value of a single work that may or may not be an exemplary case of the style that both appreciate. But there is another and reverse case; this is where somebody feels that a work, that others do not value highly at all is one of those works of supreme power that everybody ought to recognize, regardless of taste. Here agreement or disagreement in taste is not a relevant issue. So Beethoven's Ninth Symphony, over which there is some dispute, is held by many to be a supreme masterpiece and when Vaughan Williams acknowledges it,[12] despite the fact that he is not very partial to Beethoven on the whole, in their view he properly salutes a work that transcends differences of taste. Of course, the clientele in question is assumed to be generally knowledgeable about classical music. The phenomenology of all these cases is, I believe, much like the way in which I find it impossible to deny that there is a table in front of me as I work. Similarly, I believe, there are a few works of art whose status is disputed but whose power strikes its aficionados so intensely that they feel we must acknowledge it and will brook no dissent.

I take it that two listeners differing over Vaughan Williams's *A London Symphony* may both have listened carefully and without prejudice. I have said that what is important in this example is that they might share the same values in music; they like the same sorts of thing but they differ in their judgement of this work. It might, of course, sometimes be difficult to establish that they have the same values; the natural way to do this would be by seeing not only what repertoire they prefer but what considerations they adduce in defending a particular verdict, what features and what passages they point to. We would be justified in assuming that more general aspects of taste did not enter the picture if we found that they did not refer to such stylistic factors defending their differing conclusions.

Could we say that both judges are right? Well anybody who is a robust realist and thinks that the value of the work is something independent of particular judgements of it cannot entertain that conclusion. Those who do not espouse strong realism have an option. They might say that both are right in the sense that procedurally both have followed the right path prior to making a judgement. They have both paid careful attention to the work; they have both listened to different performances in different contexts; they have both tried to prepare for a listening by hearing other related works by the same composer or by those who have influenced him. If they have done all this, then you might say that both are right. If this seems rather odd, consider a parallel case in ethics. Two women in relevantly similar circumstances come to different conclusions as to whether to have an abortion. Suppose they have both been as honest as they can, neither giving too much weight to their own futures nor too little; they have both taken advice and thought hard and deeply about the complex issue. I certainly feel a strong pull to the conclusion that both are right simply because it is hard to imagine in this case what rightness could amount to other than the serious and careful attention to all aspects of the situation.[13] So why should not the same hold in the case of my musical example?

If we do think that correctness of judgement is a matter of following the right procedure, then we will draw the conclusion that in such cases not only is there no agreement as to what the "objective" status of the work is; there is, in one clear sense, no "objective" *independent* status to be determined. It does not exist. There is no right judgement prior to the enquiry. However, if the rightness of the judgement is merely a matter of the integrity of the assessor, then all judgements in this category will be satisfactory. But clearly this is not the case. If you judge that a piece of music that lies outside your taste is poor in quality, you will, if you are sensible about judgements in the arts, allow that the consensus has the last word. You may then judge that it is good even though you cannot see what is good about it. The notion that correctness in judgement is a matter of procedure can only apply to a tiny sub-class of judgements about the arts; indeed, I suspect that it applies to a tiny number of moral judgements, even though these may be peculiarly important moral judgements. They may even be those that are permanently disputable.

Do such cases of unresolvable divergence of judgement occur more frequently with respect to music than the other arts? I suspect they do, which makes a discussion of this issue more pertinent to a discussion of the particular nature of value judgements about music. Let me explain. A clash of opinion over a novel, a film or a play may often be explained in terms of differing religious or political standpoints; this is not an explanation so often encountered in differences over music. Thus an atheist might find the element of religious commitment in Dostoevsky or Gerard Manley Hopkins rebarbative. You might find the whole genre of American westerns unattractive because of an assumption that there is no problem so complicated that it cannot be solved by shooting somebody. (Of course, some westerns are more subtle or subvert the genre.) This type of explanation is less readily available in music. There are some examples; they tend to belong to music in as far as music is a mixed medium. Some find much of the music of Messiaen objectionable because of the atmosphere of incense, of religious kitsch and of an apparent certitude about dogma that, in the twentieth century, seems like a pose or worse; many musicians dislike Wagner's *Parsifal*. (One German critic remarked that the baton should be gently but firmly removed from the hand of anybody who attempted to conduct it.)

Of course, there are explanations of negative judgements of "pure" music that border on the ideological. The style of Richard Strauss offends many, partly because the late style, with its classical references, its extraordinary euphony and melisma, its allusions to the great tradition of German music, seems to have been composed in a different world from that of his fellow Germans. On the other hand, some find the combination of naiveté and a superlative technique rather endearing and what faults there are forgivable. (I can't think of another composer to whom we would apply the epithet "forgivable".)

Admittedly, differences of opinion over musical style may connect, closely or not so closely, with broader aspects of our personalities, not just with our taste but with our values elsewhere. The conspicuously bourgeois features of Strauss might not gel with radical political opinions. But such considerations are usually more remote from the judgement of music than they are from the judgement of film, theatre or fiction. In any case no such explanation accounts for the sort of divergence I have outlined over Vaughan Williams's *A London Symphony*. If we "agree to disagree" here it is with a nagging discomfort absent in the cases where it can be explained away in terms of broader divergences of taste, or moral or political commitment.

Where does this leave us? The existence of divergences of this sort leads some thinkers to say that it cannot be "a matter of fact" as to what the real status of the work is, a fact that careful and competent listeners converge upon. For that to be the case there would have to be some point at which the listener fails, either in being prejudiced against the work or in lacking the right sort of information or training in taste. She fails to grasp the true status of the work and the explanation must lie in one or other of the ways in which she is ill-prepared. But we have found examples where the listener is well-prepared, is not guilty of any prejudice nor has any distaste for the style and yet she fails to endorse what seems to be the consensus. Now the assumption that her dissenting judgement can somehow be explained away in the usual way looks more like a matter of faith than anything else.

We raise again the spectre of non-realism about judgements of merit. Fundamental disagreements become a problem for realism when they are thought to underpin the conclusion "this work is great" or "this is rubbish". One way of putting it is to say that realists who subscribe to an ideal observer theory, believing that the ideal observer grasps certain facts relevant to verdicts, require that ideal critics do not disagree. For anti-realists, such divergences are less problematic. For the more robust realist, of course, agreement alone will not guarantee that the aesthetic properties are being seen for what they are. The ever present threat of scepticism means that, for the realist, there is no automatic route from either the existence of a consensus among the qualified or from the deliverances of an ideal observer to the object really having the properties ascribed. There may still be a gap between the evidence grasped by the ideal observer and the independent "facts of the matter" as far as the work's merit is concerned. In theory, both consensus and ideal observer could be wrong. But the crucial challenge to the realist is the case where you feel that you cannot but insist on the stature of this particular work and yet you know that other competent judges disagree vehemently, and there is not much doubt that people react in these different ways to Tchaikovsky's "Pathétique" Symphony.

The crux for the realist

We have, in this final chapter, been mainly concerned with trying to understand how we can distinguish expressions of personal taste from judgements that a piece of music "really" has merit over and above such individual preferences. Let's not forget the importance of this. A teenager is told that the late Beethoven quartets rank among the supreme achievements of mankind. She does not want to miss them; she knows that her taste needs to be developed in order that she may grow into them. Her education in the arts requires the assumption that there may be works of art that are good and yet, at present, they are to her a closed book. It is the distinction between what we like and what is good that makes education in the arts both possible and desirable, an education that is made requisite by the various ways in which we can fail to understand and appreciate, some of which I listed earlier in this chapter.

So far I have mentioned various ways in which the distinction might be understood. The first was that "objective" properties of works might be linked via criteria to value judgements and that these objective criteria are what enable us to define the "real" stature of a piece of music (or of a performance, for that matter); the second was that works have a value independent of ordinary human judgement in as much as that judgement matches what an ideal listener might decide; and the third was that the consensus decides. On this third account, what the verdict of the elite gives is a decision as to the true status. But, while electing for a form of consensus theory, I only suggested that the consensus is a means of finding out what the status of the piece is. I left open the possibility that it is not equivalent to that status. Then the merit of the piece may be something over and above the way in which we settle on what that merit is. So a form of realism remains possible. But what sort of realism? What makes the work itself meritorious, distinct from the judgement of the consensus? This, I think. Works of art have causal features that involve us or move us in the way that is characteristic of our response to works of art. That is, we do not "project" on to the work of art what moves and interests us. Nor is any reductive programme tenable that turns the value of the work into what the consensus declares valuable. So I incline towards a propensity theory of artistic value. Works of stature have causal powers to produce in the prepared mind a fascination with and absorption in the object. To quote Hume, "there are certain qualities in objects which are fitted by nature to produce those particular feelings".[14] Thus they may also produce the frisson we value, *inter alia*. I construe the beauty (or whatever other artistic features are relevant) of the object as I construe "poisonous": that is a propensity to affect human beings or other mammals in the absence of whom it must be construed counterfactually, as philosophers say. (Poison isn't a bad analogy; it is a matter of independent fact that arsenic harms humans, but it also depends upon the way human beings are constituted.) That is, were I to experience this work in the right setting and with the appropriate attention and preparedness, then I would respond. Now this allows a contrast between what an object's value really is and how it might seem to an individual judge, although not, as I have said, a contrast between its real value and the consensus of judges as to its value. Certainly the first contrast has to be maintained in some form or other because, as I have insisted, it is germane to everyday thinking about the arts.

But the problem with this is obvious. We have spent some time discussing the existence of irresolvable divergences of opinion among the qualified. The way I have described a causal theory does not allow for these. For I have described the causal theory as allowing that music of merit will have certain sorts of effects upon a prepared listener. But the counter-examples we have been discussing are precisely those: where two listeners are both equally prepared but where they diverge in their responses, and, consequently, in their judgement. In fact, the causal theory fails at an even earlier stage because it does not allow for the possibility that I may agree that this music is fine even though it does nothing for me, which is precisely the feature of our life with the arts that gave rise to sophisticated forms of the consensus theory in the first place. The causal theory may seem no more than a truism, that works of art involve and impress us, but it does not seem to help with the problem at hand.

Possibly the sensibility of our culture might change so that greater unanimity occurs. An authoritative critic might persuade us to see a composer's work in a new light, foregrounding what we previously passed over, or the style of a period might become more accessible through changes in the receiving culture. A savouring of irony, parody and quotation made Mahler acceptable where he had been ignored. His influence on Britten and Shostokovich might, through the acceptance of those composers, indirectly have brought about the resurgence of his music in the 1960s. But it is hard to see how these factors could bring about the reconciliation of divergent judgements over a single work.

Perhaps the causal theory can be no more than a truism. There may be works that impress some judges but not others. If you consider the variety of ways in which art affects us – it delights, appals, challenges, disturbs, provokes a revision of fundamental values and assumptions, creates an imaginative involvement with others and so on – it seems likely that any attempt to expand the causal thesis into a form that is not simply banal will be open-ended. We cannot predict how the arts of the future will affect us nor how familiar masterworks will be understood. Perhaps music is more restricted than other arts in the range of its effects but it is certainly wide enough to preclude any informative formulation of the causal thesis.

I considered earlier the possibility that there are some works that have no "objective" status; if this is so, we need not be realists or non-realists *tout court*. Perhaps some judgements of value or, indeed, judgements about the expressive character of some works, call for a realist account while others do not. Do we have to be realists or anti-realists over the complete range of works? Perhaps not. Of course, in some areas there must be a measure of conformity. Thus a range of aesthetic judgements that are not about works of art, the sort of judgements learned by small children, "this is pretty" or "this is ugly", must show uniformity. So a child is told that this is a lovely tune and acquires thereby that use of the word "lovely". Such appraisals we learn in the same way as we learn other words like "cat" and "dog". A child who, shown a daffodil, said it was not pretty either has not learned the term properly or is a precocious brat, an infant Oscar Wilde.[15] Such basic aesthetic judgements as "the flower is pretty", which contrast with judgements of art and are themselves to be "surmounted" by developing tastes in the arts, demand a realist interpretation; they may even reflect what Wittgenstein called "primitive reactions". Wittgenstein said that the reaction to seeing that a door is too high is analogous to taking my hand away from a hot plate.[16]

Still, the problem of irreconcilable judgements won't go away. It may be true that we acquire our vocabulary of evaluation in the way I describe. It may even be that in some uses the question of whether the object really has the properties attributed will not arise. It remains the case that at a more sophisticated stage, there may be irreconcilable divergences of judgement. If music means a great deal to you, you back your taste. And then the problems begin, because other music-lovers may passionately disagree. The important consideration here is this. If the consensus of judges tells us what the "real" status of the piece of music is, then a non-realist will naturally equate the consensual verdict with the "real status". This move is what philosophers would call "reductive". When I mentioned this earlier I gave as a paradigm of reduction the phenomenalist thesis that because material bodies are not independent of their being observed, their status amounts to no more than the possibility of our having sensations of them. "Reduction" is the technical term for this and this classical move "reduces" material bodies to the possibility of sensation. Likewise, the reductive move in the philosophy of artistic value will be to reduce claims about the real value of a sonata to claims about what a weighted or qualified judgement by the connoisseurs will offer. But now, if this is so, the individual who maintains, against the tide, that Berlioz's Requiem is a work of outstanding greatness has to recognize, on pain of irrationality, that he cannot be making a claim about its real status since the consensus argues against this verdict on Berlioz. His only recourse is to say that the consensus, over time, will come around to his way of thinking. But he might not concur with that prognostication. He might allow that Berlioz will always be a controversial musician. If musicians from Donald Tovey to Pierre Boulez have denied his stature, then why should we think that another century or two will make any difference? So we are left with this impasse. The existence of irreconcilable divergences of judgement seems to rule out realism because there now seems reason to suppose that there is no independent fact of the matter on which judges will converge. And there is no other route to a verdict except through competent judges. Yet the alternative to realism, which is to "reduce" claims about the real status to claims about the judgement of the consensus, thereby preserving the important distinction between the judgement of the individual and the status of the work, requires the dissenter to allow that his claim is no longer about the real status of the work. But this he will not do. He thinks the work is *really* outstanding and demands that this judgement of his be viewed as an objective judgement.

In a way, I want to stand the realist argument on its head. If irreconcilable judgements do exist, then they have to be treated realistically. It is no good saying that all this shows is that you cannot be a realist about judgements of artistic value. For if you cannot be a realist about artistic value you cannot present irreconcilable differences as having any probative power against realism. The problem is that a non-realist reading of the judgements in question robs them of what distinguishes them from mere assertions of taste.

Are verdicts essentially particular?

One pervasive feature of most of the theories we have been discussing is that they view artistic judgement as particular. The only exception, and the theory most summarily dismissed, was the idea that the merit of music is a matter of satisfying certain general constraints that can be formulated as criteria. It seems that verdicts are ultimately subordinate to the individual judgements made by competent individual listeners. There does seem to be a divide here between moral and artistic judgements, at least given the way most philosophers characterize moral judgements. Whereas with a moral judgement, that this action is a case of stealing and falls under that general heading gives a reason why it is wrong, that this piece is melancholy or in sonata form or whatever never gives a reason for regarding it as good or bad. It never carries a polarity. The attempt to find the "real status" of a work is secondary, although its importance is undoubted. We are listeners among other listeners; we share common human responses to music and a common background in the musics of our society. Music would be a very different art were discrepancies between judgements more common than they actually are. As we have seen, in the case of most such discrepancies we have various ways of explaining why they occur. We can see that we may be missing what others find worthwhile. But we also recognize, although we are sometimes surprised by, individual differences that cannot be accounted for and this, *inter alia*, underlines the priority of the particular judgement.

So let us consider what is known as "particularism" in the judgement of art generally and music in particular.[17] Particularism has been much discussed in ethics recently, although the intense debate over particularism there seems to have had little impact on the philosophy of art, which is surprising, although it may merely reflect the regrettable fact that philosophers no longer "keep up" with developments across the board as they did forty or fifty years ago. Philosophy has become more specialized. Still, there are a sufficient number of general surveys to make ignorance of developments in neighbouring areas not entirely excusable. What I propose to do, before bringing the discussion of artistic verdicts to an end, is to examine various forms of particularism and then to try to see how general maxims might still play a part in musical criticism and practice.

Particularism I

First, a radical form of particularism maintains that there are no common features uniting the various pieces of music that we call "good" or "bad" other than that we call them such. In the same way some particularists in ethics claim that we see "straight off" that some action is wicked or immoral without first grasping the "neutral" or descriptive features that make it so, for the simple reason that there *are* no common "neutral features" underlying the application of these words. Attempting to proceed via a grasp of these neutral features is futile. For what we cannot do is to describe cruelty, for example, in terms that have no evaluative overtones. If we try to say that cruelty involves ill-treating another where there is no guilt on the victim's part, we are no nearer to a neutral specification of what is being done. The description is already replete with words like "guilt" or "ill-treatment". If we try to describe the action in terms like "hitting" we not only ignore "mental cruelty" but we omit what makes the action count as wrong. There are very considerable difficulties in making the necessary descriptions both general and neutral. In parallel, it is often argued that there are no general non-evaluative features that can be cited as grounds for any judgement about the goodness or badness of a work of art. As we saw earlier, when writers have tried to provide general characteristics, citing qualities like unity, variety or intensity, they do so in such very general terms that we are not clear as to what will count as unity, variety or intensity. In any case, it is certainly possible to find works that have these characteristics but are not very good. Too much unity is monotony, for instance. A more positive case for particularism may use the notion of "salience" or "foregrounding" here. I have argued elsewhere that this is something of great significance in the arts.[18] Your grasp of a work usually begins with something in it impressing you. What you immediately find salient then may be central to your fuller and mature grasp of the work, although it may also take a lower profile, as they say, in the light of a more complete understanding.

Another way of putting this version of particularism is to suggest that there is no shape to the underlying class of musical judgements. But in at least one form this claim is difficult to sustain. What there is is some form of commonality in judgement. The business of concert-going may well reinforce this. Our listener finds herself swept along with the enthusiasm of the rest of the audience. (When I last heard Richard Strauss's *Four Last Songs* in the concert hall, I was touched by the fact that tears were running down the cheeks of the person sitting next to me.) Although the divergent cases of irreconcilable differences of judgement may not be in any way marginal to her taste – they matter intensely to her – generally her judgements do coincide with those of the majority.

What might seem to back particularism is the argument that art can strike us with considerable force before any sort of reflective critical reasoning plays a part. Even if the music did have merit because of general features that are criterion-bound, that would play no initial part in the judgement I make. The paradigm cases of "valuing" involve those works of music that strike the prepared mind with irresistible force (or indeed, the unprepared, although these cases are of lesser significance). As I argued in the previous section of this chapter, a work of art may so impress me that no countervailing reasons you offer will make me budge. You may point out that it is derivative or that the effects are cheap or that the dramatist loads the dice in order to increase the sense of tragedy. I may not be fazed.

Characteristically in the arts, the verdict precedes the deliberation. I am "seduced" by *La Traviata* and I only resort to analysing it if I want to persuade somebody else to listen to it or if my judgement is challenged. I might then look at the ending and think that it is sentimental in the way Dickens can be sentimental. Then I might change my mind about it. I might, too, be persuaded of the merit of a work that does not appeal to me because a number of judges whom I respect form a consensus about its merit. Note that, in this case, I am not argued into appreciating it but only argued into recognizing its stature. My recognition of what my peers think about this music leads me to a judgement about the merits of the work itself. I don't say that I am never argued into appreciation, but where this does happen it happens because my attention is drawn to features that I then see to be powerful. I foreground certain sections. I may find those aspects of the work that strike others now strike me.

Of course, there might be judges who get the decision right (we know because it matches the consensus of the informed) without being able to explain why: without being able to point out the significantly relevant features of the work or its performance. I think that such an "idiot savant" is far more likely in, say, music but I would not rule out people having a sort of natural good taste in the other arts. We sometimes say "I don't see how it works but it does". Here the task of the great critic may very well be to articulate what strikes him about a work, and this is a very distinctive skill.

Let's take an example. Consider Benny Goodman's "AC-DC Current", recorded in 1939. How would you talk about this piece in an endeavour to help somebody new to swing? For a start, Charlie Christian's opening arpeggio-like figure on the guitar is constantly used at various points as a sort of punctuation; in its earlier occurrences it is often in a key remote from the main key of the piece, notably immediately preceding Goodman's hiccuping intervention (just before the cry from somebody of "Hi Ho, Bernstein!"); the main key of G is then resumed without warning or preparation. It is difficult to find "highlights" in this masterly piece, as perfect as a Mozart quartet movement, although Goodman's entry is certainly riveting enough as is his long-held note a little later, reminiscent of the long-held clarinet note in "Doctor Jazz" (just before Jelly Roll Morton's vocal). Perhaps the best you can do is to provide the new listener with a mental map so that she can keep track of what is happening. Once done, you think, she surely cannot fail to fall in love with it. Essential in this is a sort of interplay between attention to the detail, seeing through that how the piece works, and the overall judgement.

Particularism II

You may resist the argument so far on quite general grounds; you may argue that drawing parallels between morality and the arts is misguided. Ethical particularists are largely concerned with actions, with what it is right to do in a given circumstance. But judgements about aesthetic value, you may say, do not involve deciding to act; so a central issue in the philosophy of morality, that of providing a bridge from reasoning to action, has no analogue. But this view of the aesthetic as "contemplative" is somewhat parochial, certainly as far as music is concerned. First, we must recall that we are concerned with the artistic rather than the merely aesthetic and that, for a good deal of its history, performance was central to the artistic life in dance, recitation or the performing of music. The player does have to decide how something is going to be played or the actor how lines are to be spoken and even the non-participating member of the audience will be better equipped if she is aware of the constraints. Up to a point it is a matter of being right or wrong. If an inner part "carries the tune", the pianist had better be aware of it. But beyond that there are matters on which there will, of course, be a difference of opinion among the qualified and this may be, as we say, "a matter of interpretation". But active involvement is not entirely restricted to players; the reader of poetry or prose, too, pays attention; this or that passage appears salient and he may want to recommend or describe the poem or novel to somebody else in the ways we have been discussing.

It is certainly more often the case that our appreciation of the aesthetic is more completely contemplative and that the will is not involved but that this is not universally the case is shown by considering examples such as choosing a shirt, a tie to go with a suit or an arrangement of flowers in gardening or internal decor. These are all matters aesthetic rather than artistic in nature but action is called for.

Particularism III

I have suggested that we characteristically first judge a piece to be grand or mediocre and then try to find grounds for this being so. The grounds tend to be *ex post facto* and particular to the case. Although this is often the case in the arts, and my examples so far reflect this assumption, we need again to remind ourselves that music is a performing art. This priority does not seem to hold in performance, for here we commonly have to make decisions about how to play, speak lines or dance a particular passage prior to embarking on it. We have first to find grounds to do this dance, this speech or this piece of music in a particular way and we are, of course, looking for the *right* or, at least, an *illuminating* way. More importantly, these grounds may be quite general. Thus the pianist is told by her teacher that it is permissible to pedal through staccatos when playing Beethoven and Schubert; this is a general principle, although one that may have exceptions. It is more of a negative than a positive principle. Normally one does not pedal in staccato passages because, of course, the staccato effect is lost thereby; nevertheless there are passages in some composers where it is effective and proper. So, before she starts to practise, she may read through the music, noting problematic passages as far as fingering is concerned and, at this stage, make some preliminary decisions about pedalling. Of course, these initial decisions may be revised when she comes to play it and, ultimately, it is a question of "this sounds right here", although only the experienced, informed and aware performer or listener is in a position to make this judgement.

I have stated these principles about pedalling in a fairly general way and they could, of course, be relativized to the music of a particular period. Should, then, the particularist acknowledge that there are generalizations that are important in the arts? After all, if, as is generally agreed, long experience and general familiarity are crucial for artistic judgement, what form could this take if it is not general? If this is so, then it ought to be capable of being summarized in the form of maxims. Anybody who has had advanced lessons in creative writing or the performing arts or in painting, knows that the good teacher alerts you to the crucial points. At such points there may be something generalizable: "you don't do that". But it may well be that there are exceptional cases where it does work.

Take another example. Consider the common interpretative point that a *diminuendo* is better than a ritardando at the end of a Mozart slow movement whereas slowing down is legitimate at the end of a Beethoven or Schubert slow movement or even, arguably, in the last bar or so of a Bach slow movement. But we are told by all sides that rules have to be applied.

In this context this can only mean one of two things: only sometimes is it permissible to end a Mozart slow movement with a ritardando; or we have to decide just how much of a *diminuendo* is called for. So, as far as the first is concerned, you might then ask which Mozart slow movements can be ended this way: those that seem heavier and more romantic, more an anticipation of Beethoven? Once we get to this stage is there any other answer than Frank Sibley's, that we "look and see"?[19] Our decision on this might not be "arbitrary" but it might not be open to any further explanation or grounding, if, indeed, "explanation" is the proper word here.

Suppose we say that there are generalizations but they are extremely complex and have to be qualified. We have rules of thumb that we apply in the broad range of central cases and these work. One problem about the arts is the fact that rules of thumb might just be useful in the middle range of more or less competent pieces but useless when we are dealing with finer achievements. So the great pianist may get away with pedalling where I might not or with a ritardando where it would be crazy for me to try it, just as the great composer can overrule the conventions of harmony and counterpoint that the student ignores at his peril. And isn't this just our experience with great musicians? Wilhelm Furtwängler's wayward way with tempi and his uniquely flexible ensemble produces, in Bruckner or Beethoven, an effect of mystery and profundity. In the hands of ordinary musicians, this is a recipe for disaster and they had best not attempt it. Once again, our recognition of the particular majesty of Furtwängler's musicianship is the particular judgement in the light of which talk of general rules or maxims becomes subsidiary. Their range and applicability is only to the middling competent.

But suppose, you will say, a pianist copies Solomon or a conductor copies Furtwängler. This is possible. The teenage Glenn Gould copied Artur Schnabel's interpretation of Beethoven's Fourth Piano Concerto in one of his earliest concerts, only to have a local music critic snort "Who does the kid think he is, Schnabel?"[20] Here, of course, familiar considerations enter. This is a token of somebody else's interpretation where the interpretation is the type. The young Gould no more interpreted the music than a copyist composes when he writes down the notes of an existing work.

Particularism IV

Particularists may allow that there are, indeed, general considerations that go to make a work of art good or bad, but these are multifarious; they may include unity and elegance, for example, but we cannot rank them in any order. In any particular case, then, we have to judge how they apply in the given situation and whether they are relevant considerations. There seems much to be said for this, for after all unity may be often a virtue in a movement and thematic integration is something we admire, but we would not wish Mahler's symphonies, in which this is less conspicuous, to be more like those of Sibelius, in which the logical development is so striking.

Particularism V

One strong form of ethical particularism maintains that the very same factors may count in favour in some circumstances and against in others. That it produces pleasure may normally be a reason in favour of an action; that the pleasure is sadistic makes the pleasure a reason against another action. Indeed, although I don't think huntsmen are necessarily sadistic, that they take pleasure in hunting a fox to death is thought by the anti-hunt lobby to be a reason against hunting; however that they take pleasure in it is a reason *for* people playing rugby. Now, of course, the universalist who believes that there are general rules that cover morality will make the obvious reply; qualify pleasure as "sadistic pleasure" and we have no problem in seeing that this is never a good reason for doing something. "Innocent" pleasure is. The case for claiming that a factor may have one "polarity" in one context and another in another is much stronger in the arts. You cannot specify generally and in advance the situations in music where a device works as opposed to those situations in which it does not (and we return to the earlier and generally accepted point that there are no criteria for merit in the arts). This claim is not controversial in the arts. However, for the moral philosopher there are certainly problems in rejecting what have been called "switching arguments". You use a switching argument when you claim that a consideration that operates in one case ought to operate in a like case. An essential part of moral reasoning involves pointing out "special pleading". For example, imagine that a wealthy Western country was adamant that there should be no relaxation of patent rights to favour African countries that could not afford anti-HIV drugs; if they could not pay the rates demanded by drug companies, then "tough". If then, when it came to relaxing patent rights because the inhabitants of this wealthy country had insufficient medicines against anthrax, the drug companies were immediately "persuaded" by its government that they should not stand upon their rights in the face of the greater need of the people, this would be rightly damned as double standards; morality sometimes demands fairness. To reject "switching arguments" is to emasculate this type of moral objection.

But there is nothing like this in the arts. "Special pleading" is no objection to recommending a work of art and this, surely, indicates something of very considerable importance. Praising and recommending a work of art is always special pleading. So, whatever the case in ethics, switching arguments evidently do not work in the arts. The very same device may both explain why one poem works and why another fails to work. Criticism in the arts is far more specific and more completely holistic. We are interested in how this image works in this particular poem or why this harmonic change is so effective here where it is banal elsewhere. Indeed, it is true in the arts that pretty well every consideration is capable of having its polarity reversed by a change in context. Playing Schubert well requires an exact calculation of the moment of hesitation that precedes a change of phrase. Many competent players seem to lack this sense. It is akin to the slight hesitation required in playing the three-in-a-bar rhythm of a Viennese waltz. Played in strict tempo the music loses its lilt, but even where an eighteenth-century composer produces music in 3/4 time, as Handel does in his *Water Music*, it would be a gross solecism to attempt a Viennese lilt to the rhythm.

Particularism VI

It has been claimed that if the particularist is right and there were no patterns in evaluation, such that we can learn the application of "good" or "bad" the way we do elsewhere, then the judgements of artistic value have to be "expressive", involving "something about our responses". Some logical positivists claimed that moral judgements were merely expressions of their authors' approval or disapproval (which has been called the "boo–hurrah" theory of ethics). The suggestion in parallel then is that particularists ought to acknowledge that artistic judgements are not cognitive but "expressive". They reflect our reaction to the work first and foremost and not features about the work itself, save derivatively. Thus one version of what I shall call an "expressivist" account of a judgement of a piece of music as exhilarating would base the rightness of the use of that description on the fact that the speaker is herself exhilarated by the music. Likewise, if the music is described by her as moving, she is moved by it. Both these are theories I considered in Chapter 3.

All this needs unwrapping. So far, I have expounded "expressivist accounts" as though they were about first-person judgements, similar to "I am in pain", perhaps. When Wittgenstein suggested that these judgements might be like taking my hand away from a hot plate, he seemed to have this analogue in mind. I observed earlier that there is a certain sort of commonality in our judgements of works of art. There are patterns in reactions in as much as there is art that appeals across societies, sub-cultures and tastes and across generations. A child can see, perhaps with puzzlement, that somebody is moved by a piece of music or a play or a poem. She sees that many are moved at a performance of *Messiah*. She learns thereby that terms like "wonderful", "moving", "great" or "over-whelming" are used to apply to that work, but she may not necessarily be moved herself. If a response is idiosyncratic, she will discover this in time. Then, by listening to what adults say or by reading, she finds that there is a canon of works of art that most people admire. It is not hard to see how such words expressing valuations can be picked up and, once we see this, the enquiry as to whether value-judgements in aesthetics are expressivist or cognitive looks like a false antithesis. They may be both on different occasions, and, indeed, their expressivist use is usually consequent to their being picked up in the way I suggested, even though they might be learned through the experience of the child herself. I can imagine a child being flushed and excited and her father saying "I can see that you found the music wonderful"; she thereby learns this application of the word "won-derful" partly through her own experience but with the help of another person's usage. But more often, I suspect, a child learns to use these words initially in contexts where no experience of her own is involved. Since she may begin by learning to use the words to describe a work of art that moves adults but passes her by, when she uses these words it is not expressivist, if by "expressivism" is meant that their use stands to the child's experience just as a cry of pain or an expression of delight does.

Of course, once acquired, they may be used expressively. But the fact that they can be used in early usages to record verdicts or other aesthetic assessments that are not reactive shows that there is a non-expressivist usage. The fact is that the use of these appraisals is complicated and it takes some time to learn them thoroughly. They are certainly not generally purely expressive, for if they were, the distinction, which I have insisted is so crucial in the arts, between thinking something good and liking it, would disappear. This strikes me as the crucial rejoinder to an expressivist treatment. Perhaps it is the case that there is a primitive use of these words as "interjections" as Wittgenstein thought, but the mastery of these words goes well beyond this.[21]

The concept of "interest"

So far we have concentrated on the single judgement and, by implication, the response to a single work. We need to redress this by bringing out an aspect of our engagement with the arts that is often neglected. A passion for the music of a composer, a performer or a period raises new issues. Important here is the way that pleasure gives way to interest.[22] Having heard a piece by a particular musician and enjoyed it, you seek out others; perhaps you buy an anthology or a disc of "greatest hits", hoping that other music will appeal. This gradually turns into something different: an interest. For education in the arts is typically a progress from pleasure to interest. Certainly one's first interest in the arts may come from the sheer pleasure in wordplay, in a rhythm or melody or in a patch of colour. I shall give an example of the first, Harry Champion's music hall song, "I'm Henery the Eighth, I Am", although I suspect that readers won't thank me. (You probably won't be able to dislodge it from your mind for a week or two.)

I'm Henery the Eighth, I am,
Henery the Eighth I am, I am!
I got married to the widow next door,
She's been married seven times before.
Every one was a Henery [Audience: Henery];
She wouldn't have a Willie or a Sam.
I'm her eighth old man named Henery;
I'm Henery the Eighth I am!

The neatness of the rhymes, of the scanning and the inversion in the penultimate line, not to say the humour in the surprise denouement, make this delectable, at least for an hour or two. Music offers many parallel examples. The best I can do is to refer you to music by Joan Cererois, Loyset Compère and Stefano Landi in the discography.

Now the first powerful impact of music may well be in the sheer sound quality of an instrument or a voice, or, perhaps, a tune in a Tchaikovsky ballet that lodges itself in the mind like the music hall song I have just quoted. Proust memorably reflects on "the little phrase" of Vinteuil.[23] Then you notice other things or have them drawn to your attention. You decide to read about Tchaikovsky's music or listen to talks on it. You want to hear more of his music so you try something else. At first it will be because you are anxious not to miss out on a new source of pleasure. But later you begin to prize the individuality of his voice and from this point

161

on what matters is that it grips your attention; even as this is happening you might not realize that your enjoyment has gone beyond mere pleasure. Then you try other composers. You even might find something absorbing while wishing that it would end. It has become an ordeal yet one you willingly put yourself through. At the same time this becomes a process towards the development of an individual taste.

Philosophy of art has been locked into a sort of infantilism. Many philosophers still think that the explanation and justification of an interest in music, if not the other arts, lies in the pleasure we take. Either their own interest in music is superficial or, more often, they do not pay enough attention to the ways their own tastes have developed. A concentration on pleasure misplaces the nature of our interest of music. Certainly there is much in the arts that gives pleasure and to which pleasure is the proper response. Nobody goes to see a Gilbert and Sullivan operetta or *Guys and Dolls* to be exercised over profound issues. But Rembrandt portraits or Shakespeare tragedies are different, and to say that you enjoyed them sounds as though your response is pretty inadequate. Similarly with late Beethoven. You can, if you like, expand the concept of pleasure or enjoyment to cover such cases, but an implicit redefinition denatures the original claim. What would be the point?

So we need to make distinctions, distinctions being the centre of philosophy as they are the centre of art, as Iris Murdoch once observed. We may say of something "it gives me great pleasure" or "it was a pleasant experience". But we do not often speak this way when talking of the arts. More often we will say "I enjoyed that". We delight in the combination of Ira Gershwin's lyrics and George Gershwin's tunes. Do we "enjoy" *Tosca*? Well, "enjoy" is certainly not *le mot juste*. Am I stirred by it? Unless I am one of those who despises Puccini's "shabby little shocker",[24] I am. Would it then be true to say that I enjoy being stirred? I think I do, although pursuing this path leads into dangerous waters; it tempts us to say that we go to see *Tosca* because we enjoy being stirred and that is not so. The work, not the experience, is the proper focus of attention. Something is wrong if you go to a concert or to the theatre in search of a particular experience, much as there is something wrong if you give to a charity because it makes you feel good and because you prize that feeling, rather than giving to the charity because there is a need. Of course, just as the good person is one who is pleased to give to charity so the musical person is one who is stirred by music. That is the major part of what it is to be musical. But we must not be confused about the motivation. That she is pleased to give to charity is not why she gives and that she is stirred by the music may not be the reason why she attends the concert.

The pleasure of the connoisseur, in the view of many aestheticians, implies and is implied by the recognition of merit. But we need to make a distinction between getting pleasure from listening to a work and thinking the music is good. It is important for you to be able to say that you love the music of Richard Strauss but do not think it of the very highest quality. It might be that you love it because it gives you pleasure but "pleasure", as I argue, is not the only thing that matters here; it is a mistake to assume that it is integrally tied in with judgements of value. The music of Strauss might please you even while you recognize the over-use of effective but stock devices that makes Strauss a little suspect.

There are more extreme cases still than those we have been considering. A friend of Billie Holliday, who much admired her art, said that he found her singing of "Strange Fruit" too disturbing: "It was revolting listening to it; I don't even like to think about it". ("Strange Fruit" is about the lynching of blacks in the American South.) Now this is in no sense at all a negative judgement. Many feel this way about *King Lear*, of course. These are works neither liked nor loved. But they are admired.

If you are seriously interested in drama, you don't expect to enjoy *Wozzeck* or for that matter, *Saved* or *Trainspotting*: you endure them. Even some of Bach's cantatas, we are told, were intended to harrow the congregation rather than to titillate their ears. Philosophers puzzle over this and look for explanations in terms of education for life or some such. But you only need such an explanation because of a residual and insistent utilitarian account of human motive in the background: the supposition that there is an ulterior motive such as pleasure or satisfaction. We see these operas because we want to know what is there; these may be some of mankind's greatest achievements and we do not want to miss them no matter how harrowing they may be. We lose ourselves in them; we cease to look at the time or at the other members of the audience, wonder at what they are doing or where and how they live. The great work of music, finely performed, absorbs us. To be interested is usually to have gone beyond the stage where pleasure is a motive. Likewise some readers of this book will be deeply interested in philosophy. If you are, then do you enjoy doing philosophy? The answer will almost certainly be "sometimes but more often not". Somehow the question is inappropriate. Philosophy is what you do. In the same way the pursuit of the arts is central to the life many of us lead.

The verdict on verdicts

So should we endorse particularism or not? It is sometimes difficult to give straight answers in philosophy. President Johnson once sighed "Oh for a one-armed lawyer". Equally in philosophy we may be liable to end with the conclusion, "on the one hand this, and on the other hand that". Although I shall recommend particularism in the end for some yet more general reasons, considerations run both ways. These considerations commend particularism:

- There are no precise and general criteria for merit in music that do not fall foul of exceptions. Those that have been offered tend to be either too vague to be very helpful or positively or negatively evaluative from the outset. They may, too, be overridden by other factors that make an overall verdict different from the *pro tanto* judgement.
- Switching arguments do not work in the arts. What can be a merit in one work may be a fault in another.
- Even the consensus is constructed from single judgements made by experienced and qualified listeners. The single judgement is thus epistemologically and ontologically prior and divergences of judgement may remain.

This consideration runs against particularism. For run-of-the-mill, more or less competent writing, there are general considerations that may rule in favour of or against a particular work. These may, in modest work, give way to a negative judgement in a case where the rules are defied; in general, only the master is equipped to defy the rules. I should add that the defiance is not total. Even the revolutionary is revolutionary in terms of adding to or adjusting an existing tradition.

In as much as we are not required to offer a philosophical theory that removes difficulties that are part of our life in the arts, we must recognize that unremovable differences of opinion are part of the data on which we reflect. I merely say that particularism is an account of value that sits fairly happily with the existence of unresolvable differences of opinion in the arts. But this need not require us to deny the existence of maxims or rules providing that their location and function is clearly recognized.

In an earlier book on the aesthetics of music[25] I argued that an agreed and consistent analysis of what a work of music is could not be obtained because the different ideologies with which different musicians and music-lovers approach music ensured differences over its identity. I pointed out that some take the performance of an interesting interpretation as basic while others give allegiance to the score. My arguments in this chapter strongly suggest, in addition, that it may be impossible to make our account of artistic value internally consistent. The existence of irreconcilable disputes seems to rule out realism. A non-realist account "reduces" claims about "objective value" to claims about what the consensus says. But if, then, the claims made for or against the work in question are "reduced", they turn out to be no more than expressions of personal taste. But then they have been stripped of their force. The advocate of Berlioz is not merely saying "I like Berlioz's work although I admit it isn't very good"; she claims that his music really is masterly and ought to be recognized as such.

Ideology raises its head again, for you may well argue that a culture in which individual experience is rated as highly as it is in ours will certainly allow that experience to play a more dominant role in determining value than a culture in which general and public standards of goodness and badness in the arts are assumed in advance and where individual judgements are presumed to be subservient to these. Those cultures would have no truck with particularism. The fact that we can neither subscribe to realism nor relinquish it is likely to be a result of competing ideological strains. That divergences of opinion have to be expressed realistically reflects our reluctance to surrender reactive judgements and such reactive judgements are privileged in an ideology that places a premium on the personal reaction. We are stuck with a demotic metaphysics that cannot be made consistent.

Do we just acknowledge that this is how it is and jettison any attempt at philosophically motivated reform of our concepts? Certainly I lean this way. Indeed, it is not surprising that this sphere should harbour contradictions. After all, we certainly hold contradictory beliefs elsewhere so why might not the rationale that seems to lie behind our judgement of the value of music be internally inconsistent? Many systems of belief are. Theologies often are. Like theologies and ideologies, philosophies of the arts try to encompass varying interests and considerations. We might, of course, simply acknowledge that we are irrational in refusing to qualify some reactive judgements much as we think that a parent's blindness about his or her child's faults is a rather lovable irrationality without which the world would be a worse place. The difference, though, is that we do acknowledge that the parent's judgement is erroneous by reference to some agreed facts. But there is no parallel to this in the arts, nothing accessible beyond the judgements that we make, no independent facts of the matter about value that can be inspected.

The indications of inconsistency or incoherence in our conceptualization of the arts that I have collected are piecemeal. The analytic philosopher in me would like there to be more general arguments showing why we cannot get a coherent picture of the arts and where strains are likely to occur. But dull experience shows that our concepts arise as the results of different pressures and different interests. Here and there inconsistencies may poke through the surface. But I have no intuitions as to how this gives a basis for predicting the eruptions of incoherence. What is important is to recognize that our concepts of music and of the arts in general, are concepts with a history, concepts which change with other changes in society, in its values and its most general concepts. A result of this is that, at any one time, a concept may contain, in its sediment, ideas of different ancestry that may conflict.

Coda

I began this book with a list of the philosophical problems most likely to strike thoughtful musicians and music-lovers: questions about music's power, whether it can have meaning, what counts as art music and questions about the divergence of taste. I said then that these are questions that relate to the value that music has for us. My approach has been "problem-orientated" and the nature of those problems made it natural that I should conclude with a discussion of value. Other writers have viewed music primarily as a branch of metaphysics,[1] raising questions about sounds, tones and musical movement. My approach has been to introduce only such ontology as is requisite to help with the problems at hand and I think it fair to say that most recent writers on music share this approach.

My conclusions favour particularism and I shall close by making a more general case for it. In my previous book on the philosophy of music, *Music and Humanism*, I suggested that for four centuries language has been a model in terms of which we understand music, a model which we use, consciously or unconsciously, in approaching Western classical music. We use metaphors drawn from language, we speak of musical paragraphs and, most significantly, music can be followed and it can be followed over a long period. As we saw, for a long time it was a cliché that music is a language of the emotions. Western music has performed a sort of arc from being a decorative art to being what is sometimes called a fine art and back to a decorative art again; for it is a familiar difficulty with most "advanced" Western music, beginning with the second Viennese school, that it cannot be followed in the way that music of the past can, even after we have familiarized ourselves with the style. When music was constructed and understood on linguistic analogies, with rhetoric as a model, it was an art that I would describe as a "humanist art". Three characteristics are essential here. First, it can be described in expressive terms as "grave", "exuberant" and the like. Secondly, it can be interpreted, not just in the sense that performers interpret the music from a score, but in the sense that it can be given a meaning. Thirdly, it can be followed. I have discussed these claims in the previous chapters. Not all music that we classify as fine art offers much to those who approach it in these terms but the very finest music of the Western classical era does, and it is this that gives us the essence of the art of that place and time. In this respect great art is stereotypical. It provides a paradigm and the paradigm defines the art no matter how small a proportion of the music rewards the effort of being thought of in these terms.

Part of what I have called a "humanist" element is the individuality we prize in a composer. For many listeners the music of Tallis speaks across the centuries as, more than any other composer of his generation, the voice of an individual and for that reason we love his music above that of his contemporaries. Thus in one respect, and at a very general level, particularism seems to accord with the way judgements are made. Yes, we look for unity and diversity, for technical accomplishment in the layout for instruments and voices, but we also look for imaginative ideas and imagination in their treatment and in this respect the crucial features of our engagement with music (and, *pari passu*, with other arts) begin to emerge. For what we prize, all things being equal, and what makes the difference between the great master and the smaller talent, is the individuality of voice. In the same way, when your friends die it comes as a shock to realize that you miss more those whose wit and intelligence took you by surprise. The death of a Mercutio distresses us in the way that the death of a Polonius does not. Distinctiveness is the mark of the master. Whatever role is played by generalizations fades into the background. And the roles of beauty or grace or the giving of pleasure matter less. Of course, we could hardly dispute that there is a generalization – that we prize originality – nor would I dispute that originality is merely one virtue among many and one that could be counter-balanced by defects. But I do suggest that individuality is the most prized of artistic virtues in our culture. It informs our current concept of art and it explains a great deal. For we cannot prize what is individual without prizing what makes it different from others; it is this that, at the summits of the art of music, makes the search for critical generalities fruitless.

I suggested that in some ways this is akin to the way we value our friends. Earlier I quoted Hume:

> We choose our favourite author as we do our friend, from a conformity of humour and disposition. Mirth or passion, sentiment or

reflection; whichever of these most predominates in our temper, it gives us a peculiar sympathy with the writer who resembles us.[2]

But in some ways friendship is not an apt parallel. It matters to me that I do not miss the opportunity of hearing a piece of music or a performance that is said to be outstanding and, in the pursuit of this, I am prepared to encounter some boredom. But I do not seek out people who might interest me because, of course, I cannot make such demands of others. In fact, to prosecute an acquaintance on the assumption that I might find her interesting would give her a reason not to regard me as a friend. For friendship should have no such ulterior motive. I cannot make a claim on her because I think, in advance, that she might interest me. Those who nurture acquaintances in this way, like Mme. Verdurin in Proust's *Remembrance of Things Past*, are suspect. For there to be anything like an analogy with music there would need to be something like the operation of a consensus advising me which people to pursue or advice from somebody who knows more people than I do as to who to endeavour to meet. But friendships are far more the product of accident and it is in the nature of friendship that this should be so.

For all this, friendship is not so bad an analogy. Charles Lamb wrote about the death of a friend:

One sees a picture, reads an anecdote, starts a casual fancy, and thinks to tell it to this person in preference to every other – the person is gone whom it would have peculiarly suited ... Common natures do not suffice me. Good people, as they are called, won't serve. I want individuals.

As with friends, so with music.

Notes

Introduction

1. Charles Rosen, *Piano Notes* (London: Allen Lane, 2003).
2. Critical discussions of these two thinkers will be found in Malcolm Budd, *Music and the Emotions* (London: Routledge & Kegan Paul, 1985). Roger Scruton, who is a sympathetic critic, discusses Schopenhauer in *Death Devoted Heart* (Oxford: Oxford University Press, 2004).

Chapter 1: Overture and beginnings

1. W. Wordsworth, *Lyrical Ballads*, Preface to second edition.
2. See Lydia Goehr, *The Imaginary Museum of Musical Works* (Oxford: Clarendon Press, 1992).
3. Enrico Fubini, *A History of Musical Aesthetics*, M. Hatwell (trans.) (London: Macmillan, 1990) gives an excellent account of the subject up to about 1975. It does not cover recent work.
4. E. Hanslick, *On the Musically Beautiful*, G. Payzant (trans.) (Indianapolis, IN: Hackett, 1986).
5. See *ibid.*, 3.
6. See *ibid.*, xxiii, 3.
7. *Ibid.*, 32.
8. *Ibid.*, 9.
9. See *ibid.*, 8–9.
10. *Ibid.*, 22 and see p. 14.
11. *Ibid.*, 6–7.
12. *Ibid.*, 19.
13. *Ibid.*, 9–10.
14. *Ibid.*, 11.
15. *Ibid.*, 80.
16. *Ibid.*, 64.
17. *Ibid.*, 59.
18. *Ibid.*, 49.

19. *Ibid.*, 1.
20. Edmund Gurney, *The Power of Sound* (New York: Basic Books, 1966 [1880]), 202.
21. *Ibid.*, 226n.
22. *Ibid.*, 296.
23. *Ibid.*, 246n.
24. *Ibid.*, 43.
25. *Ibid.*, 369.
26. *Ibid.*, 91.
27. *Ibid.*, 204ff. This aspect of his thought is defended by Jerrold Levinson, *Music in the Moment* (Ithaca, NY: Cornell University Press, 1997).
28. *Ibid.*, 165.
29. *Ibid.*, 375.
30. *Ibid.*, 339, 342.
31. *Ibid.*, 340.
32. *Ibid.*, 345.
33. *Ibid.*, 324–5.
34. *Ibid.*, 140.
35. *Ibid.*, 177.
36. *Ibid.*, 344.

Chapter 2: The work of music

1. The quotation from John Cage comes from Noel Carroll, "Cage and Philosophy", in *Musical Worlds*, Philip Alperson (ed.) (University Park, PA: Pennsylvania State University Press, 1998). There is an excellent discussion of Cage's *Silent Music* in Stephen Davies, *Themes in the Philosophy of Music* (Oxford: Oxford University Press, 2003).
2. Stanley Cavell, *Must We Mean What We Say?* (Cambridge: Cambridge University Press, 1976).
3. See Calvin Tomkins, *The Bride and the Bachelors* (London: Weidenfield & Nicolson, 1965) on this and much else that is relevant.
4. W. B. Gallie was responsible for the idea of "essentially contested concepts". See his *Philosophy and the Historical Understanding* (London: Chatto & Windus, 1964), Ch. 8.
5. Wittgenstein, *Philosophical Investigations* (Oxford: Blackwell, 1953), §142.
6. For discussions of procedural definitions, and so on, see Stephen Davies, *Definitions of Art* (Ithaca, NY: Cornell University Press, 1991). See also Berys Gaut, "'Art' as a Cluster Concept", in *Theories of Art Today*, Noel Carroll (ed.), 25–44 (Madison, WI: University of Wisconsin Press, 2000).
7. See Robert Stecker, *Artworks* (University Park, PA: Pennsylvania State University Press, 1997).
8. Wittgenstein, *Lectures and Conversations on Aesthetics, Psychology and Religious Belief*, Cyril Barrett (ed.) (Oxford: Blackwell, 1966), 34.
9. On "historical accounts", the *locus classicus* is Jerrold Levinson, *Music, Art and Metaphysics* (Ithaca, NY: Cornell University Press, 1990).
10. T. J. Diffey, "The Republic of Art", *British Journal of Aesthetics* **9** (1969), 145–56.
11. Kenneth Clark, *Civilization* (London: The Folio Society, 1999), 152–4.
12. R. A. Sharpe, *Contemporary Aesthetics* (Hassocks: Harvester, 1983, reprinted Aldershot: Gregg Revivals, 1990).
13. Love-spoons are a Welsh tradition; a love-spoon was carved for a partner and the various devices on the spoon symbolized such marital virtues as care and fidelity.

14. See Stan Godlovitch, *Musical Performance* (London: Routledge, 1998).

15. On the distinctive nature of the work of "rock" see John Andrew Fisher, "Rock 'n' Recording: The Ontological Complexity of Rock Music", in Alperson (ed.), *Musical Worlds*, 109–23. Glenn Gould's ideas on classical recording are relevant here. See *The Glenn Gould Reader*, Tim Page (ed.) (London: Faber and Faber, 1987). Andy Hamilton has a well-informed article on these issues: "The Art of Recording and the Aesthetics of Perfection", *British Journal of Aesthetics* 43(4) (2003), 345–62. See also Stephen Davies, "So You Want to Sing with the Beatles? Too late!", in *Themes in the Philosophy of Music*, 94–107 (Oxford: Oxford University Press, 2003).

16. See Goehr, *The Imaginary Museum of Musical Works*.

17. *Complete Pianoforte Sonatas, Volume III: Beethoven*, H. Craxton (ed.), D. F. Tovey (ann.) (London: ABRSM Publishing), 217.

18. A version that distinguishes the composer's instructions from editorial additions.

19. See Nicholas Wolterstorff, *Worlds and Works of Art* (Oxford: Clarendon Press, 1980).

20. I have not acknowledged many articles in these notes, preferring to keep references to those that are easily obtainable and readable by beginners, but I have learned from the lively debate initiated by Julian Dodd's "Musical Works as Eternal Types", *British Journal of Aesthetics* 40 (2000), 424–40. But there is by now a considerable literature on this. For a start consult Stephen Davies, *Musical Works and Performances* (Oxford: Oxford University Press, 2001). Much that is relevant to the question of discovery is to be found in Peter Kivy, *The Fine Art of Repetition* (Cambridge: Cambridge University Press, 1993), Essays II, III and IV.

21. The debate on constructivism has been lively. See Michael Krausz, *Rightness and Reasons: Interpretations in Cultural Practices* (Ithaca, NY: Cornell University Press, 1993). There was a discussion in the late 1990s conducted through the pages of the *Journal of Aesthetics and Art Criticism*. See Robert Stecker, *Interpretation and Construction* (Oxford: Blackwell, 2003) for a far more detailed account of the arguments than I have space for here.

22. See Peter Kivy, *Authenticities* (Ithaca, NY: Cornell University Press, 1995), Randall Dipert, "The Composer's Intentions: An Examination of their Relevance for Performance", *Musical Quarterly* 66 (1980) and T. S. Kuhn, *The Structure of Scientific Revolutions* (Chicago, IL: University of Chicago Press, 1962).

23. See Peter Kivy, *The Possessor and the Possessed* (New Haven, CT: Yale University Press, 2001).

24. On Janáček's *Jenůfa* see John Tyrell, *Janáček's Operas* (London: Faber and Faber, 1992), 100–7.

25. My information on Toscanini and on the orchestration of Prokofiev's *Romeo and Juliet* comes from Erich Leinsdorf, *The Composer's Advocate* (New Haven, CT: Yale University Press, 1981), 200.

Chapter 3: Meaning

1. Igor Stravinsky, *Autobiography* (London: Calder and Boyars, 1975), 53–4.

2. *The Best of the Two Ronnies* (BBC Video: M and S 2224633).

3. Deryck Cooke, *The Language of Music* (Oxford: Oxford University Press, 1959) gives a famous glossary linking phrases and expressive descriptions within a basically expressionist aesthetics of music.

4. See Gregory Karl and Jenefer Robinson, "Shostakovich's Tenth Symphony and the Musical Expression of Cognitively Complex Emotions", in *Music and Meaning*, Jenefer Robinson (ed.) (Ithaca, NY: Cornell University Press, 1997).

5. Leo Tolstoy, *What is Art and Essays on Art*, A. Maude (trans.) (Oxford: Oxford University Press, 1930).

6. See Colin Radford, "Emotions and Music: A Reply to the Cognitivists", *Journal of Aesthetics and Art Criticism* **47** (1989), 69–76 and "Muddy Waters", *Journal of Aesthetics and Art Criticism* **49** (1991), 247–52, Aaron Ridley, *Music, Value and the Passions* (Ithaca, NY: Cornell University Press, 1995) and Derek Matravers, *Art and Emotion* (Oxford: Clarendon Press, 1998). There are, naturally, some differences between them.

7. Martha Nussbaum, *Upheavals of Thought* (Cambridge: Cambridge University Press, 2001), Ch. 5 and see esp. 249, 251.

8. Wittgenstein's thoughts about the relevance of gesture are best investigated via *Zettel* (Oxford: Blackwell, 1967) para. 157–75, rather than the more commonly used *Lectures and Conversations*, Cyril Barrett (ed.) (Oxford: Blackwell, 1966), which are based on student notes. I find it hard to think that Wittgenstein would have said that the expression of emotion is a gesture (see *Lectures and Conversations*, 37).

9. In a famous paper by O. K. Bouwsma, "The Expression Theory of Art", in *Aesthetics and Language*, William Elton (ed.) (Oxford: Blackwell, 1959).

10. D. F. Tovey, *Essays in Musical Analysis III: The Concerto* (Oxford: Oxford University Press, 1946), 143.

11. Lionel Pike, *Beethoven, Sibelius and "the Profound Logic"* (London: Athlone, 1978).

12. Peter Cooke and Dudley Moore, *The Dagenham Dialogues* (London: Methuen, 1971).

13. R. Graves, "The Challenge", in *Collected Poems* (London: Cassell, 1938).

14. See Miranda Seymour, *Robert Graves: Life on the Edge* (London: Doubleday, 1996), 235.

15. E. T. Cone, "Schubert's Promissory Note; an Exercise in Musical Hermeneutics", *Nineteenth Century Music* **5**(3) (1982), 233–41.

16. See Lawrence Kramer, *Musical Meaning* (Berkeley, CA: University of California Press, 2002).

17. See Jerrold Levinson, "Performative vs. Critical Interpretation in Music", in *The Interpretation of Music*, Michael Krausz (ed.) (Oxford: Oxford University Press, 1993).

18. On the "new musicology", see Peter Kivy, *New Essays on Musical Understanding* (Oxford: Clarendon Press, 2001), Ch. 8.

19. Edward J. Dent, *Mozart's Operas* (Oxford: Oxford University Press, 1970), 177.

20. See E. T. Cone, *The Composer's Voice* (Berkeley, CA: University of California Press, 1974), Ch. 7 and Nicholas Cook, *Analysing Musical Multi-Media* (Oxford: Oxford University Press, 1998).

21. Samuel Johnson, "The Idler no. 51", in *Selected Essays*, W. J. Bate (ed.) (New Haven, CT: Yale University Press, 1968), 319.

Chapter 4: Value

1. John Mackie, *Ethics: Inventing Right and Wrong* (Harmondsworth: Penguin, 1977).

2. On these topics see Frank Sibley, *Approach to Aesthetics* (Oxford: Oxford University Press, 2001).

3. Arnold Schoenberg, *Theory of Harmony*, R. Carter (trans.) (London: Faber and Faber, 1978), 60ff.

4. On the ideal observer theory see Charles Taliaferro, "The Ideal Aesthetic Observer Revisited", *British Journal of Aesthetics* **30**(1) (1990), 1–13 and John Hospers, "The Ideal Aesthetic Observer", *British Journal of Aesthetics* **2**(2) (1962), 99–111.

5. Oscar Wilde, "The Critic as Artist", in *Intentions* (London: Methuen, 1927), 189.

6. David Hume, "Of the Standard of Taste", *Selected Essays* (Oxford: Oxford University Press, 1993 [1741]), 150.
7. Sibley, *Approach to Aesthetics*, 77.
8. Samuel Alexander, *Beauty and other Forms of Value* (London: Macmillan, 1933), 176.
9. See Alan Goldman, *Aesthetic Value* (Boulder, CO: Westview, 1995), Ch. 2.
10. Isaiah Berlin, *The Proper Study of Mankind* (London: Chatto & Windus, 1997).
11. The "storm and stress" movement of German literature in the 1760s and 1770s, notable in the work of Goethe and Schiller, had a musical parallel in the dramatic style of Haydn and J. C. Bach in the early 1770s.
12. R. Vaughan Williams, "Some Thoughts on Beethoven's Choral Symphony", in *National Music and Other Essays* (Oxford: Oxford University Press, 1963).
13. The influence of Peter Winch's "The Universalizability of Moral Judgements", in *Ethics and Action*, 151–70 (London: Routledge & Kegan Paul, 1972) will be obvious to philosophers.
14. Hume, "Of the Standard of Taste", 141.
15. When Wilde described a sunset as a third-rate Turner, the joke is, of course, that concepts of taste are normally inapplicable in these cases. We *do* develop tastes in landscape but this is a sophistication which strikes us as a little pretentious and it was exactly in this way that Wilde was, of course, sending himself up.
16. Wittgenstein, *Lectures and Conversations*, 14.
17. I have found Brad Hooker and Margaret Little, *Moral Particularism* (Oxford: Oxford University Press, 2000) helpful, especially the essays by Jonathan Dancy and Margaret Little. Many of the forms of particularism I note here are discussed in their moral guise in the various essays that make up this collection.
18. In R. A. Sharpe, *Contemporary Aesthetics* (Hassocks: Harvester, 1983).
19. Sibley, *Approach to Aesthetics*, 76.
20. "A Desert Island Discography", in *The Glenn Gould Reader*, Tim Page (ed.), 437–40 (London: Faber and Faber, 1987).
21. Wittgenstein, *Lectures and Conversations*, 3.
22. See Stephen Davies, "Why Listen to Sad Music if it Makes One Feel Sad?", in *Music and Meaning*, Jenefer Robinson (ed.), 242–53 (Ithaca, NY: Cornell University Press, 1997).
23. Marcel Proust, *Swann's Way* (Harmondsworth: Penguin, 1999), 378–84.
24. Joseph Kerman, *Opera as Drama* (New York: Vintage Books, 1956), 254.
25. R. A. Sharpe, *Music and Humanism* (Oxford: Oxford University Press, 2000).

Coda

1. For example, see Roger Scruton, *The Aesthetics of Music* (Oxford: Clarendon Press, 1997).
2. Hume, "Of the Standard of Taste", 150.

Bibliography and discography

Further reading

If, as I hope, you are encouraged to delve deeper into the extensive contemporary literature on the aesthetics of music, you may find this bibliography useful. Over the past decade, publications in the area of the philosophy of music have increased dramatically; significant contributions are largely to be found in the two major journals in aesthetics, *The British Journal of Aesthetics* and the *Journal of Aesthetics and Art Criticism*. The books I have recommended share one thing in common; they are well written, indeed some of the authors have a very considerable feeling for the shape and rhythms of English prose and they are accessible to the general reader. If you have approached this subject from, say, literary theory or from some other branch of philosophy such as the philosophy of language or philosophy of mind, the aesthetics of music will prove, in that respect, a pleasant surprise.

Alperson, P. (ed.) 1998. *Musical Worlds*. University Park, PA: Pennsylvania State University Press.
Cook, N. 1990. *Music, Imagination and Culture*. Oxford: Oxford University Press.
Davies, S. 1994. *Musical Meaning and Expression*. Ithaca, NY: Cornell University Press.
Davies, S. 2001. *Musical Works and Performance*. Oxford: Oxford University Press. [Davies offers exhaustive surveys of the recent literature but these books are not just a matter of who says what. There are many acute criticisms and keen observations here.]
Fubini, E. 1990. *A History of Musical Aesthetics*, M. Hatwell (trans.). London: Macmillan.
Godlovich, S. 1998. *Musical Performance*. London: Routledge.
Goehr, L. 1992. *The Imaginary Museum of Musical Works*. Oxford: Clarendon Press.
Kivy, P. 1989. *Sound Sentiment*. Philadelphia, PA: Temple University Press.
Kivy, P. 1990. *Music Alone*. Ithaca, NY: Cornell University Press.
Kivy, P. 1993. *The Fine Art of Repetition*. Cambridge: Cambridge University Press.
Kivy, P. 1995. *Authenticities*. Ithaca, NY: Cornell University Press.

Kivy, P. 2001. *New Essays on Musical Understanding*. Oxford: Clarendon Press.
Kivy, P. 2002. *Introduction to a Philosophy of Music*. Oxford: Oxford University Press. [A useful general account of Kivy's views.]
Ridley, A. 1995. *Music, Value and the Passions*. Ithaca, NY: Cornell University Press.
Sharpe, R. A. 2000. *Music and Humanism*. Oxford: Oxford University Press.

References

Alexander, S. 1933. *Beauty and other Forms of Value*. London: Macmillan.
Alperson, P. (ed.) 1998. *Musical Worlds*. University Park, PA: Pennsylvania State University Press.
Berlin, I. 1997. *The Proper Study of Mankind*. London: Chatto & Windus.
Bouswma, O. K. 1959. "The Expression Theory of Art". In *Aesthetics and Language*, W. Elton (ed.), 73–99. Oxford: Blackwell.
Budd, M. 1985. *Music and the Emotions*. London: Routledge & Kegan Paul.
Carroll, N. 1998. "Cage and Philosophy". In *Musical Worlds*, P. Alperson (ed.), 125–30. University Park, PA: Pennsylvania State University Press.
Cavell, S. 1976. *Must We Mean What We Say?* Cambridge: Cambridge University Press.
Cone, E. T. 1974. *The Composer's Voice*. Berkeley, CA: University of California Press.
Cone, E. T. 1982. "Schubert's Promissory Note: An Exercise in Musical Hermeneutics", *Nineteenth Century Music* 5(3), 233–41.
Cook, N. 1998. *Analysing Musical Multi-Media*. Oxford: Oxford University Press.
Cooke, D. 1959. *The Language of Music*. Oxford: Oxford University Press.
Davies, S. 1991. *Definitions of Art*. Ithaca, NY: Cornell University Press.
Davies, S. 1997. "Why Listen to Sad Music if it Makes One Feel Sad?". In *Music and Meaning*, J. Robinson (ed.), 242–53. Ithaca, NY: Cornell University Press.
Davies, S. 2001. *Musical Works and Performance*. Oxford: Oxford University Press.
Davies, S. 2003. *Themes in the Philosophy of Music*. Oxford: Oxford University Press.
Dent, E. J. 1970. *Mozart's Operas*. Oxford: Oxford University Press.
Diffey, T. J. 1969. "The Republic of Art", *British Journal of Aesthetics* 9, 145–56.
Dipert, R. 1980. "The Composer's Intentions: An Examination of their Relevance for Performance", *Musical Quarterly* 66, 205–18.
Dodd, J. 2000. "Musical Works as Eternal Types", *British Journal of Aesthetics* 40, 424–40.
Fisher, J. A. 1998. "Rock 'n' Recording: The Ontological Complexity of Rock Music". In *Musical Worlds*, P. Alperson (ed.), 109–23. University Park, PA: Pennsylvania State University Press.
Fubini, E. 1990. *A History of Musical Aesthetics*, M. Hatwell (trans.). London: Macmillan.
Gallie, W. B. 1964. *Philosophy and the Historical Understanding*. London: Chatto & Windus.
Gaut, B. 2000. "'Art' as a Cluster Concept". In *Theories of Art Today*, N. Carroll (ed.), 25–44. Madison, WI: University of Wisconsin Press.
Godlovich, S. 1998. *Musical Performance*, London: Routledge.
Goehr, L. 1992. *The Imaginary Museum of Musical Works*. Oxford: Clarendon Press.
Goldman, A. 1995. *Aesthetic Value*. Boulder, CO: Westview.
Gould, G. 1987. *The Glenn Gould Reader*, T. Page (ed.). London: Faber and Faber.
Gurney, E. 1966. *The Power of Sound*. New York: Basic Books.
Hamilton, A. 2003. "The Art of Recording and the Aesthetics of Perfection", *British Journal of Aesthetics* 43(4), 345–62.
Hanslick, E. 1986. "On the Musically Beautiful", G. Payzant (trans.). Indianapolis, IN: Hackett.

Hooker, B. & M. Little (eds) 2000. *Moral Particularism*. Oxford: Oxford University Press.
Hospers, J. 1962. "The Ideal Aesthetic Observer", *British Journal of Aesthetics* 2(2), 99–111.
Hume, D. "Of the Standard of Taste", in *Selected Essays*, 133–53. Oxford: Oxford University Press, 1993 [1741].
Karl, G. & J. Robinson 1997. "Shostakovitch's Tenth Symphony and the Musical Expression of Cognitively Complex Emotions". In *Music and Meaning*, J. Robinson (ed.), 154–78. Ithaca, NY: Cornell University Press.
Kivy, P. 1993. *The Fine Art of Repetition*. Cambridge: Cambridge University Press.
Kivy, P. 1995. *Authenticities*. Ithaca, NY: Cornell University Press.
Kivy, P. 2001. *New Essays on Musical Understanding*. Oxford: Clarendon Press.
Kivy, P. 2001. *The Possessor and the Possessed*. New Haven, CT: Yale University Press.
Kramer, L. 2002. *Musical Meaning*. Berkeley, CA: University of California Press.
Krausz, M. 1993. *Rightness and Reasons: Interpretations in Cultural Practices*. Ithaca, NY: Cornell University Press.
Kuhn, T. S. 1962. *The Structure of Scientific Revolutions*. Chicago, IL: University of Chicago Press.
Leinsdorf, E. 1981. *The Composer's Advocate*. New Haven, CT: Yale University Press.
Levinson, J. 1990. *Music, Art and Metaphysics*. Ithaca, NY: Cornell University Press.
Levinson, J. 1993. "Performative vs. Critical Interpretations in Music". In *The Interpretation of Music*, M. Krausz (ed.), 33–60. Oxford: Clarendon Press.
Levinson, J. 1997. *Music in the Moment*. Ithaca, NY: Cornell University Press.
Mackie, J. 1977. *Ethics: Inventing Right and Wrong*. Harmondsworth: Penguin.
Matravers, D. 1998. *Art and Emotion*. Oxford: Clarendon Press.
Nussbaum, M. 2001. *Upheavals of Thought*. Cambridge: Cambridge University Press.
Pike, L. 1978. *Beethoven, Sibelius and "the Profound Logic"*. London: Athlone.
Radford, C. 1989. "Emotions and Music: A Reply to the Cognitivists", *Journal of Aesthetics and Art Criticism* 47, 69–76.
Radford, C. 1991. "Muddy Waters", *Journal of Aesthetics and Art Criticism* 49, 247–52.
Ridley, A. 1995. *Music, Value and the Passions*. Ithaca, NY: Cornell University Press.
Rosen, C. 2003. *Piano Notes*. London: Allen Lane.
Schoenberg, A. 1978. *Theory of Harmony*, R. Carter (trans.). London: Faber and Faber.
Scruton, R. 1997. *The Aesthetics of Music*. Oxford: Clarendon Press.
Scruton, R. 2004. *Death Devoted Heart*. Oxford: Oxford University Press.
Seymour, M. 1996. *Robert Graves: Life on the Edge*. London: Doubleday.
Sharpe, R. A. 1983. *Contemporary Aesthetics*. Hassocks: Harvester.
Sharpe, R. A. 2000. *Music and Humanism*. Oxford: Oxford University Press.
Sibley, F. 2001. *Approach to Aesthetics*. Oxford: Oxford University Press.
Stecker, R. 1997. *Artworks*. University Park, PA: Pennsylvania State University Press.
Stecker, R. 2003. *Interpretation and Construction*. Oxford: Blackwell.
Stravinsky, I. 1975. *Autobiography*. London: Calder and Boyars.
Taliaferro, C. 1990. "The Ideal Aesthetic Observer Revisited", *British Journal of Aesthetics* 30(1), 1–13.
Tolstoy, L. 1930. *What is Art and Essays on Art*, A. Maude (trans.). Oxford: Oxford University Press.
Tomkins, C. 1965. *The Bride and the Bachelors*. London: Weidenfeld & Nicolson.
Tovey, D. F. 1946. *Essays in Musical Analysis III: The Concerto*. Oxford: Oxford University Press.
Tyrell, J. 1992. *Janáček's Operas*. London: Faber and Faber.
Vaughan Williams, R. 1963. "Some Thoughts on Beethoven's Choral Symphony". In *National Music and Other Essays*, 83–120. Oxford: Oxford University Press.
Wilde, O. 1927. "The Critic as Artist". In *Intentions*, 95–217. London: Methuen.

Winch, P. 1972. "The Universalizability of Moral Judgements". In *Ethics and Action*, 151–70. London: Routledge & Kegan Paul.
Wittgenstein, 1953. *Philosophical Investigations*, E. Anscombe (trans.). Oxford: Blackwell.
Wittgenstein, 1966. *Lectures and Conversations on Aesthetics, Psychology and Religious Belief*, Cyril Barrett (ed.). Oxford: Blackwell.
Wittgenstein, 1967. *Zettel*, E. Anscombe (trans.). Oxford: Blackwell.
Wolterstorff, N. 1980. *Worlds and Works of Art*. Oxford: Clarendon Press.

Discography

I list recordings that may need some tracking down or where certain versions seem to me very much to be preferred. There are several excellent versions of, say, the symphonies of Shostakovich or Prokofiev and advice is readily available.

Count Basie, "Lester Leaps In", on *Count Basie* (Bluenite BN005, 1996). [Unfortunately the CD has no details of the musicians and date save the information that it is, remarkably, a live recording.]
Beethoven, Piano Sonatas Nos. 23, 28, 30, 31, Solomon (Testament SBT 1192, 2000).
Benjamin Britten, *Sacred and Profane*, The Sixteen, Harry Christophers (cond.) (Collins Classics 13432, 1993).
Holst, *Hymns from the Rig Veda*, on a CD including *Two Eastern Pictures* and *Hymn to Dionysus*, Royal Philharmonic Orchestra and Royal College of Music Chamber Choir, Sir David Willcocks (cond.) (Unicorn-Kanchana DKP(CD) 9046, 1985). [Unfortunately, the CD is not helpfully banded.]
Joan Cererois, "Seráfin, que con dulce harmoníá", sung by Emily Van Evera and Timothy Wilson [the incomparable counter-tenor], on *The Christmas Album*, Taverner Consort, and Choir Players, Andrew Parrott (cond.) (EMI CDC 7 54529 2, 1992; reissued Veritas VC5451552, 2002). [There is another version of this on a more recent, much lauded, disc: *Missa Mexicana*, The Harp Consort, Andrew Lawrence-King (cond.) (Harmonia Mundi HMU 907283, 2002). I rather prefer the first.]
Loyset Compère, "Le grant Desir", sung by Catherine Bott and Catherine King, on *Renaissance Love Songs* (BBC MM54, 1997). [This is a disc that was issued to accompany the *BBC Music Magazine* V(6). You will need to track it down through secondhand dealers.]
Dvořák. *Slavonic Dances* Series I op. 46, Series II op. 72, Czech Philharmonic Orchestra, Karel Sejna (cond.) (Supraphon SU1916-2-011 (1995) [recorded 1959]).
B. Goodman, L. Hampton, C. Christian, "AC-DC Current", Benny Goodman Sextet: Benny Goodman (clarinet), Lionel Hampton (vibes), Fletcher Henderson (piano), Charlie Christian (guitar), Artie Bernstein (bass), Nick Fatool (drums). [Recorded live in 1939 and available on various albums.]
Jimmy Guiffre Trio, "The Train and the River", on *Sound of Jazz* (Columbia CK 45234).
Janáček. *Jenůfa*, Chorus and Orchestra of the National Theatre Prague, Bohumil Gregor (cond.) (EMI CMS 7 243 5 65476 29, 1995). [This performance embodies the Kovarovic alterations.]
Stefano Landi. *Homo Fugit velut umbra . . .* L'Arpeggiata, Christina Pluhar (cond.) (Alpha 020, 2002). [This is very much a version for twenty-first century ears, I suspect.]
Richard Strauss, "Gesang der Apollonpriesterin" op. 33 no. 2, on *Orchestral Songs vol. 2*,

Felicity Lott with Royal Scottish National Orchestra, Neeme Järvi (cond.) (Chandos CHAN 9159, 1993).

Tallis, *Spem in alium*. Of the many recordings, two stand out. For a cathedral acoustic find *Tallis: Sacred Choral Works*, with Winchester Cathedral Choir, Winchester College Quiristers and Vocal Arts, David Hill (cond.) (Hyperion CDA66400, 1990). For a less reverberant acoustic but perhaps a more authentic one, if it is true that it was first performed in the Long Gallery at Arundel House, listen to the recording by the Tallis Scholars, Peter Phillips (cond.) (Gimell 454906-2, 1985; reissued 1994). Imagine dying before you had a chance to hear this music.

Index